BUCKNELL REVIEW

Classics and Cinema

STATEMENT OF POLICY

BUCKNELL REVIEW is a scholarly interdisciplinary journal. Each issue is devoted to a major theme or movement in the humanities or sciences, or to two or three closely related topics. The editors invite heterodox, orthodox, and speculative ideas and welcome manuscripts from any enterprising scholar in the humanities and sciences.

This journal is a member of the Conference of Editors of Learned Journals

BUCKNELL REVIEW

A Scholarly Journal of Letters, Arts, and Sciences

Editor
PAULINE FLETCHER

Associate Editor
DOROTHY L. BAUMWOLL

Assistant Editor
STEVEN W. STYERS

Editorial Board
PATRICK BRADY
WILLIAM E. CAIN
JAMES M. HEATH
STEVEN MAILLOUX
JOHN WHEATCROFT

Contributors should send manuscripts with a self-addressed stamped envelope to the Editor, Bucknell University, Lewisburg, Pennsylvania, 17837.

BUCKNELL REVIEW

Classics and Cinema

Edited by
MARTIN M. WINKLER

LEWISBURG:
BUCKNELL UNIVERSITY PRESS
LONDON AND TORONTO: ASSOCIATED UNIVERSITY PRESSES

Associated University Presses
440 Forsgate Drive
Cranbury, NJ 08512

Associated University Presses
25 Sicilian Avenue
London WC1A 2QH, England

Associated University Presses
P.O. Box 39, Clarkson Pstl. Stn.
Mississauga, Ontario,
L5J 3X9 Canada

The paper used in this publication meets the
requirements of the American National Standard for
Permanence of Paper for Printed Library Materials Z39.48-1984.

Library of Congress Cataloging-in-Publication Data

Classics and cinema / edited by Martin M. Winkler.
    p.   cm. — (Bucknell review : v. 35, no. 1)
  Includes bibliographical references.
  ISBN 0-8387-5198-9 (alk. paper)
  1. Historical films—History and criticism.   2. Mythology,
Classical in motion pictures.   3. Civilization, Greco-Roman in
motion pictures.   4. Classical literature in motion pictures.
I. Winkler, Martin M.   II. Series.
AP2.B887   vol. 35, no. 1
[PN1995.9.H5]
051—dc20
[s791.43′658]   90-55651
                                                                              CIP

(Volume XXXV, Number 1)

m.R.

PRINTED IN THE UNITED STATES OF AMERICA

Contents

Recent Issues of BUCKNELL REVIEW

Introduction

The first picture I worked on at Metro was *Quo Vadis?*, with [studio producer] Arthur Hornblow. Considerable research had been done for this film by a classics scholar named Hugh Gray, who happened to be in the research department. He might just as well have been an Oxford don. He was an exceptionally cultivated man with a delightful personality. I requested that he collaborate with me. We wrote about half the script, and I thought it was quite good, but it wasn't what L. B. Mayer wanted. Mayer was after a De Mille-like religious epic. . . . I told him I wasn't at all sure I could give him what he wanted. He said, "You can only try! Try, John! Try!" I left the house in a cold sweat and went straight to Arthur's. I told him I was sure they'd never buy our version of the picture. . . .

From there on, it was out of our hands. L. B. assigned producer Sam Zimbalist and director Mervyn LeRoy, and got the story he had wanted all along. It was another dreadful spectacle, catering to the audience L. B. thought was there. L. B. was right; the audience *was* there.

—John Huston, *An Open Book*

BOEULDIEU:	Do you mind? Your dictionaries are going to be in my way.
DEMOLDER:	I'm sorry, but it's such difficult work. Pindar has always been so badly translated.
BOEULDIEU:	Really? I'm sorry to hear it. Rotten shame!
MARECHAL:	I never asked you before because basically I couldn't care less, but who is this chap of yours, Pindar?
DEMOLDER:	You can make fun of it if you like, but to me it's the most important thing in the whole world. No joking, I care about it more than about the war or even my own life. Pindar is the greatest of the Greek poets!
MARECHAL:	The greatest Greek poet? Well, I never!

—*Grand Illusion*

From Hollywood's "dreadful spectacle" to the moving mention of Pindar in one of the most humane achievements of the cinema, the history, mythology, and literature of ancient Greece and Rome have been a staple of the medium since its earliest beginnings. In between the extremes of unabashed embraces of the lurid and the ridiculous on the one hand and committed attempts at the accurate and even the sublime on the other, films dealing with antiquity or reflecting ancient literary or mythical archetypes

9

have in their own ways managed to express the fascination which the ancient world has always exerted on popular imagination. The new lease on life outside the ivory towers of academia which the cinema has given to antiquity has, however, generally been ignored or disdained by the cultural establishment, at least until recently. Academic compartmentalization is now making way for less confined comparative approaches to the study and teaching of the humanities.

The present volume of the *Bucknell Review* is intended to illustrate the interdisciplinary nature of classical studies by focusing on some of the connections between antiquity and our own society as revealed in the medium of film. Ancient myths and archetypes recurring in the cinema attest to the vitality of our cultural tradition, and film versions of classical texts usually contain features worth examining. Retellings of classical stories on film may show that their creators have used the old material consciously in order to comment on their own times or unconsciously reflect cultural trends. For example, a Greek director may bring classical tragedies to the screen or an Italian director may present a highly personal version of a Roman novel, while ancient myths can provide instances of more or less imaginative entertainment. The ancient material may become imbued with a creative art and intelligence not readily apparent to a casual viewer. Openly commercial films set in antiquity, whose historical or mythological accuracy may leave much to be desired, can still reward a close engagement with their underlying qualities. But even genre films, which at first sight have nothing in common with the ancient world, may adapt archetypes familiar from antiquity, particularly those relating to heroic myths. As American philosopher Stanley Cavell observes in *The World Viewed,* there is "a significant fact about movies: that there is always something to find." In *Themes Out of School* Cavell calls for our "ability to move between high and low, caring about each from the advantage of the other." The present book both adopts and extends this idea: for "high and low" read also "then and now." Popular culture, both ancient and modern, is today a legitimate field of academic inquiry, and we are justified to attempt to bridge, in Cavell's words, "the division between the commodity and the serious work."

Classics and Cinema contains contributions on films which overtly deal with antiquity and on those which have recourse to archetypal mythical or literary themes. The contributors, all classicists, are aware that they have not exhausted the possibilities of this area of inquiry; we intend our papers to be representative of different approaches to the subject at hand and to give an indication of the range such explorations may take. The book is thus in the nature of a *satura lanx*, a "well-filled dish" containing a variety of items. But this does not make it a mere mélange. Readers will easily be able to trace thematic connections among the papers. While the choice for individual topics was left to the authors, my concern as editor was to ensure that they fit an overall design. My goal was to demonstrate, in the specific area indicated by the book's title, that classics is a versatile and exciting discipline, capable of combining methods of traditional scholarship with an openness to modern critical thought in its approaches to the ancient cultures and to the classical tradition. There now exists widespread interest among classicists, not least in the United States, in such endeavors. In colleges and universities throughout the country, courses on classical civilization, especially on mythology, regularly incorporate film screenings. The programs of national and regional classics associations list topics involving film more and more frequently. Panels devoted to classics and film were organized by me for the Classical Association of the Middle West and South and by Jon Solomon, author of *The Ancient World in the Cinema*, for the American Philological Association. Most of the papers read on these occasions appear in these pages, extensively reworked; they are accompanied by others written especially for this volume. At a time when humanities in general and classics in particular are no longer the bedrock of education they once were, the use of film within a traditional and largely nonvisual curriculum can provide an excellent means to reach students. If, at the same time, appreciation of our own culture— and this includes popular culture—can be enhanced by an examination, from a classical perspective, of the cinema, which is our primary visual art form, then the rationale for opening the curriculum to include film need not be questioned; the educational as well as aesthetic rewards to teachers and students can only increase. Incorporating feature films, especially the works of acknowledged filmmakers, into classical course offerings need not represent a "selling out" to the lowest common denominator or a trivialization of the tradition of Western culture; rather, it is an effective means to make antiquity more readily accessible and to throw light on our own age as well. Conversations with colleagues and my own experience in the classroom over several years have convinced me of this; ultimately, these provided the impulse for the present book. All its contributors hope that the work presented here will suggest further avenues of teaching and of research and publication.

Not the least reward for this kind of undertaking is a change of pace from standard academic procedure. As will be readily apparent, we deal with films as cultural artifacts deserving consideration as works of high or popular art or, sometimes, both. Our primary intent is interpretive, and we approach the films we discuss with certain thematic concerns. We emphasize film's importance as a form of narrative and apply methods of literary scholarship to analyze what Cavell has called "movies worth possessing and questioning." That is to say, we "read" films as "texts." In this, of course, we each have different perspectives and priorities. But the very diversity of both content and approach in our papers will, we believe, make them interesting not only to academic specialists in classics and related areas within the humanities, such as English, comparative literature, and film studies, but also to general readers and to amateurs (in the original sense of the word) of literature and film.

The absence of film stills from the papers in this book deserves a word of explanation. This was a deliberate choice on the part of the authors regarding their "texts." Moreover, from a practical point of view, the cost of even black-and-white illustrations to accompany the papers was prohibitive, to say nothing of color plates. While this is an unfortunate aspect of academic publishing, the increasing availability of films on videotape has somewhat compensated for any regrets about excluding stills. We are aware that watching a videotape is far from the ideal way of approaching an artistic film which, for its full impact and beauty to be appreciated, should be watched on the big screen, its original format intact. If our papers send readers to the films we discuss, to watch a particular work again or for the first time—or even to think anew about some of the classical texts—then we will have succeeded in our purpose.

Nevertheless, an entire book about film, whatever its approaches and objectives may be, without any visuals at all did not seem to me to be a well-rounded entity, either. The idea for a special photo section to broaden its range thus suggested itself. I therefore asked Greek writer-director Michael Cacoyannis to contribute a visual essay based on one of his films. The result is his selection of fifteen stills, accompanied by brief captions, from *Iphigenia,* one of the most accomplished translations of Greek tragedy to the screen. The photo essay in turn led to my wish to involve an experienced filmmaker even more closely in this project and to obtain some firsthand information about the process of filming ancient literature. This resulted in the interviews with Michael Cacoyannis and Irene Papas, the foremost interpreter of classical characters on the screen, whose presence in Cacoyannis's films is essential to the artistic achievement they represent. I would like to thank both Ms. Papas and Mr. Cacoyannis for their participation in spite of very busy schedules. My thanks go also to Marianne McDonald, who helped me approach them and who collaborated with me on the interviews. Finally, I thank my contributors for a pleasant and rewarding experience. Without their enthusiasm and the patience with which they responded to my occasionally less than gentle interference in the development of their papers I could not have realized what had long been a favorite project.

MARTIN M. WINKLER

BUCKNELL REVIEW

Classics and Cinema

Teaching Greek Myth and Confronting Contemporary Myths

Peter W. Rose

Miami University of Ohio

I have used contemporary films for a number of years now in teaching Greek mythology.[1] In the following essay I will explore and interrogate my own rationale in doing so, describe how I present Greek myth, and offer a detailed account of the uses to which I put some specific films (*Clash of the Titans, Jason and the Argonauts, Return of the Jedi,* and *Superman*), two films based on Greek myths and two which evoke on the screen contemporary American myths. Finally, I will attempt to sum up the implications of this sort of pedagogy. Since one's pedagogical practice is an eminently personal as well as a political act imbedded in the concrete specificities of time and place, I make wider use of the first person pronoun than would be relevant in a critical analysis of a text. The relevance of what I have done or would now do needs to be assessed by each reader in the light of his or her own specific pedagogical circumstances and goals.

In classics, apart from heated discussions of the various options available in teaching beginning and intermediate language, pedagogy is rarely discussed. Certainly the explicit use of popular cultural objects—while not unheard of—is equally rare. Indeed, educational theorist Henry Giroux points to this parallel between pedagogy and popular culture:

> Pedagogy is often theorized as what is left after curriculum content is determined. It is what follows the selection of ideologically correct content. . . . Popular culture is still largely defined in the dominant discourse as the cultural residue which remains when high culture is subtracted from the overall totality of cultural practices; it is the trivial and the insignificant of everyday life, a form of popular taste often deemed unworthy of both academic legitimation and high social affirmation.[2]

The first question I pose to myself in this connection is, What am I doing when I teach a course in ancient Greek mythology?

Mythology was certainly not something most classicists were taught in graduate school, nor did it occur to most classics departments to offer it as an undergraduate option until the late sixties and early seventies when more standard offerings had been decimated by the call for "relevance." Today, though I have not seen hard statistical data, I suspect on the basis of my direct experience in a variety of institutions that at a great many colleges and universities mythology courses draw the largest number of students taught by classicists. They thus constitute not only a deeply invested bread-and-butter issue for classicists' material well-being, but for a great many students represent their *only* exposure to the civilization of ancient Greece. The first factor has tended to foster a certain meretricious mindlessness in some presentations of the subject.[3] The second is a consideration that should recall us to our moral responsibilities as educators of future citizens.[4]

In the decade of the eighties, the political significance of teaching the classics in general has come under considerable scrutiny. On the one hand, classics are a key component in the educational agenda of the New Right, most clearly identifiable in the positions taken by former President Reagan's Secretary of Education, William Bennett, and in the very popular best-seller by Allan Bloom, *The Closing of the American Mind*.[5] For both Bennett and Bloom the classics constitute immutable reservoirs of fixed truth about a fixed human nature, a fixed human condition. So taught, the classics can convey to students precisely the message of the *severe limits of possibility* which it has been the goal of the New Right to impart to the dominated majorities of the world.[6] On the other hand, subordinated groups such as women, Afro-Americans, and other ethnic minorities whose relation historically to "Western Civilization" is by no means unequivocally positive, have raised serious and legitimate questions about the misogynistic, patriarchal, and ethnocentric strains imbedded in the classical texts. All of these developments have made it, I hope, somewhat more difficult for classicists to see their pedagogical activities as devoid of political implications. What John Sullivan said about the teaching of history is equally true of the teaching of the classics: there can be no unideological teaching of classics. The question is whether the teacher is consciously aware of her or his approach and perspective.[7] Although Greek literature as such has been more directly implicated in this debate, Greek mythology, which we know primarily from Greek literary texts, can, depending on how we present it, also be enlisted in support of a certain politics of a critically unexamined, allegedly monolithic Western tradition. We all know of mythology courses in which the students learn a few hundred names in the interest of "cultural literacy," see some fleshy Renaissance nudes to bring home the continuity of the tradition, and perhaps even listen to an opera or two—all without the slightest hint that there is anything distinctly *odd*, distinctly *different*, about Greek myth seen from the perspective of the twentieth-century United States.

For me the liberatory potential for students of an encounter with Greek civilization in general and with Greek myth in particular is first and foremost the possibility for engaging with the culturally Other. Not that there are no continuities or similarities available or worthy of study. But I see my first responsibility as challenging the massive bias of most of my students' cultural experience toward inculcating the belief that anything different from what they know is either undesirable or unattainable. The profoundly ahistorical or antihistorical cast of most of what constitutes students' cultural experience—and which therefore deeply constructs their own subjectivities, their own perceptions of their individual and collective life options—seems to me the chief obstacle to the transformation of our society into a truly democratic and humanely decent society.[8] To put it differently, if I ask myself why so many students seem so easily to consent to a view of the future characterized by an escalating threat of human extinction through war and environmental pollution, by ever more bitter divisions between the self-centered rich and the desperate poor, between the First World and the Third World, between the white minority and the colored majority, between the empowered male half and the exploited female half of humanity, it seems to me due in the final analysis to the success of their cultural environment in conveying to them the message that they are powerless to change a world whose parameters are dictated by an immutable human nature. Of course, to call this posture "ahistorical" or "antihistorical" is to invoke a notion of history as precisely the realm of possibility where a whole set of choices from the most individual to the most broadly societal have directly constructed the conditions of possibility in any particular social and historical context. A serious encounter with a *different* civilization can be liberating not simply in presenting that other civilization as a repository of *better* choices but rather as a model of a social totality in which the *consequences* of choices in various spheres—economic, political, social, educational, cultural—introduce students to the very fact of choice and thus break the chain of "natural" necessity.

Such an encounter cannot, I believe, be readily processed by students if it is completely divorced from the mechanisms by which they process the rest of their daily experience. This seems to me the most relevant context for understanding broadly the role of "popular" culture in the experience of students. It is not a matter of seeking a level of "relevance" that merely confirms their current individual perceptions of what matters. In differing degrees and differing contexts depending on a whole array of socio-economic factors, rock music, advertisements of all sorts, games, toys, "street" practices (e.g., males casting remarks at passing females), TV, and film play a decisive role in students' attempt to forge a sense of themselves, their moral values, and their life options.[9] By incorporating elements of that culture in a course on ancient mythology, I hope to engage the students in a double, if not exactly simultaneous, interrogation of their own cultural practices as well as those of a radically different society.

There is, I believe, a particular similarity between popular culture and mythology which constitutes both an additional pedagogical attraction in the combination and, at the same time, a special problem. Both myth and popular culture appeal, when they do appeal, on a particularly visceral level that students are extremely reluctant to subject to "cold" intellectual scrutiny. With both sorts of cultural experience students are especially likely to complain, Why can't we just *enjoy* the stories? Why do we have to *ruin* them by *analyzing* them? Not just concepts or systems of beliefs are at stake: *pleasure* is at stake.[10] Of course the degree of particular students' emotional investments in any given cultural object will depend on a host of very specific factors—economic level, class background, and gender most obviously. There are some students who are particularly resistant to the appeals of Greek mythology and some who may be particularly resistant to the sorts of films I have tried to use. I can only say that the particular students I teach do seem, by and large, to feel rather strongly the visceral attraction of both myth and film.[11]

Since everyone who teaches Greek myth seems to do it very differently and since any assessment of the usefulness of my approach to film implies in part at least an assessment of the context in which I use it, I will try to describe as briefly as I can the overall structure of my course and the assumptions that inform its structure.

The most basic problem I perceive in presenting Greek myth

may be summed up in the tension between—to use Lévi-Strauss's terms—the synchronic approach and the diachronic approach, between, on the one hand, treating Greek myth in its entirety as a meaningful, internally self-reinforcing system of narratives and, on the other, presenting mythic narrative as itself an historical problem—a problem to which Greek culture offered in the course of time a variety of solutions.[12] Many contemporary critical approaches which I find engaging in various degrees are radically ahistorical and treat myth in general as precisely a mode of discourse that precedes historical consciousness. Accepting, so to speak, myth's own philosophy of time, they proceed to analyze particular myths with little or no interest in the impact of historical changes on the meanings of myths. Among these I would cite Freudian and Jungian psychoanalytic approaches, Lévi-Straussian structuralist analyses and—with a few equivocations—the work of such figures as Malinowski, Dumézil, and Eliade.[13] For them history is at best an intrusion; the interpretative enterprise consists in getting at the atemporal cores of meaning. On the other hand, one of the traditional fascinations of a history of the *written* remnants of Greek culture involves tracing the emergence of an ever-growing self-consciousness in the poets about narrative as itself a problem and the parallel forging of an increasingly abstract language.[14] Side by side we find either the attempt to force narrative to bear an ever heavier burden of abstractly conceived meaning or the movement toward a nonnarrative alternative, signaled by the development of strident critiques of Homer and Hesiod in the Presocratics and culminating in Plato's head-on assault on narrative and poetry.

My course attempts to introduce students to both ahistorical and historical dimensions of the study of myth by, in a sense, covering the ground twice. In the first half of the course I use Tripp's *Handbook* to present the major stories in as detailed and interpretatively neutral a manner as possible.[15] At the same time I introduce students to three critical approaches. The psychoanalytic approach (Bettelheim, Freud, Slater) stresses the parallels between myth and dreams as a radically *narrative* means of dealing with what the society defines as unacceptable desires and fears.[16] The structuralist approach (Lévi-Strauss) offers both a methodology for grasping the *grammar*, so to speak, of these peculiar narratives and an account of their *function*, namely, to overcome unresolvable intellectual contradictions in a spurious repetitive spiral of narrative mediations.[17] Finally, the overtly political approach (Malinowski and Marx) stresses the role of myth as a self-interested source of validation for actual social and political institutions, in short as *ideology*.[18] Students are invariably shocked at the relatively heavy theoretical component in a course which many of them take precisely because, as suggested above, they associate myth with painlessly "self-evident" stories. The variety of theoretical perspectives I offer not only reflects what I genuinely find most relevant to the study of myth, but aims in itself to introduce students to the very fact of theoretical variety. At least in my university, students are rarely confronted with more than one point of view and even that one view is rarely situated within the theoretical background that has formed their teacher's pedagogical practice. Yet the possibility of genuine *critical* thinking requires that future citizens develop precisely the capacity to grasp the significant presuppositions of the intellectual, moral, and political options offered them.

In the second half of the course I include a necessarily abbreviated historical survey from Homer to Plato. Film plays a key role in my attempt to effect a transition between the halves of the course—to suggest the explanatory power of some ahistorical approaches (psychoanalytic and structuralist) and at the same time to confront the students with the reality of historical change. The primary vehicle for this encounter has been a film based on the Perseus myth, *Clash of the Titans*.

After the students have read a considerable number of myths in Tripp's *Handbook*, and read all the critical approaches including Slater's analysis of the ambiguity of snake symbolism as part of the "oral narcissistic dilemma," I ask them to read Slater's analysis of the Perseus myth and view the film *Clash of the Titans*, a videotape of which is available in a learning lab so that they can view the film more than once. I then ask them to analyze the film's and Slater's contemporary approaches in the light of the ancient data on the myth available in Tripp's *Handbook*. The vehicle for their response has sometimes been an in-class hour test, sometimes an outside essay. I must point out in this connection that the size of my classes, usually fifty to sixty students, has seemed to me virtually to preclude the more gradually dialogic explorations of popular culture advocated by progressive theorists.[19] At the same time, I see distinct advantages in asking the students to write about the film *before* I have anything at all to say about it. Not only do I write abundant comments and questions on their texts, but I attempt to give at least a full class after the hour-test summarizing the range of their comments, offering my own "reading" of the film, and inviting their comments. Precisely because they have already engaged with the film on their own, they are often readier to speak up on these occasions despite the inhibiting size of the class.

Slater's general thesis presupposes Freud's view that the emotional life of adults is significantly determined by their earliest relationships to those who bring them up.[20] He argues that the circumstances of Greek society which dictated the relative seclusion of legally married women and encouraged the relative nonparticipation of fathers in the rearing of young children led to a deeply ambivalent mother-son relationship. This pattern is reflected in the misogyny and male narcissim prevalent in Greek myth. In the absence of a strong husband/father the mother simultaneously pushes the male child to be an overachiever and makes emotional demands upon him which fill him with a sense of terror and doom. He wants complete possession of the mother to nurture him literally and, metaphorically, to foster his ideal self-image. But it is precisely the intensity of her emotional concentration upon him which fills him with fear of being "engulfed" by the mother. Slater calls this ambivalence the "oral narcissistic dilemma" and seeks to organize the major hero figures of Greek myth as, in effect, a system of different attempts to overcome this dilemma. Zeus' exaggerated displays of sexual prowess are one way of attempting to deny the threat by overcompensation. Orestes' or Alcmaeon's mother-murder is another extreme solution, echoed in various more muted slayings of female monsters. Dionysus illustrates "identification with the aggressor," i.e., becoming like the threatening mother in hopes of dispelling her threat. Lame Hephaestus—variously rejected by both parents—represents symbolic self-emasculation in the hopes of ingratiating himself with his ferocious mother. Apollo is presented as primarily dealing with the threatening female by "antisepsis"—by a posture, not always successfully maintained, of hostile distance from all hints of female fertility. Heracles, whose name furnishes Slater with his title, *The Glory of Hera*, illustrates the richest variety of responses—vast displays of male potency, repeated triumphs over female monsters, transvestism with Omphale, homosexuality with Hylas, and finally tragic defeat at the hands of Deianeira, whose name means "man/husband-destroyer."

Within this configuration Perseus is presented by Slater under the rubric of "maternal desexualization." Perseus, completely deprived of any positive adult male role models, perceives males solely as sexual competitors for his mother's attentions. Acrisius,

Danae's father, who imprisons her in a tower or underground to keep away suitors, especially his brother Proetus, out of fear that the child will kill him as predicted by a prophecy, only mirrors Perseus' own obsessive concern with his mother's chastity—the motive force behind his "heroic" quest for the Medusa head and his subsequent murder of Polydectes and company. Perseus' fascination with his mother's sexuality is further evidenced by the strong emphasis on looking at the forbidden place—"scopophilia" in Freudian terms—at the same time that he is terrified by the prospect of the ferocious return gaze should he be caught looking. Here the parallels of Actaeon, torn to shreds for seeing forbidden female nakedness, or Teiresias, blinded on some accounts for the same crime, come to mind.[21] Perseus' radical solution to the dilemma of a mother he wants desperately to keep but whose sexuality is frightening for him is to cut off the offending part.

Slater's identification of the Medusa head with the mother's genitalia is the centerpiece of his analysis. Those who find in Medusa's paralyzing look quaint folklore of the evil eye or the Sartrean horror of the reifying stare of the Other will not be moved by Slater's citation of a sexual psychopath's dream in which the pubic hair of an adult woman is perceived as menacing snakes.[22] The same skepticism will perhaps greet the rest of his argument on this point, which I will not summarize here. I only note that he sees the sexual nature of the assault on Medusa confirmed by the resulting births of Pegasus, Chrysaor, and various snakes from the drops of Medusa's blood.

Perseus' rescue of Andromeda and eventual marriage to her are interpreted by Slater as essentially replays of his relationship with his mother. Slater emphasizes the visual element in his falling in love in consequence of seeing her enchained naked body, another fight with a monster again using a sword, another encounter with an older suitor—Andromeda's uncle—and another use of the Medusa head to immobilize the opposition. He sees as deeply significant the fact that Perseus brings both his mother and his new bride back with him to Argos. Slater's general assessment of the "heroic" pattern of Perseus' career emphasizes the hero's real helplessness—his constant reliance on help from the desexualized Athena and from multiplied magic devices—and the brutal violence of his solution to the problem of maternal sexuality.

Finally Slater focuses briefly on the myth of Bellerophon—a figure also connected with Proetus and with the winged horse born at the decapitation of Medusa. Slater finds confirmation of the motif of fear of the mother's sexuality in Bellerophon's disastrous encounter with Proetus' wife, who seeks his death when he declines her sexual advances. He also notes that Plutarch preserves a story that the hero was stopped cold in his assault on a city when the women of the city came out and displayed their genitals to the bashful hero.[23]

Clash of the Titans, released in 1981, starring Harry Hamlin as Perseus, Judi Bowker as Andromeda, Laurence Olivier as Zeus, and a variety of well-known names in cameo roles as goddesses and ghouls (Maggie Smith, Ursula Andress, Claire Bloom, Flora Robson), was generally panned by those critics who took any note of it but did reasonably well at the box office.[24] The screenplay was written by Beverley Cross and directed by Desmond Davis, whose films in the sixties (e.g., *Girl With Green Eyes* and *A Nice Girl Like Me*) earned him a reputation for "an empathy for women's plight in modern society."[25] Special effects were done by "Wizard" Ray Harryhausen, whom reviewers often saw as the sole source of any interest the film has. At the time I first introduced it into the course, usually about half of my students had already seen it on their own. I prefer to discuss the details of the film's plot primarily in the context of the students' observations. But for those who have not seen it, I would only point out that the most striking innovation of the film version is the near suppression of Danae from the plot: she is out of the picture after some five minutes. Secondly, the female monster, Medusa, though still narratively central to the plot of the film, is presented as dramatically secondary to a male sea monster, the Kraken, the only alleged "Titan" in the film and not even a figure from Greek myth.[26]

In asking students to compare Tripp, Slater, and *Clash of the Titans,* I juxtapose three very different entities: the already heterogeneous ancient evidence distilled in an eclectic handbook, an analytic academic discourse, and a popular film. I wish I could say that I substantially advanced the students' appreciation of the specificity of those different modes. Film literacy for a modern student should be a fundamental component of any "cultural literacy" worthy of the name, but apart from a scattering of comments directed at elements in the myth which are compatible or incompatible with translation to the filmic medium, I did not attempt to teach them film literacy.[27]

What did I want and what did I get from the students? On the simplest level I wanted to see the extent to which they recognized how the film version radically cut, selected, transformed, and supplemented the available narrative data, most of which Slater had at least attempted to account for. On a deeper level I hoped that they would explore the ideological implications of the most blatant omissions and additions in the film with a view to gaining some historical perspective on their own society's cultural production by contrasting it with that of ancient Greece. I did not expect, but would have welcomed, some exploration of the ideological aspect of Slater's emphases in using the ancient data. Bracketing social and political aspects of myth interpretation in favor of an exclusive focus on the sexual dynamics of the nuclear family, alas, comes as naturally to contemporary students as it does to Slater.

My actual instructions read as follows:

> Choose at least FIVE mythemes (i.e., an action linked with a subject, a symbolic object, creature, or significant event) from the narrative material associated with Perseus (i.e., everything in the Handbook about the royal line of Argos). Consider whether these mythemes are typical of Greek myth as you've studied it (i.e., do you see any suggestive parallels? what sorts of concerns seem to be associated with these motifs?). Examine what happens to these mythemes in Slater and in Clash of the Titans. What role do they play in Slater's interpretation? Are they included, altered, or omitted from the film? What are the CONSEQUENCES FOR THE MEANING of the myth of the treatment of these elements in the film? Consider the changes—omissions, transformations, additions—and ask yourself what these reveal about the differences between Greek society and our own society. How much of the original meaning (as you and/or Slater interpret it) is left in the film? If the meaning of the film is different, what does it mean?
>
> The POINT of this exercise is to make as concrete as possible a comparison between Slater's and the filmmakers' use of the same material, to find out what you've learned about analyzing Greek myth and the myths of your own culture.

On the whole the most successful aspect of the experiment was the application of the psychoanalytic approach to the film. While there were those who inevitably explained the relative absence of the mother as due to the fact that the Greeks liked incest whereas it is not so popular in America, many recognized the ways in which the film demonstrated the de facto return of the repressed unconscious material. They noted the relentless imagery of flying which begins with the credits and includes the addition of a monstrous turkey-vulture carrying the virgin Andromeda through the air, Pegasus imported from the Bellerophon story, and the magic mechanical owl (an obvious import from Star Wars). Cumulatively this emphasis tended to confirm for many students Slater's focus on the element of phallic display in the myth and his insistence on the relevance of Bellerophon to the Perseus narrative material. The repeated losses of the hero's sword—particularly to a snake—suggest the pervasive fear of inadequacy stressed by Slater. Despite the heavy shift toward the "romance" of Perseus and Andromeda, some noted the carry-over of misogyny in the film, focused precisely in the mother obsessed with her son (Thetis and Calibos) and echoed in the vain mother Cassiopeia, who boasts not of her own beauty, as in the ancient version, but of her daughter's. Medusa is still a terrifying female, and the seemingly gratuitous addition of a phallic weapon (the bow and arrows) escalates the threat she poses and shifts it from the myth's exclusive interest in her stare.

At the same time many noticed the centrality of unobserved staring with clearly erotic overtones in Perseus' spying upon Andromeda asleep—not to mention the audience's spying on her bathing. The frightening stare of Medusa is echoed in the ferocious stare of the living stone of Thetis' statue. The panic of the cannibalistic Graiae when they lose their eye is vividly evoked in the film and was noted by students. Despite the relative absence of the mother, a few noticed that her sexual attractiveness is heavily stressed in Oedipal terms by the visual evocation of her nude nursing of her son and the flamboyantly nude stroll of mother and son along the sounding surf. Built into the narrative of the film, as opposed to the ancient material, is the precondition of the hero's "facing" the explicitly devouring Graiae and an explicitly immobilizing Medusa before sexually consummating his relationship with Andromeda, whose appearance is most like the mother's precisely when she is seen nude in her bath. In fact, some students even speculated on the possibility that a heavier-breasted actress than Judi Bowker, perhaps even the same actress who played Danae, stands in for Bowker in the nude bathing scene where the actress's face is invisible. Most noted the striking emphasis in the film on Zeus' relentless involvement in the fate of his son, whereas for Slater, Zeus in the ancient myth is the quintessential *absent* father. Most attributed this to the superiority of modern American fathers. Some noted that the addition of Ammon, not a god but a ham tragedian played by Burgess Meredith, insists on the availability of a nonthreatening father figure, who repeatedly offers decisive advice and encouragement. Indeed the film, which multiplies hostile and/or dangerous females (all the goddesses but especially Thetis, the Graiae, Cassiopeia) while omitting the "maternal" role of Athena and limiting "positive" female images to the dubious examples of Danae and Andromeda, is arguably more patriarchal and misogynistic than the Greek myth. One student noted that Andromeda's dream of flying with a bird to meet her former suitor suggests the danger of female sexuality even in this most innocuous-seeming of virgins.

But despite the suppression in the film of the lecherous uncles Proetus and Phineus as well as the major motivating threatening male in the myth, Polydectes, the suitor of Danae, there are hostile males (Acrisius, Calibos, the Kraken) whose function is, as in the myth, to block Perseus' access to the female object of desire. One student even argued that Calibos' association with downing winged horses—an element completely lacking in the ancient material—confirmed his symbolic role as a potentially castrating father figure.

The appeal to the students of psychoanalytic elements was clear in their perceptive focus on the repetition of snake symbols: they noted that snakes are at the base of Zeus' throne; the snake that glides over Perseus' sword temporarily renders him impotent and is allied with the doubled devouring threat of Cerberus; Medusa, in addition to her writhing coiffure of snakes, has a long snaky tail; Calibos not only has a long, frequently undulating tail, but uses a long whip as his prime weapon; the Kraken too uses his enormous tail as a weapon against Perseus on his winged horse. To be sure, some of these are associated with clearly male phallic conflict. But Slater's insistence on the ambiguity of the snake symbol to include as well the engulfing female threat seems confirmed in some of these instances.

The most characteristic disappointment for me in the responses of students was their relative lack of critical distance from the contemporary ideology pervading the film. Despite hopes raised for a more enlightened perspective from a director noted for his empathy with women, the film celebrates traditional heterosexual romance in terms which totally objectify the nubile female while denigrating adult women. It celebrates American fatherhood under conditions which little justify it.[28] It reinforces the fetishism of mechanical gimmicks as the solution to all problems and indulges in blatant racism by adding the embodiment of evil in the only black character in the film (Calibos). At the same time, commenting on the students' analyses and discussing the film in class offered an opportunity to explore some of these issues.

The pedagogical advantages of a film of an ancient Greek myth are more or less comparable in *Jason and the Argonauts*, though I found there were fewer psychoanalytically interesting details to which the students might respond. There is a close parallel in the film's censorship of the "uncanny" elements[29]—the powerful female and helpless dependent hero are replaced by a typical Hollywood helpless (and vacuous) female and an assertive macho hero. The philandering of the hero and the revenge of Medea are completely repressed from the purely "romantic" narrative of the film while both the psychoanalytic and political motivations for the quest for the golden fleece—its symbolic role in the fusion of sibling rivalry and dynastic intrigue so striking in the ancient mythic material—are omitted. Thus, like *Clash of the Titans,* it allows students an opportunity for assessing the concrete *differences* between the ideological norms of gender relations in their own society and those explored in ancient Greek myth. At the same time I must acknowledge that the inherently transhistorical claims of the Freudian approach tend to undermine attempts to historicize gender relations. Though Slater presents his study of Greek myth as a cautionary tale to suburbanized America with a clear sense that there are *choices* in how societies organize sexuality and gender identities, the intellectual excitement of a Freudian approach—particularly to those who are encountering it for the first time—derives in great measure from the discovery of *similarities* in human psychic responses to similar situations.[30]

In a sense, choosing a modern remake of an ancient myth, while it initially seemed a privileged example because it offered such clear grounds for comparison and contrast, had a number of other potential drawbacks. The distancing implicit in an ancient myth where human royalty and the omnipotence of pagan gods are "natural" assumptions and where the primary focus is on issues of family romance, makes it difficult to raise issues of ideology apart from those of gender roles without incorporating a far more serious study of ancient Greek society and history than I found possible in a single semester. Thus there seemed a built-in limitation to the private sphere in sticking with these modern versions of ancient myths. This difficulty seems to me due only in part to the exclusion, in my course, of an in-depth account of the political functions of ancient myth. In part too I think it stems from the heavy bias of ancient Greek myth toward the dynamics of personal affective relations. Perhaps because the close intertwining of the personal and political in the initial Mycenaean context was as unrecoverable for the Greeks of the historical period as it is for us, the reworking of the old stories was primarily on the conscious level ethical and on the unconscious level a vehicle for exploring in fantasy the tensions of Greek gender relations.[31]

In any case, focusing on contemporary mythic films like *Super-*

man (1978) or *Return of the Jedi* (1983), which more explicitly subordinate the private sphere to the public sphere, had the advantage of inviting students to take seriously the more overt political implications of contemporary myth-making. Moreover, their introduction to psychoanalytic approaches enabled them to see critically sorts of relationships in these films which they had previously taken as "natural." I was also interested to find in the case of these films from their own cultural context, the students were less resistant to analysis than with their initial experience with *Clash of the Titans.* I am not sure whether I had just worn down their resistance or, as I prefer to believe, they were beginning to reap some of the *pleasure* of understanding how myths are trying to "think through us"—to echo Lévi-Strauss's famous formulation.[32] There is, I hope, some compensation for the lost pleasure of spontaneous ideological recognition, that unconscious assent to the image of ourselves seductively proffered in the film, in the empowerment of exercising some critical control over the images that beckon us to subjection.[33] What we lose in the assurance of a familiar world we gain in a new freedom to reject proffered versions of our identity which invite us to acquiesce in an unsatisfactory status quo—"summonses" which Althusser calls ideological "interpellations" (from the Latin *interpellare*).[34]

As in *Clash of the Titans* and *Jason and the Argonauts,* the "mythic" element in *Return of the Jedi* and *Superman* is most obvious in the special effects that transcend normal expectations and take us into a realm beyond the rules of everyday reality. At the same time a number of more or less obvious signs point to referents in an historically real world, and it is not difficult, once the question is posed, for students to recognize some of them. In *Return of the Jedi* the helmets of Darth Vader and soldiers of the Evil Empire echo Nazi uniforms.[35] In conjunction with the authoritarian tone of those in power and the abject—"robotlike"—obedience of the ruled these visual elements reinforce other associations with the images of twentieth-century totalitarian societies. The focus on an ultimate weapon (the Death Star) to quell all resistance resonates with the origins of the atomic bomb and the ever-more menacing promises of the military industrial complex. Students readily associate the "rebels" with various media images of Nicaraguan "Freedom Fighters" against "totalitarian communism." Depending on their knowledge (often minimal) of the sixties, they can see links between the centrality of the Force and the "consciousness revolutionaries" of that era. Most, however, saw the Force as a direct analogue to Christian faith asserting itself against godless communism. To this extent students can feel a largely comforting recognition of the eternal verities of the cold war's standard repertory of ideological representations.

When, however, one raises the issues of Vietnam, Central American insurgency in El Salvador or Guatemala against U.S.-backed oligarchies, or the long record of U.S. support for apartheid in South Africa, the discussion can grow more heated and confused. What is the referent, for example, of the Ewoks, primitive peoples who triumph over the high-tech agents of empire both by stealing their own weapons and by imaginative acts of daring? If the rebellion stands for American democracy, why is it led by a *royal princess* and why is the Force restricted to a *hereditary* elite? Discussion along these lines can at least introduce students to the whole phenomenon of ideological messages which seem to be intentionally mixed in order to tap audience awareness of various contradictions in the world and allay anxieties by the sheer confusion of clear and unclear referents to their own world.

A particularly striking instance of this mixed-message phenomenon may be illustrated by the echoes of American race relations in the film. On the one hand, Lando Calrissian (played by a popular black actor, Billy Dee Williams) is a loyal friend who is given the prestigious command of the attack on the Death Star. We seem to have a clear "liberal" image of complete and unproblematic integration of black people into white middle-class society as projected in many TV soaps. Yet the same character is portrayed as a cynical traitor in an earlier episode *(Star Wars)*. Moreover, some explanation needs to be given for the choice of James Earl Jones, one of the finest black actors in America, to do the voice of the very essence of evil, Darth Vader, who is always clothed in black from tip to toe. The racist symbolism seems all the more blatant when we see a *white* actor with a distinctly different, vaguely English, voice representing the *redeemed* Vader (renamed Anaken). Students who notice or are confronted with these issues inevitably produce very different explanations. But the entire experience introduces them to a level of consciousness about their own entertainment which is quite new for them.

Furthermore, their rather extensive immersion in Freudian analysis from the earlier part of the course enables them to recognize the symbolism of Sarlacc, a very fleshy-looking hole in the sand which is surrounded by rows of teeth reminiscent of the Scylla. The parallel toothy, devouring mouth of the monster Rancor combined with the hideously elaborated mouth of Jabba the Hutt can give rise to a more elaborate interrogation of family and gender politics of the film. Luke Skywalker, like Perseus, is a young man without a father; but, unlike Perseus, he has no mother figure in his life. His *only* female interest is Princess Leia, who turns out to be his sister, and students cannot miss the film's tantalizing play with the motif of incest so familiar from Greek myth. Beside the extreme paucity of females in the film there is the heavy proliferation of father figures (Obi-Wan Kenobi, Yoda, and Anaken—the good, i.e., "white," side of Darth Vader) and the strong male bonding of Luke and Han Solo—troubled only by the ambivalence of the only *female* figure's love for both. Luke's initial mission is to save Han; this is the portion of the film where Luke is most threatened by huge, toothy, devouring mouths and where the sexual aspect of Leia—heretofore predominantly arrogant and stereotypically "bitchy" in a full-length white dress—is heavily emphasized by her reduction to a scantily clad, chained adjunct of Jabba the Hutt. On the other hand, several women students saw in Leia's power and initiative, together with the position of authority assigned a black woman in the rebel army command, a clear and positive reflection of the impact of the women's movement on popular culture.

Luke's climactic confrontation—his "destiny"—is with the evil father Darth Vader, and students repeatedly noted the strongly Oedipal pattern in this major narrative focus. Some pointed out that the phallic Jedi weapon given Luke by another father figure (Obi-Wan Kenobi) allows him to retaliate precisely for Darth's earlier symbolic castration of him (cutting off his right hand in an earlier encounter in *Star Wars*) by cutting off the same body-part from his father. Exploration of this configuration invites the students to consider just how "healthy" or "natural" an image of American family and gender roles are evoked by this particular myth, one which clearly was enormously popular.

At the same time they are made extremely uncomfortable by any discussion of the "male bonding" between Han Solo and Luke; and most found preposterous the idea that C3PO, with his high voice, slender, glitzy form, self-conscious display of his vast knowledge, and constant "maternal" chiding of his companion, the fellow droid R2D2, makes fun of a certain gay stereotype. The patronizing stereotype, however, of the "primitive" Ewoks, who mistake this fancy golden machine (C3PO) for a god, escaped no one. However, those students who attempted to analyze this juxtaposition of cultures tended to ignore any contemporary reference to the relations of "Third World" and "First World" in favor of a completely unhistoricized invocation of Lévi-Strauss's opposi-

tion between Nature and Culture. This response suggests some of
the difficulty of introducing an unfamiliar and powerful critical
model, then attempting to offer some qualification or critique of
that same model. If the students get it at all, they tend to adopt it
hook, line, and sinker.

Finally, *Superman* is particularly useful for stressing the histor-
icization of myth. Indeed, one might even say that the film is in
some sense about the historicity of myth. Beginning with a black-
and-white evocation of the original appearance of the comic strip
in 1938, the film constantly invites its older viewers to savor—
however ironically—the historical disjuncture between the ideology of the thirties and the realities of the late seventies. On the
simple narrative level the comedy of Clark Kent's befuddled
search for a phone booth, the traditional site of his quick-change
act to emerge as Superman, in an age when phone booths have
been replaced by little see-through plastic windshields, invites the
audience to register the change. Similarly, the comic irony of Lois
Lane's first comment on Clark Kent when she overhears him
arranging to have half his salary sent to his old mother in Kansas
("Are there any more like you back home?"—to which the answer
of course is a calculatedly simple "No") confronts an audience of
the "sophisticated" present with the unabashed "hoakieness" of
the original concept of Superman. Finally, in her penthouse patio
interview with Superman the full weight of the historical gap is
spelled out when Superman offers his famous credo, "Truth,
Justice, and the American Way." Lois comments, "You'd have to
come up against every politician in the country." An audience
which has lived through the hasty disappearance of Spiro Agnew
from the vice-presidency in the face of serious fraud charges, the
revelations of Watergate, the Saturday night "massacre" of the
special prosecutor, the resignation of Richard Nixon in the face of
certain impeachment, and the hasty pardon from his old ally
Gerald Ford is invited here to an ideological "recognition" that is
not entirely reassuring.

On the other hand, observing the reactions of students in the
eighties to this film suggests just how deeply the film's nostalgia
for what seemed the simpler politics of a bygone era anticipates
the willful simplemindedness of politics in the eighties. A younger
audience does not "get" the little ironic reminders of the changed
and corrupted present. They are inclined to participate in the
simple Manichaean dualism of criminals on the one side and good
policemen and prison wardens on the other. Nothing in the
explicit politics of the film undercuts the public role of Superman

as the helpful adjunct of the status quo, which, apart from Lois Lane's cynical comment cited above, is presented as unequivocally good.

However, the sexual politics of the film—especially with the aid of juxtaposition to comparable Greek myth—can suggest an historical slippage from the initial Superman "myth" that in turn sheds light on other sorts of politics. If one asks students for the nearest Greek parallel to Superman, it is usually only a matter of seconds before they bring up the name of Heracles. If then they are asked for the clearest differences between the two, especially if they have read Sophocles' *Trachiniae*, a perception of the radically different role of sex in the careers of the two heroes virtually imposes itself. The original conception of Superman relentlessly underlines his "real-life" repression as a shy Milquetoast, never able to communicate effectively with the ever-inaccessible Lois Lane.[36] As such he is the direct antithesis of the relentlessly sexual Heracles, whose hyperbolic sexual "accomplishments" included intercourse with fifty virgins in a single night, the murder of his host, and the destruction of an entire city to win the object of his lust. On the psychoanalytic level, both Heracles and Superman appear as classic instances of overcompensation in fantasy for the hopeless inadequacy of real-life performance. But whereas Heracles' violent ambivalence toward an organized social role is a key component of his traditional mythic interest, the Superman/Clark Kent of the comic book is the epitome of desexualized submission to the order of his society. A contradiction, however, emerges fairly clearly in the first Superman film and is made explicit in the second, when Superman has to surrender his superpowers to have intercourse with Lois Lane. It would appear that by 1978 some explicit sex is so crucial an element in selling a film—even one presumably directed primarily at a preteen audience—that the filmmakers had to scrap what is perhaps the single most essential feature of the original "mythic" conception, Superman's desexualization. Students who had studied Slater's analysis of the flying motif in the Perseus myth were quick to see the sexual symbolism of Superman's long flight with Lois. The use of his X-ray vision shortly before to indicate the color of Lois's underpants only confirmed the strategic departure from the wimpy Puritanism of the original "hero." Asking why these changes were necessary leads directly to questioning a society in which the overwhelmingly dominant ethical imperative is to make a profit— the American Way far more clearly than anything to do with Truth and Justice. It is the economic imperatives of film produc-

tion itself which in the last instance contradict both the loving
ironies of juxtaposed eras in the film and the unlovely nostalgia
for an era of overwhelming violence in support of simpleminded
pieties. Needless to say, the students were by no means inclined to
acquiesce passively in such a reading of the film. The point was
not simply to convince them of my own views of the film, but
rather to engage them in a level of critical questioning about
contemporary myths which for most of them was essentially absent from the rest of their education. As one student wrote on her
paper with obvious satisfaction: "For the first time, I've actually
thought about what is important to us as Americans, instead of
just sitting passively in front of a television screen and watching a
movie as I would normally do."

To sum up. If twentieth-century linguistic theory has taught us
anything, it is that meaning is not inherent in isolated objects of
perception but arises from a linguistically mediated system of
differences. I believe the same principle is relevant to the study of
cultures. A genuine appreciation and critical assimilation of classical culture is only possible within the framework of an explicit
juxtaposition to what it is *not,* a clear exploration of the ways
Greek culture *differs* from our own. This implies neither an
idealization of Greek values nor a naive chauvinism about our
own contemporary values. On the contrary, the responsibility to
contribute in whatever way we can to the formation of citizens
capable of full participation in a true democracy requires that we
take every opportunity to engage our students in an ongoing
critical dialogue with the received conglomerate of ideas, beliefs,
and ideological practices into which they are born and which are
constantly reinforced and adjusted both in most of their schooling
and in all forms of popular culture. To me, film seems a particularly fruitful vehicle for helping students assess the otherness
of Greek culture at the same time that they are empowered to use
that otherness to take a fresh look at their own culture. In particular, films which either use explicitly Greek mythic material or
offer self-consciously mythic narratives extrapolated from contemporary American culture offer teachers who are so inclined a
valuable tool for engaging their students in this critical enterprise.
Though my own inclinations have led me toward Freudian and
Marxist models of ideological critique, I do not think the pedagogical usefulness of juxtaposing films with ancient myths requires acceptance of those models—unless of course one accepts

the proposition that only these models provide a ground from which to engage in a *critical* dialogue with the culture surrounding us and which we as teachers must choose either to perpetuate or to interrogate.

NOTES

1. My thanks to Steven A. Nimis for comments and suggestions on an earlier draft of this essay. Thanks too to many perceptive students who have helped enlighten me over the years.
2. Henry A. Giroux, Roger I. Simon, and Contributors, *Popular Culture, Schooling, and Everyday Life* (Granby, Mass.: Bergin & Garvey, 1989), 221. I am grateful to Professor Giroux for kindly lending me his manuscript prior to publication.
3. See John J. Peradotto, "Myth and Other Languages: A Paedagogic Exercise, with a Preface on Interpretative Theory in the Undergraduate Classroom," *Classical World* 77 (1984):209–28. He begins his meditation on the problem of teaching theory in the classroom with an ironic allusion to the passing of a "Golden Age . . . in which classical mythology could be taught in innocent disregard of interpretative theory, by the simple dissemination of the data" (209).
4. On the issue of educating for citizenship see especially Henry A. Giroux, *Schooling and the Struggle for Public Life: Critical Pedagogy in the Modern Age* (Minneapolis: University of Minnesota Press, 1988), especially chap. 1, "Schooling, Citizenship, and the Struggle for Democracy," 3–36.
5. Bennett's general views may most clearly be seen in William Bennett, *A Nation at Risk: The Imperative for Educational Reform* (Washington, D.C.: United States Department of Education, 1983), report of The National Commission on Excellence in Education. See also Allan Bloom, *The Closing of the American Mind* (New York: Simon & Schuster, 1987). For some assessments of the pedagogical implications of such an agenda see Stanley Aronowitz and Henry Giroux, "Schooling, Culture, and Literacy in the Age of Broken Dreams: A Review of Bloom and Hirsch," *Harvard Educational Review* 58, no. 2 (May 1988):172–94, and in the same issue Peter L. McClaren, "Culture or Canon? Critical Pedagogy and the Politics of Literacy," 213–34.
6. Giroux has a succinct summary of the constituent elements, implications, and positions of this phenomenon in his *Schooling*, 220–21.
7. John P. Sullivan, "Editorial," *Arethusa* 8, no. 1 (1975):6.
8. Giroux, *Schooling*, 15, cites a recent survey: "The majority of young people in grades seven through twelve believed that some form of global catastrophe would take place in their lifetimes. [In] discussions with high school students across the country, very few of them believed that adults can effect any changes in democracy working as collective citizens. . . . None of them had studied an interpretation of history in which trade union struggles, civil rights struggles, or feminist struggles had any impact on changing the course of human history."
9. See Giroux, *Popular Culture*, 18: "The popular cannot be ignored because it points to a category of meanings and affective investments that shape the very identities, politics, and cultures of the students we deal with."
10. This point is made especially well by Lawrence Grossberg, "Teaching the Popular," in *Theory in the Classroom*, ed. Cary Nelson (Urbana: University of Illinois Press, 1986), 177–200. For a more radically skeptical view of the pleasure of spectacle in cinema see Dana B. Polan, "'Above All Else to Make You See': Cinema and the Ideology of Spectacle," in

Postmodernism and Politics, ed. Jonathan Arac (Minneapolis: University of Minnesota Press, 1986), 55–69.

11. Miami University is part of the Ohio state system, but its rural location and exclusive entrance mechanisms have brought an extremely homogenized, well-to-do, white middle-class student body. The proportion of minority students is among the lowest in the country at a tax-supported school.

12. Claude Lévi-Strauss, "The Structural Study of Myth," in his *Structural Anthropology,* trans. Claire Jacobson and Brooke Grundfest Schoepf (Garden City, N.Y.: Doubleday, 1967), 202–28. The familiar theme of the movement from *mythos* to *logos* has been set on a different footing from the simple progression envisioned by its original German propounders—e.g., Wilhelm Nestle, *Vom Mythos zum Logos,* 2d ed. (Stuttgart: Kröner, 1942; reprint, New York: Arno, 1978)—by the research of Milman Parry, *The Making of Homeric Verse,* ed. Adam Parry (Oxford: Oxford University Press, 1971), and Albert B. Lord, *The Singer of Tales* (New York: Atheneum, 1965) on the oral nature of Homeric verse.

13. Jungians include the enormously prolific Joseph Campbell and Erich Neumann. For bibliography and a brief assessment of these and others named in the text see John Peradotto, *Classical Mythology: An Annotated Bibliography* (Urbana, Ill.: American Philological Association, 1973).

14. See especially Eric A. Havelock's numerous works, in particular, *A Preface to Plato* (Cambridge: Harvard University Press, 1963), and *The Literate Revolution in Greece and Its Cultural Consequences* (Princeton: Princeton University Press, 1982).

15. Edward Tripp, *Crowell's Handbook of Classical Mythology* (New York: Crowell, 1970).

16. From the voluminous output of Sigmund Freud, I have usually assigned selections from *The Interpretation of Dreams,* vols. 4 and 5 of *The Standard Edition of the Complete Psychological Works of Sigmund Freud,* ed. James Strachey (London: Hogarth Press, 1953), and selections from *The Ego and the Id* (vol. 19). Bruno Bettelheim, *The Uses of Enchantment* (New York: Knopf, 1976) is a rather eclectic Freudian. I find his analysis of "Jack and the Beanstalk" (183–93) not only a relatively painless introduction to Freud but, because of his insightful use of the repetitions in the story, a nice anticipation of the approach of Lévi-Strauss. Philip E. Slater, *The Glory of Hera: Greek Mythology and the Greek Family* (Boston: Beacon Press, 1968), has an implicit historicizing dimension despite the primary emphasis on applying Freudian categories to ancient Greek myth.

17. See Lévi-Strauss, *Structural Anthropology,* 226.

18. I usually assign the famous essay by Bronislaw Malinowski, "Myth in Primitive Psychology" (1926), reprinted in his *Magic, Science, and Religion and Other Essays* (Garden City, N.Y.: Doubleday, 1955), and, under separate covers, as *Myth in Primitive Psychology* (Westport, Conn.: Negro Universities Press, 1971). For Marx I usually assign the selections and comments in Burton Feldman and Robert Richardson, *The Rise of Modern Mythology 1680–1860* (Bloomington: Indiana University Press, 1972), 426–504.

19. E.g., Giroux and Paul Smith in *Popular Culture,* chaps. 1 and 2.

20. I am well aware that perhaps a majority of classicists who know of Slater's work do not like it; and in general Freudian approaches to classical mythology have met with indifference at best, active scorn at worst. I doubt anything I could say in this context would convert the committed anti-Freudian, so I must address my brief comments to those willing to entertain the possibility that there is something of value in it. Personally I can only endorse Peradotto's assessment of Slater: "Classical specialists will find here and there points of misplaced emphasis over which to argue, but to merit the right to criticize Slater as he deserves they must be prepared to venture into his bailiwick at least as deeply as he has come into theirs" (*Classical Mythology,* 29).

21. These are not cited directly by Slater, but see *Glory of Hera,* 327. See also Richard S.

Caldwell, "The Blindness of Oedipus," *The International Review of Psychoanalysis* 1 (Spring 1974):207–18. The "equivalence of Oedipus and Teiresias" (208) is a key element in his analysis.

22. For alternative interpretations of the myth see Edward Phinney, Jr., "Perseus' Battle with the Gorgons," *Transactions of the American Philological Association* 102 (1971):445–63; Thalia Feldman, "Gorgo and the Origins of Fear," *Arion* 4, no. 3 (Autumn 1965):484–94; Hazel Barnes, "The Look of the Gorgon," in her *The Meddling Gods: Four Essays on Classical Themes* (Lincoln: University of Nebraska Press, 1974), 3–51. Cf. Slater, *Glory of Hera*, 318–19.

23. Slater, *Glory of Hera*, 333–36.

24. Heavily ironic review titles were typical: e.g., David Ansen, "Andromeda Strained," *Newsweek*, 6 July 1981, 75–76; Richard Corliss, "For Eyes Only," *Time*, 22 June 1981, 22; John Coleman, "Near Myth," *Statesman*, 3 July 1981, 22–24.

25. Ephraim Katz, *The Film Encyclopedia* (New York: Perigee, 1979), 311.

26. *Kraken* is a German word for a giant octopus. One appears in Jules Verne's novel *Twenty Thousand Leagues under the Sea*.

27. I recommend, however, for some basics James Monaco, *How to Read a Film: The Art, Technology, Language, History, and Theory of Film and Media*, rev. ed. (New York: Oxford University Press, 1981), and Bill Nichols, *Ideology and the Image: Social Representation in Cinema and Other Media* (Bloomington: Indiana University Press, 1981). See also *Movies and Methods: An Anthology*, ed. Bill Nichols (Berkeley: University of California Press, 1976), and *Movies and Methods, Vol. II: An Anthology* (Berkeley: University of California Press, 1985) as well as *Studies in Entertainment: Critical Approaches to Mass Culture*, ed. Tania Modleski (Bloomington: Indiana University Press, 1986).

28. A study done in 1972 of the amount of time spent on child care in twelve countries came up with the startling conclusion that American fathers spend an average of *twelve minutes per day* on child care. See Carol Travis and Carole Wade, *The Longest War: Sex Difference in Perspective*, 2d ed. (San Diego: Harcourt Brace Jovanovich, 1984), 287. One would like to believe there has been a dramatic improvement since that date, but there is room for doubt. Travis and Wade found the same twelve-minute figure in a 1978 study and comparable evidence in one from 1983. I am indebted to Judith de Luce for bringing this data to my attention.

29. I allude here in particular to Freud's 1919 essay, "The 'Uncanny'," *Complete Works*, 17:217–52.

30. For a nuanced attempt to confront the ahistoricism of Freud while retaining some of Freud's insights see Page DuBois, *Sowing the Body: Psychoanalysis and Ancient Representations of Women* (Chicago: University of Chicago Press, 1988).

31. For an intriguing, if rather fanciful, attempt to reconstruct an historical Perseus see Cornelia Steketee Hulst, *Perseus and the Gorgon* (La Salle, Ill.: Open Court, 1946). In the wake of Martin Bernal, *Black Athena* (New Brunswick: Rutgers University Press, 1987), the attempt to find an Egyptian connection seems somewhat less fanciful. For the more blatant political uses of myth among the Greeks see Martin P. Nilsson, *Cults, Myths, Oracles, and Politics in Ancient Greece* (New York: Cooper Square Publishers, 1972). For the Mycenaean foundations of Greek myths see his *The Mycenaean Origin of Greek Mythology* (Berkeley: University of California Press, 1972).

32. See Claude Lévi-Strauss, *The Raw and the Cooked: Introduction to a Science of Mythology: I*, trans. John and Doreen Weightman (New York: Harper & Row, 1969), 12.

33. See Nichols' discussion of "The Aesthetics and Politics of Recognition" in *Ideology and the Image*, 36–42.

34. See his famous essay, "Ideology and Ideological State Apparatuses: Notes towards an Investigation," in his *Lenin and Philosophy*, trans. Ben Brewster (New York: Monthly

Review Press, 1971), 127–86, where he spells out how educational, cultural, and political institutions constantly present us with invitations to define ourselves in terms favorable to the interests of those institutions.

35. Obviously much of what I say about *Return of the Jedi* holds true of the earlier film *Star Wars* (1977), which inspired former President Reagan to dub the Soviet Union the "evil empire" and his critics in turn to dub his fantasy-ridden Strategic Defense Iniative precisely "Star Wars." My choice of the later film is partly the fortuitous consequence of its being popular at the time I was working out my approach to myth and partly due to the greater complexities arising from the presence of the Ewoks and the more elaborate focus on the Rebellion.

36. I am indebted to Bobby Seale, former leader of the Black Panther Party, for first bringing to my attention this aspect of Superman in an address delivered at Yale University in 1970.

Classical Gods and the Demonic in Film

Frederick Ahl

Cornell University

T HE number of English-language films in which we find Zeus, Jupiter, or others of the Greco-Roman pantheon present in person is limited indeed. Most, at least until 1977, are listed in Jon Solomon's thorough *The Ancient World in the Cinema*, still the only complete survey of classical themes in film.[1] Yet the absence of Greco-Roman deities should not surprise us. Hollywood has traditionally shied away from substantial treatments of gods in whatever form, as Andrew Greeley observed in his well-known article: "Why Hollywood Never Asks the God Question."[2] The widespread hostile reaction to Martin Scorsese's film of Nikos Kazantzakis's *The Last Temptation of Christ* reminds us how fragile and sensitive religious feelings are. And Salman Rushdie's critique on Islam in *The Satanic Verses* has left him in hiding, under sentence of death by the Iranians.

Nonetheless, Cecil B. DeMille's great "religious" epics do tackle the "god question" to at least some extent, although John May objects that DeMille's *The Ten Commandments*, "for all its literal fidelity to the Book of Exodus, does little more than create the impression that God is the Divine Impresario."[3] But even construing God as a Divine Impresario offers an answer of sorts. It makes God a mirror image of the artist, a notion that can claim a certain scriptural authority from Genesis. There is no doubt, however, that DeMille pursues a more cautious path in the later version than in the original where, following the example of D. W. Griffith's *Intolerance*, he relates the story from Exodus to the breakdown of morality in modern times. Such overt parallelism was more inadvisable in the social and political environment of America in the 1950s than it had been in the teens, twenties, and thirties, when American film was a major voice in social and political comment. In the days of Senator McCarthy, such comment could get one into deep trouble.[4]

40

Ingmar Bergman, in the more safely secular atmosphere of Sweden, asked the "god question" more often than most film-makers in the 1950s and 1960s. Usually his complaint was, as in *The Silence* (1962), about the failure of God to respond to humans. His artistic, questioning agnosticism recalls that of the priest Ab-salon in Carl Theodor Dreyer's *Day of Wrath* (1943):

> *Absalon.* Look at the sky, the clouds . . . they're like some strange writing on the wall.
> *Parish Clerk.* It's the Lord's hand that writes.
> *Absalon.* But where is he who can read the writing?[5]

Bergman, in fact, projects his own despair about the futility of life and of the quest for God not only onto the screen but back into his reading of ancient literature. Of Euripides' *Bacchae* he observes: "Euripides' weighty sculpture represents mankind, the gods and the world in merciless and meaningless movement beneath an empty sky."[6]

In his autobiography, *The Magic Lantern,* Bergman discusses his film for television, *From the Life of the Marionettes* (1980), that he carved (like a steak, he says) from an unsuccessful six-hour film-script. Part of the material jettisoned from the original script, he notes, was a paraphrase of Ovid's narrative of Philemon and Baucis (*Metamorphoses* 8.611–724), which he had inserted "as a counterweight to the basic structure." His decision to scrap the Ovidian paraphrase seems also to be a rejection of what he takes to be Ovid's fantastical optimism. Ovid's story, we will recall, tells of Jupiter wandering in disguise upon earth and being hospitably received by an old couple, Philemon and Baucis. In return for their kindness he grants them their wish not to be separated at death. "The god," Bergman declares, "responds to their wish and turns them into a huge tree to shade the farm." The rub is, however, Bergman continues, that although "my wife and I live near each other . . . I have no means of describing our af-finity. . . . one problem is insoluble. One day the blow will fall and separate us. No friendly god will turn us into a tree to shade the farm."[7]

Bergman's agnosticism is an angry, unsatisfied hunger for god (or gods), not a rejection of god. And he has oversimplified Ovid, whose Jupiter is anything but a "friendly god" on the whole, and whose transformation of Philemon and Baucis' farm into a temple honoring himself is hardly an unselfish act of generosity. Ar-boreal metamorphosis, too, is something of a mixed blessing.

THE DEMONIC AND THE MAGICIAN

Demons have, on the whole, been easier to find and to treat than God or gods. In a powerful scene in *The Seventh Seal* (1957), Bergman's Knight takes the opportunity to question a fourteen-year-old girl, condemned as a witch, whether she is really in league with the devil. "Why do you ask?" she inquires of him. "I too want to meet him," the Knight explains. "Why?" the poor child Tyan persists. "I want to ask him about God," the Knight adds, "He, if anyone, must know."[8] American directors, too, usually approach the "god question," if they approach it at all, through the devil. Europeans and Americans have fewer problems accepting the reality of the devil even when they have doubts about God. May suggests that "the demon as person is all but absent from normative American literature."[9] Yet he and the forces of evil are vividly (and often appealingly) present in Marlowe's or Goethe's Mephistopheles, not to mention Milton's Satan. Christianity, once clear of theologians, retains a strongly dualist, Manichean base with a clear sense of the devil.

Film has always had a particular affinity for the demonic. In its earliest days, film was, in its own way, a kind of sorcery or magic, and thus evoked strong and sometimes negative reactions to its morality. Indeed, it was traveling magicians, the masters of optical and other illusion such as Carl Hertz, who often introduced audiences around the world to film. Yet Erik Barnouw notes: "The role of the magician in early cinema has been neglected by film scholars . . . Many people find it difficult to think of film in the context of magic. But the first viewers . . . knew they were seeing things that could not be. . . . They knew they were seeing magic." For this reason, magicians were careful to ensure that their audiences understood they were witnessing tricks, not miracles: the magicians were not really raising demons or ghosts. Barnouw adds: "the transfer to the screen of the magician's most sensational illusions . . . proved ultimately catastrophic for magicians. Anyone with a camera and a splicer could produce the same miracles, and did."[10] The innovator, of course, needed to be cautious about his secrets. That modern cinematic master of special effects, Ray Harryhausen (on whom more later), describes himself as a magician who guards his techniques carefully: "You'll no longer be interested in a magician if he gives away all of his secrets."[11] Time and advancing technology, of course, eventually betray the magician's secrets. The demonic special effects of early film often seem ludicrous nowadays, since general understanding of what technical magic does (if not of what it is and how it works) eventually catches up with the special effects artists of film as it does with practitioners of stage magic and unveils the "illusion." When we look back at past film "magic," therefore, it is necessary to see it with a certain historical sympathy.

The stage masters of magic lanterns and other visual illusions "laid the foundations for the field of 'special effects' in the modern cinema."[12] Sometimes their influence was even more general and powerful. Bergman attests to the influence exercised on him by the magic lantern pictures and by the devil they brought before his eyes when he was a child:

> The devil became an early acquaintance, and, in the way of a child, it was necessary to render him concrete. It was here the magic lantern came in, a little tin box with a kerosene lamp (I can still remember the smell of hot sheet metal) and the gaily colored glass slides. Little Red Riding Hood and the Wolf, among others. And the wolf was the devil, a devil without horns, but with a tail and wide, red jaws, strangely tangible, but still impalpable, the very representative of evil and seduction on the nursery's flowery wallpaper.[13]

In *Fanny and Alexander* (1982), a film which, he says, "most directly draws on my own childhood memories," Bergman makes a place of special importance for the magic lantern. And, not surprisingly, he has entitled his autobiography *Laterna Magica*.[14] One of his most powerful films of the sixties, *Ansiktet* (*The Face* or *The Magician* [1958]), shows how delicate the line can be between religious imposture and technical wizardry when it comes to the magician's magic lantern. "Our *laterna magica*," a character protests, is "a ridiculous and harmless toy."[15] Yet the master of magic acquires a following of believers, regardless of his protests, and sometimes becomes a believer himself. Even the skeptical host in *The Magician* is disappointed to learn that everything is no more than a cheap trick.

Although film can, magically, "realize" the demonic, it can also leave its audience uncertain as to why the demonic is being realized. Is it just "for effect," to frighten us, or does it convey some deeper thoughts on the nature of life as it did in the hands of the German expressionists in the years following the first world war?[16] The monsters of the horror films, endowed with subhuman instincts and superhuman power, can be, as they are in Robert Louis Stevenson's *Dr. Jekyll and Mr. Hyde,* an expression of the struggle between what Plato described in the *Republic* as the rational and the tyrannical elements in the human soul. The tyrannical elements are, Socrates says:

Those that awaken when we sleep . . . when one part of our soul is at
rest—the part that approaches things reasonably and verbally, with
gentle clarity, the part that rules the other element of the soul. That
other element is like a wild and ferocious animal, gorged on food and
drink. It leaps up, pushes sleep away from it, and goes off on a lively
search to satisfy the call of its particular nature. You know it is bold
and stops at nothing at these times: for it is freed from—and unbur-
dened by—morality and thought. Its lust, in fantasy, does not shrink
at intercourse with its mother or with anything human, divine, or
animal. It will kill anything and has no taboos against any kind of
food. To put it in one succinct statement: it will stop at nothing we
would regard as mindless or disgusting.[17]

Film has greater power than any other artistic medium to represent the irrational, tyrannic soul in its most grotesque manifesta-
tions, to show us both the external and the internal demons of our
dreams, fantasies, and societies.

Robin Wood argues (wrongly, I think) that "what the horror
film now insists upon is the *impossibility* (not just desirability) of a
society founded upon monogamy and family and their inherent
repressiveness."[18] Wood adduces, by way of example, Larry Cohen's *Demon* (first released in 1982 as *God Told Me To*), which tells
of a detective, reared a strict Catholic, who has both a mistress and
a wife. The detective, as he investigates a series of apparently
random killings of people who are themselves assassins, traces
them to the inspiration of a young god, born of a human virgin
impregnated by light from a spacecraft. He also discovers, however, that he himself is another "god" of the same kind—though
in him the supernatural force has been repressed by his Catholic
upbringing. He kills or seems to kill his unrepressed "brother"
god, and ends convicted of murder, repeating as explanation of
his motive the phrase used earlier by each of the assassins: "God
told me to."

The god is conceived as both beautiful and vicious. Cohen
compares him to "the snake of D. H. Lawrence's famous poem . . .
associated with danger, energy, and fire—with forces that society
cannot encompass and therefore decrees must be destroyed."[19]
The classicist will surely also see in that god born of a flame the
Dionysos of Euripides' *Bacchae*. Cohen's detective, like Euripides'
Pentheus, discovers his bisexuality through his ultimately destructive encounter with the god. Yet in Cohen's film the Pentheus
figure destroys the Dionysos figure: the force of repression is
greater than that of the dangerous energy it confronts. The
young god whom the protagonist kills is a curiously androgynous
being whose complete bisexuality justifies, even in a Catholic

sense, his sexual allure to a man. Although the god's appearance is male he is, simultaneously, sexually female—he has a vagina and a womb and invites the detective to father his child. Wood comments: "The new world envisaged is, by implication, a world in which the division of sexual roles will cease to exist."[20]

I would state the matter differently: Cohen has created a kind of Ovidian fantasy, a male version of the tale of Iphis and Ianthe, which legitimizes homosexual love by making it, miraculously, sexually productive. In Ovid, the female Iphis, who has been raised as if she were a boy, falls in love with, and eventually marries, a girl named Ianthe. The goddess Isis transforms Iphis into a man on her wedding night so the marriage can be consummated.[21] Since the Church declares the purpose of sex to be procreation, the invitation to procreate (rather than simply to indulge in sexual gratification) endows a relationship with a kind of sanctity even when both partners appear to be of the same sex.

Cohen's protagonist, however, finally kills the Dionysian "god figure." Repression triumphs. Thus the detective resembles Ovid's Cinyras, rather than Ovid's Iphis. Cinyras is enticed into an affair with a young girl who, he is told, is the same age as his daughter, Myrrha, but eventually finds out that his lover is, in fact, Myrrha herself. In response to his discovery he attempts to destroy his daughter, the object of his socially unsanctioned sexual passion, and becomes, like Cohen's detective, an agent of the very repression he does not wish to admit openly to himself.[22] Hence Wood, I think, misses the point when he suggests that the horror film, such as Cohen's *Demon*, shows the *impossibility* of a society based on repressive family structures. On the contrary, the horror film generally shows the inescapability of such structures, and reasserts the suppression of the irrational, sleeping, "tyrannic" soul, to use Plato's image, by the waking, rational soul: Dr. Van Helsing triumphs (yet again) over Dracula. As Bergman points out: "The *Bacchae* bears witness to the courage to break the moulds."[23] The horror film, generally, does not.

Nonetheless Cohen's *Demon* is an attack on Christian monotheism and on the assumption of God's masculinity and goodness. While there may be, in horror films, some sort of talismanic power in Christian symbols, as we see again and again in the protection afforded to potential victims of Dracula by the sign of the cross, the cross is certainly no *more* effective against the Dracula of film than, perhaps not even as effective as, folk remedies such as wreaths of garlic, or the universal power of the living sunrise, which forces the mythic and demonic back into its subservience to daylight, history, logic, and time. The Dracula of film is not so much a reincarnation of the notorious Romanian king, Vlad the Impaler, nor even of Bram Stoker's curious villain, as he is a kind of countergod, a darker interpretation of Christ, who offers his own version of eternal life in a communion of blood: a different and more macabre restatement of "the resurrection of the body."

The fascination the Dracula of film exercises over the pure maiden chosen as his bride or "victim" becomes a strong indication of the seductive power of evil and night fantasy in the dark irrational side of even the most conventionally virginal and chaste heroine: the awakening of Plato's tyrannical soul. The heroine responds to Dracula's biting kiss, as in Werner Herzog's *Nosferatu the Vampyre*, with a look of carnal pleasure which is, of course, reconciled with her more "normal," waking, repressed behavior, on the grounds that she is in a dreaming or mesmerized state: not fully in control of herself.

We should also remember that ancient Greek and Roman tragedy both make use of the idea that there is a kinship between the human sacrifice of a virgin and the ritual of marriage. In Euripides' *Iphigenia in Aulis* and Seneca's *Trojan Women*, for example, the pretext for the sacrifice of the virgins Iphigenia and Polyxena is marriage with Achilles—in Polyxena's case, a posthumous marriage, since Achilles is already dead.[24] Ancient dramatists, particularly Seneca, were well aware of the curious sexuality of death. When, in *Phaedra*, Hippolytus rejects his stepmother's sexual overtures and threatens to kill her with his sword as a sacrifice to Diana, the goddess of the hunt and of chastity, Phaedra reacts with pleasure:

> Hippolytus, you consummate my dreams,
> cure my madness. Yet in my wildest dreams
> I never thought I'd loose my soul in death
> beneath your grip, yet keep my chastity.[25]

Sometimes, too, the sacrificer may be drawn to, even overcome by, the beauty of his victim, much as Satan is in Milton's *Paradise Lost* 9.465–66, when he sees Eve and loses, albeit temporarily, his evil:

> Stupidly good, of enmity disarm'd,
> Of guile, of hate, of envy, of revenge . . . .

Satan is, as Irene Samuel points out, "disarmed . . . of all that makes him Satan" at this moment.[26]

The elements which make Dracula a counter-Christ make him Satanic—and thus not altogether different from the pagan Pluto, god of the dead, or, rather, the pagan Pluto as viewed by medieval Christianity.[27] In Dante's *Divine Comedy*, the lower city of `hell, Satan's fortress, is *la città c' ha nome Dite*, "the city which is named Dis" (*Inferno* 8.68). And Dis, of course, is one of the several Roman names for the more familiar Pluto and Hades of mythological handbooks.[28] Dis' fortified city is, in fact, the center of the universe: "è 'l punto dell' universo," as Dante's Vergil explains to him (*Inferno* 11.64–65).

The pagan Pluto or Dis, however forbidding he and his world may be, however much he prides himself in his own pitilessness, sometimes has a compassion and understanding that extend beyond that of gods above. In the *Thebaid*, the epic written by Statius, Dante's guide to purgatory in the *Divine Comedy*, a seer, Amphiaraus, begs Pluto to pity him and be *better than* the gods (*Thebaid* 8.119–20). The stern Pluto "accepts his plea, but hates himself for being moved" (*Thebaid* 8.123). Perhaps he, like Milton's Satan, is being "stupidly good." But it is this involuntary goodness that so often humanizes a Prince of Darkness, be it Pluto or Dracula, and makes him at least more appealing, if not, as Amphiaraus hopes, better than the gods of light.

TRAGIC GODS

Larry Cohen does no more than other directors when he combines the genres of detective fiction and science fiction with the monstrous and the religious to give us the horror film. Overtones of classical divinities are understandably present. The pre-Christian religions of Greece and Rome with their goddesses and gods, embodying evil as well as good and tolerating, even assuming, homosexual attraction and activity, naturally provide the modern Western world with a model for social and sexual mores more open than the Judeo-Christian model of male monotheism and heterosexuality. Hence the shadows of Apollo and Dionysos in *Demons*. Christianity never did wrench the world of astrology and astronomy from Greco-Roman pluralist hands. It left the zodiac untouched (and even unadjusted to the Gregorian calendar). While chasing the Roman gods from their earthly temples, Christianity left them firmly in command of the skies. Scientists added further mythic figures to the heavens with new astronomical discoveries and named the spacecraft which explored the solar system after classical deities, not Christian saints: Saturn, Apollo.

Scientific thought has sought and found its vocabulary, its essential pluralism, among the ancient Greeks—what Gary Zukav calls the preference for the "both/and" to the Christian (and Kierkegaardian) binary opposition of "either/or."[29] Science, it might be argued, never really lost sight of the pluralistic universe: that loss of vision occurred among philosophers, humanists, and theologians who sought to separate God or gods from phenomena. As the twentieth century began, Planck, Einstein, Bohr, and Heisenberg brought pagan pluralism back to physics, rediscovered the disorder beneath apparent order. Annette Kuhn observes: "The courtship, successful or otherwise, of cinema by science at a certain historical moment may be seen as a bid to advance the epistemological claims of science against those of religion."[30]

Neither scientist nor filmmaker has any particular quarrel with the old gods, who have a very modern "feel" about them. It is Christianity that seems rooted in the dust of the past, the world of ox carts, galleys, and amphitheaters, rather than the Olympian pantheon. The determined struggle of Christian apologists to establish the historicity of Jesus has, ironically, trapped him in antiquity, at least in the popular mind. DeMille's biblical epics pit a rustic Christianity against a mechanized, materialistic, and modern Rome. And what enables Ben-Hur to survive, before ever he feels the "touch" of religion, is not only his determination to have his revenge but also the love and admiration bestowed upon him by his adoptive, skeptically pagan Roman father, the consul Arrius.

If, then, the old gods are those of modern science or of skeptical civilization, why do we not see more direct portrayals of them in American or European film? We may, in part, find the answer in the reductionist views of Greek and Roman myth, exemplified by Bergman's sense that Ovid's Jupiter is a "friendly god," which treat them as generally innocuous, fairy-tale creatures with magical powers. We classicists are largely responsible for such misapprehensions. As the twentieth century ends, we are just beginning to discover Einstein and Heisenberg—and still teach the ancient gods as relics of a primitive, pluralistic past rightly superseded by the binary monism of Christianity or (until recently) Marx. Zeus as a persona is, like DeMille's Old-Testament God, a Great Impresario in the sky, most notable for his spectacular destructive outbursts.

Filmmakers deeply versed in the classics approach the gods

reluctantly, even in the films made of or around Greek tragedy. With the exception of the two Greek Prometheus films, *Prometheus in Chains* (1927) and *Prometheus Second Person Singular* (1975), no tragedy filmed in performance or adapted for the screen has any gods. The closest would be Chiron the Centaur in Pasolini's *Medea* (1970). In Jules Dassin's *Phaedra* (1961), where deities might be expected, "the gods," Kenneth McKinnon comments, "are only statuary and not overtly mentioned."[31] In Michael Cacoyannis's *Iphigenia* (1976), perhaps the most dramatically successful film based on Greek tragedy, the closest we come to god is the sinister priest Calchas, who seems to have devised his own oracles through motives of personal vengeance against Agamemnon and who appears to represent, at least partially, the Greek Orthodox Church upset at the seizure of its properties by the state rather than anything in Greek tragedy. Indeed, the gods and priests of Greek tragedy, when interpreted for the screen, seem more Roman than Greek, more Senecan than Euripidean, the by-product of an agnostic, intellectual pessimism. Bergman comments:

> I lack the means of imagining the moment of separation. As I am neither able nor willing to imagine another life, some kind of life beyond the frontier, the perspective is appalling. From a somebody I will become a nobody. That nobody will not even have the memory of an affinity.[32]

The thought and the intensity of this expression recall the despairing chorus of Seneca's *Trojan Women* when they meditate on death:

> Death cannot be divided:
> it destroys the body,
> does not spare the soul—
>
> There is no Hell, no savage god who rules the dead,
> no guardian dog to hinder your escape—
> These are just idle folktales, empty words,
> myth, woven into nightmare—
>
> "Where will I lie when I am dead?" you ask—
>
> You will lie among things never born.[33]

THE EPIC GODS

While modern treatment of ancient tragedy avoids the gods, the divinities of ancient epic have enjoyed a rather prominent existence. Two English-language films almost twenty years apart give us perhaps the best visual sense of Olympus in film: *Jason and the Argonauts* (1963) and *Clash of the Titans* (1981). Both were based on screenplays by the British writer Beverley Cross (in collaboration with Jan Read, in the case of *Jason*). Both were under British direction (Don Chaffey and Desmond Davis, respectively) and have predominantly British casts, yet both have a strongly American flavor, and not just because they were released through Columbia Pictures and United Artists. Their "heroes" are played by Americans: Todd Armstrong is Jason, and the ultimate Californian, Harry Hamlin, is Perseus.

The contrast between the British environment and the American intruder-hero is particularly effective in *Clash of the Titans*, whose Olympus is, with the exception of Ursula Andress, the Olympus of the English stage and theater, with Zeus played by the late Sir Laurence Olivier, Thetis by Maggie Smith, Hera by Claire Bloom, and Flora Robson as one of the Graiae. The less populous Olympus of *Jason and the Argonauts* is similarly British, with Niall MacGinnis as Zeus, Michael Gwynn as Hermes, and Honor Blackman as Hera. In a broad, artistic sense, the opposition of British gods and American heroes is an interesting comment on the theatrical tradition of the English-speaking world, whose traditions and whose dominant actors were so long British. British stage traditions define, to a large extent, the theatrical norms in terms of which the young American must succeed. Thus form and tradition are themselves, in a sense, controlling forces, gods which govern the actions of those who agree to be players. They are, as Pindar says, the "law which is ruler of all things."

There is, then, a delicious irony in Jason's constant denial of the reality of the gods in *Jason and the Argonauts*, even when he is, quite literally, in the hands of one of them. The American who defies tradition is following it even as he defies it. He is a *contemptor deorum*, a "despiser of the gods," as is Mezentius in Vergil's *Aeneid* or Capaneus in Statius' *Thebaid*. But a despiser of the gods is no atheist. In order to challenge them, he must acknowledge their existence.

The divine exists on two distinct levels in these films. Most obviously, there is the bright, beautiful, anthropomorphic, Olympian world. Separate from but akin to it is the world of the monstrous and deformed, linked with the world of the dead and their power. This second world is seen more clearly in *Clash of the Titans* than in *Jason and the Argonauts*. And it is in this world of the divine and monstrous that the films particularly excel, thanks to the artistry of the other American elements in the films: the special effects of Ray Harryhausen in collaboration with producer Charles Schneer. Both men are pioneers in what is usually called superdynamation: the use of animated puppet figures in sequences with real actors, as distinct from cel animation, the more familiar Walt Disney variety. They are the heirs of the magicians whose "trick" photography and use of models dazzled audiences during the infancy of film.[34] Richard Meyers, in *The World of Fantasy Films*, calls Harryhausen the "model animation dean."[35] There is no question that *Jason and the Argonauts* is, as Jon Solomon observed, "best known for the superb effects of Ray Harryhausen. Thanks to him, the film surpasses all others in recreating the fantastic aspects of Greek myth."[36] Until *Clash of the Titans*, we should now add. Nor should we underrate the artistic ingenuity of his magic even though, since the "Star Wars" films, techniques have advanced further in details if not always in quality of conception. In *Jason and the Argonauts* "the complex sword fight between seven skeletons and three live actors took four and one half months to animate. Harryhausen sometimes finished as few as *thirteen frames* a day."[37]

Harryhausen is not only an expert in superdynamation but also a professional sculptor who, in a Promethean sense, probably has a better feeling for the complex artistic relationship between gods and men than most of us do. In *Jason and the Argonauts* there are numerous shots of humans approaching huge statues of the gods and praying to them. The film's gods, true to their ancient models, do not necessarily protect their suppliants, although they punish those who violate the sanctity of shrines. Acrisius, Jason's grandfather, errs because he believes that since the gods have permitted him to get away with many crimes they must therefore approve his actions completely.

Thanks, however, to Harryhausen's influence, the comment on the relationship of gods to man in *Jason and the Argonauts* is more that of the sculptor than the moralist. Perhaps the best illustration of my point is the sequence showing Jason visiting, as a tourist might, a temple with ruined columns and a fallen statue of Hermes. Jason, we realize, belongs to *our* world and *our* time. He is a young American tourist in the world of myth, naive and unsure of himself, but not unlearned. He recognizes the identity of the gigantic bronze at his feet and says the name, "Hermes," aloud. A person we take to be a priest in attendance seems to think Jason is calling on Hermes, not simply naming him. And the tone of the priest's response is ambiguous enough to suggest that he may himself be Hermes in some mortal form, as proves to be the case shortly afterwards when he becomes Hermes and grows to full, "divine" size.

Jason, having been accorded a view of Hermes in his hugeness as a god, is transported to an Olympus which is as architecturally perfect as the earthly shrine is ruined and imperfect. It is built in heavenly white, its columns and buildings intact. The effect recalls Lucian's ancient burlesque, *Zeus the Opera Star (Zeus Tragôidopoios):* it is mortal statues, buildings, and beliefs that are in ruins, not the gods themselves and the ideas they represent. And while men make models of the gods to worship or destroy, the gods make models of men. Zeus, we find, has not only been watching human characters from above through a reflecting pool suggestive of closed-circuit television monitors, but has been playing a kind of chess game with Hera. Jason, after arriving on Olympus, is discovered to be the missing piece in the game. Suddenly he sees that he now is an artifact, albeit an independent-minded one. There is, then, at least some free will within the overall deterministic structure.

As Zeus sends Jason away, he gives him a small clay model of a god which is as small in Jason's hand as he is in Hermes'. Later, threatened by the Clashing Rocks and despairing of, indeed disgusted with, the gods, Jason hurls the model into the water. There it is transformed into a huge Poseidon, complete with crown and fishy tail, who holds the rocks apart in one of the film's most spectacular moments. Those tempted to react with a sneer to this invention might first recall the even more spectacular appearance of Neptune in Vergil's *Aeneid* (1.124–56) who emerges from the sea in his chariot and scuds over the waves prying ships from the rocks with his trident.

In *Jason and the Argonauts*, then, as in the *Aeneid*, man is simultaneously greater and smaller than the gods. In *Aeneid* 1.102–24, the winds despatched by Aeolus on Juno's orders try to smash Aeneas' fleet upon the rocks appropriately enough called Altars *(Arae)*. But when Aeneas and his men land, after being saved by Neptune's intervention, they take up the implements for grinding their grain, their cereal, and roast Ceres, then pound her on a rock to make bread (*Aeneid* 1.177–79):

> Next, exhausted by events, they hurry to set out
> first Ceres, ravaged by the waves, then weapons to attack
> the cereal grain. So having saved earth's fruit they now prepare
> to roast it upon flames and crack it open upon rock.

Once the men have finished cooking, we find them "poured *(fusi)* across the grass" and filling themselves with "old Bacchus" *(Aeneid* 1.214–15). Scholarly convention since ancient times dismisses such usage as metonymy: the usages are nothing more than "poetic" diction for "grain" and "wine," respectively.[38] But the vigorous language of their contexts reinforces the full power of the underlying concepts: Ceres is violently attacked; the men who drink "Bacchus" are themselves "poured" upon the grass. The god is identical with what it represents.

What classicists may perceive as Harryhausen's "exaggerated" representation of Greek and Roman divinities arises mostly from our scholarly tendency toward minimalist reading and interpretation of ancient epic language. Harryhausen shares with Vergil and Ovid the notion that god is as much an artifact of man as man is an artifact of god.[39] What makes his Jason a hero is that he is specially selected by Zeus for the task he is to perform and is endowed with the power to create a god from a model. Indeed, it is hard to resist the thought that Harryhausen and Schneer are commenting on their own artistic works as well as recreating myth. For they know perfectly well that to obtain their special effects of superdynamation they must work with multiple models of different sizes: at some moments the good ship Argo must be a toy in the hand of the giant Talos, at others, a large vessel containing not only heroes but a talking figurehead of the goddess Hera herself.

In *Jason and the Argonauts* the gods are, on the whole, kindly if somewhat absentminded and negligent, much as they are in Apollonius' *Argonautica*. Zeus and Hera have an amiably bourgeois—and thus competitive—relationship. Hermes seems quite benign. Zeus keeps an occasionally watchful eye on chosen humans through his Olympian reflecting pool. True, these gods sometimes fail to prevent humans from criminal acts, but ultimately we are left with a strong sense that men choose their own destinies. There is little to suggest the darker order of divine power except in the kingdom of the treacherous Aeetes, king of Colchis.

In *Clash of the Titans*, Beverley Cross, now writing on his own, shows man almost entirely at the mercy of the gods and the destinies they devise for him. The gods are less agreeable, and the metaphors of their relationships with humans are harsher. Men are punished and deformed because of the private rivalries of Zeus and Hera and for the sins of the gods themselves. There is no sense of personal concern on their part for men. Zeus, we learn, has loved Danae and fathered Perseus. But it is hard to imagine that this unrelenting, aloof, and humorless tyrant could find room for any passion but anger. Zeus reshapes, controls, and destroys mankind through his models, which are arranged in little niches in his Olympian "office." His set is that of a theater where the director rules supreme, not a cosmic chessboard with regulated moves as in *Jason and the Argonauts*. And he is prepared to release more demonic, subhuman forces than his counterpart did in the earlier film.

The Zeus of *Clash of the Titans* is more suggestive of the Roman epic Jupiter than of the Greek god. He sits high above the other gods on a lofty throne, ready, as in Ovid's or Statius' supreme deity in the first books of the *Metamorphoses* and the *Thebaid*, to create or unleash the bestial, to use the forces of nature to overwhelm entire cities when his will is flouted. His consort Hera is not pleasant and "wifely," as in *Jason and the Argonauts*, but a cold and bitter opponent who berates him for his bias, just as her counterpart rails at Jupiter in Statius' *Thebaid* (1.250–82). Like Statius' divine queen, Hera proves every bit as cruel as her husband and uses her powers to thwart her husband's will for as long as she can. When Zeus deforms Hera's son, Calibos, pledged to marry Andromeda, she retaliates by forcing Andromeda's suitors to answer a riddle posed by Calibos. When Andromeda's suitors fail, as they invariably do until Perseus arrives, they are publicly burned to death. Perseus' success in solving the riddle with divine help adds a nice touch from the Oedipus tradition. But Calibos, unknown to Greco-Roman tradition, seems to be derived from the deformed Caliban of Shakespeare's *The Tempest*, the would-be lover of Prospero's daughter, Miranda, Calibos' cruel treatment by the gods gives us a certain sympathy for him, or at least a sense that his anger and brutality have comprehensible and explicable causes. He does love Andromeda, who seems to have returned his affection before his transformation into a monster.

Given the tyranny and injustice of Zeus and the destiny he claims to serve, a sense of man's isolation and helplessness permeates *Clash of the Titans*. Perseus does not choose his heroic destiny, he has it thrust upon him and must encounter most of the dangers alone. He faces a darker and more forbidding world than Jason, who is always surrounded by adventuresome, "heroic" companions. True, Jason must fight with a Hydra to gain the Golden Fleece, contend with the "Sown Men" that spring from the serpent's teeth, and overwhelm the tormenting, but not lethal, Harpies. Yet his struggles are in the open and in daylight, not in the darker reaches that Perseus must explore.

Perseus must "break," at night, the marvelous winged horse Pegasus in one of the film's most surprising sequences, replete with visual "quotations" from the Western.[40] In his search for the Gorgon Medusa, he must cross in a Felliniesque sunset to the Land of the Dead in a boat manned by a skeletal Charon, he must politely meet the gruesome Graiae, who are given humorous touches of Macbethian witchdom, he must confront and kill a ferociously effective Cerberus before encountering and beheading Medusa herself in a dark, shadowy shrine. In this last tense scene Harryhausen has further opportunities to explore his theme of the relationship between the living entity and the model: the humans whom Medusa turns to stone look very much like the archaeologists' casts of the corpses found at Pompeii and Herculaneum. Harryhausen also reminds his audience that he has additional, American, parallels in mind by making the killing of Medusa a kind of Western "showdown." Medusa shoots at Perseus with a bow and arrow, and the snakes on her head are, nicely, American rattlesnakes.

Perseus and Jason are classic American film "heroes" in their openness, candor, and naiveté. Like the Westerner, they are attractive to women, but not womanizers. They are also, simultaneously, ancient epic heroes in that they triumph, paradoxically, because of and despite their connections with the divine. Although strong youths in their prime, neither is like Steve Reeves or Gordon Scott of the Italian muscleman epics, made in the mold of Heracles, reliant on their own strength and righteousness. In *Jason and the Argonauts,* in fact, the strong-man Heracles hero-type is consciously rejected, as he was also, in a way, by Apollonius of Rhodes in his epic *Argonautica.* Apollonius' Heracles is a forthright but somewhat oafish character, so disproportionately strong (even in a company of heroes) that he cannot easily operate as part of a team of rowers. In fact, Heracles breaks his oar and leaves the Argonautic expedition when his male lover Hylas vanishes while Heracles attempts to find a suitable length of wood to replace the broken oar (*Argonautica* 1. 1164–1272). From then on, Heracles goes his own, separate way. Heracles is played in *Jason and the Argonauts* by a forty-year-old, genteel English "tough guy," Nigel Green, whose hair is studiously tinged with gray and who is no match in either musculature or honesty for the Steve Reeves heroes or for Apollonius.' His theft of a spear from the gods' treasury leads to the awakening of the bronze giant, Talos, and to the death of his ever-so-slightly effeminate friend, Hylas.

Since the dominant presence of the monstrous and the divine

dwarfs humanity in both *Jason and the Argonauts* and *Clash of the Titans,* as it does in Vergil's *Aeneid,* I think it misleading to call Jason "utterly colorless."[41] Jason's understated, often skeptical, attitudes recall the *amēchania* (inability to cope) of Apollonius' equally understated hero (or anti-hero).[42] He is still doubtful about the gods after meeting them face to face. Medea is similarly calm and composed, for all her supposed passion for Jason. She, too, makes her decisions with a clear independence of mind, even when this involves betraying her family and the cult of her favorite goddess, Hecate. It is hard to see in their behavior the seeds of the disastrous passion and cruelty which make their subsequent relationship one of horror and slaughter. It is a pity that Schneer and Harryhausen never made the sequel to which they allude at the end of the film, where the audience is, in effect, promised that it will see Jason and Medea again in, perhaps, less agreeable circumstances. Would they, too, have become monsters?

It is unjust to dismiss these two films as a mishmash of Greek myth, enlivened only by Harryhausen's technical wizardry. The Perseus of *Clash of the Titans* is, obviously, a deliberate and dramatically effective blend of Perseus, who killed Medusa from whose blood the winged horse Pegasus emerges, and Bellerophon, who bridles and rides Pegasus. The use of myth is creative and poetic, as it was among ancient poets. After all, the filmmaker is the poet, as fully entitled to fulfill his creative, Promethean role as were his ancient predecessors. Harryhausen himself is the "Titan" of these two films—neither of which, despite the latter's title, has any Titans in it. *Clash of the Titans,* in fact, has quite studied suggestions of a more modern world: the bureaucratic, despotic Zeus, the Caliban-like Calibos, and the monstrous Kraken, the ominously Northern European beast satirized by Anatole France in *Penguin Island.*

The variations on "handbook" Greek myth in *Jason and the Argonauts* and *Clash of the Titans* stem from artistic choice, not from scholarly ignorance. Beverley Cross knew myth very well. And both films achieve better than any of the solemnly produced screen versions of Greek tragedy a real visual sense of the power, intensity, and range of myth's creative, poetic imagination, particularly in their treatment of the divine. They go beyond the binary thinking which leaves us with "god" or "no god," and beyond Bergman's fierce agnosticism which has left him heavily defined by the protestantism against which he struggles. Rather, they touch on the most neglected aspect of the "god question" or, better, the "god questions." Is god also the devil, plural as well as singular, female as well as male? Are we gods and are gods us, as Larry Cohen suggests in *Demon?* To what extent is humankind free to make its own decisions? Why does god, or rather why do the gods, allow us to make evil decisions? And to what extent are we the pawns, or perhaps the puppets, in a larger game orchestrated by an ingenious Harryhausen-like master of special effects?

Such thoughts had certainly occurred to Frank Baum when he wrote *The Wizard of Oz* and to Victor Fleming when he directed its film version in 1939. The Wizard manipulates images but is himself hollow, a magician, a master of illusion for the sake of illusion. God and the gods have no answers, even if they are not as silent as Bergman complains. No doubt the same image of god as magician or Wizard-like impresario occurred to DeMille, for all his religious upbringing, when he sought to describe the effects of the Judeo-Christian God upon the world of *Exodus*.

The ability and desire to represent divinities and divine power in visual terms allows Harryhausen and other such "sculptural" artists to recreate the gods, as Jason recreates Poseidon from his tiny model, and to bring the epic nature of myth before our eyes with their own technical magic. Harryhausen, in his own Promethean way, does in *Jason and the Argonauts* and *Clash of the Titans* what Shakespeare does in the pagan world of *The Tempest* and what Ovid does in his *Metamorphoses*. Unlike Bergman, who pessimistically excises Ovid from his film as being, in a sense, irrelevant to "real" life, Harryhausen brings the Ovidian world to visual realization and with it the optimistic sense that somehow art will triumph over death. Ovid understood that his art was his claim to and hope of eternal life: that art was his god. He cries, triumphantly, at the end of his *Metamorphoses* (15.879): *Vivam!*—"I shall live!" or "Long live me!" He has metamorphosed himself into his work. He is his art, and his art has defined the gods, not they him. That is the way he transcends his mortality and the powers that destroy his physical existence.[43] Such artistic immortality is already within Bergman's grasp. Perhaps, one day, it will be within Harryhausen's, too, when we are culturally readier to take another look at pagan pluralism.

NOTES

1. Jon Solomon, *The Ancient World in the Cinema* (New York: Barnes, 1978), 72. I owe Jon Solomon a special debt of gratitude for his help and advice in the preparation of this paper.

2. Andrew Greeley, "Why Hollywood Never Asks the God Question," New York Times, 18 January 1976, sec. 2, 1 and 13.

3. John R. May, "Visual Story and the Religious Interpretation of Film," in Religion in Film, ed. J. R. May and Michael Bird (Knoxville: University of Tennessee Press, 1982), 23. May seems to be thinking of the 1956 remake rather than the original 1923 version of Ten Commandments.

4. See, e.g., Hollywood and the Catholic Church (Chicago: Loyola University Press, 1984), 179–80; also Alvah Bessie, Inquisition into Eden (Berlin: Seven Seas Books, 1967).

5. Carl Theodor Dreyer, Fire Film (Copenhagen: Gyldendal, 1964), from Vredens Dag (Day of Wrath). The English translation is cited from Carl Theodor Dreyer: Four Screenplays, trans. Oliver Stallybrass (London: Thames & Hudson, 1970), 209. Dreyer's film (itself based on Hans Wiers-Jenssen's Anne Pedersdotter) seems to have directly influenced Bergman's Smiles of a Summer Night (1955) which also treats the love of a son by a previous marriage (named Martin, as is the son in Day of Wrath) for the father's young second wife, also named Anne.

6. Ingmar Bergman, The Magic Lantern: An Autobiography, trans. Joan Tate (New York: Viking Penguin, 1988), 256.

7. The quotations are from The Magic Lantern, 264–65.

8. Four Screenplays of Ingmar Bergman, trans. Lars Malmstrom and David Kushner (New York: Simon & Schuster, 1965), 145.

9. John R. May, "The Demonic in American Cinema," in Religion in Film, 81.

10. Erik Barnouw, The Magician and the Cinema (New York: Oxford University Press, 1981), 5.

11. FXRH 4 (1974): 15; see also S. S. Wilson, Puppets and People: Dimensional Animation Combined with Live Action in the Cinema (New York: Barnes, 1980), 105.

12. FXRH 4:6–7.

13. Bergman, cited in Jörn Donner, The Personal Vision of Ingmar Bergman, trans. Holger Lundbergh (Bloomington: Indiana University Press, 1966), 239–40. We would have a better sense of the force of this experience if the English title were closer to the Swedish: The Devil's Faces (Djävalens ansikte: Ingmar Bergmans filmer [Stockholm, 1962]). The powerful image of the magic lantern has made a strong impression on other Scandinavian writers, notably the Faroese William Heinesen, who published a collection of short stories under the title Laterna Magica (Copenhagen: Vindrose, 1985), now translated into English by Tiina Nunnally (Seattle: Fjord Press, 1987).

14. The comment on Fanny and Alexander is found in The Magic Lantern among the illustrations between pages 116 and 117.

15. Four Screenplays, 262.

16. See Lotte H. Eisner, The Haunted Screen: Expressionism in the German Cinema and the Influence of Max Reinhardt, trans. Roger Greaves (Berkeley: University of California Press, 1969).

17. Republic 571c–d; the translation is mine. For a more detailed discussion of this passage see my Metaformations: Soundplay and Wordplay in Ovid and Other Classical Poets (Ithaca: Cornell University Press, 1985), 69–89.

18. Robin Wood, "Gods and Monsters," Film Comment 14 (September–October 1978): 19–25.

19. Cited by Wood, 22.

20. Ibid., 23.

21. Ovid, Metamorphoses 9.666–797. See also my Metaformations, 151–54.

22. Metamorphoses 10.298–518, on which see Metaformations, 213–18.

23. Bergman, The Magic Lantern, 256.

24. Iphigenia in Aulis, 97–105; The Trojan Women, 191–202, 360–70, and 1118–64.

25. Seneca, *Phaedra*, 710–12. The translation is mine from *Seneca: Phaedra* (Ithaca: Cornell University Press, 1986), 76.

26. Irene Samuel, *Dante and Milton: "The Commedia" and "Paradise Lost"* (Ithaca: Cornell University Press, 1966), 127.

27. For further discussion of Pluto as a countergod see my "Statius' *Thebaid*: A Reconsideration," *Aufstieg und Niedergang der römischen Welt* (Berlin and New York: De Gruyter, 1986), Part 2, vol. 32.5, 2803–2912, esp. 2858–63.

28. As Apuleius' Lucius and Isis note in *The Golden Ass* 11.2 and 5, a god may be known by many different names.

29. Gary Zukav, *The Dancing Wu Li Masters: An Overview of the New Physics* (New York: Morrow, 1979), esp. 175–76.

30. Annette Kuhn, *Cinema, Censorship and Sexuality 1909–1925* (New York: Routledge, 1988), 102.

31. Kenneth McKinnon, *Greek Tragedy into Film* (Rutherford, N.J.: Fairleigh Dickinson University Press, 1986), 102.

32. Bergman, *The Magic Lantern*, 265.

33. *The Trojan Women*, 401–8; the translation is mine from *Seneca: Trojan Women* (Ithaca: Cornell University Press, 1986), 64.

34. Harryhausen himself belongs to the world of myth in some respects. His date of birth is given in *The Filmgoer's Companion* as "circa 1920," and he holds such an honored place in the world of special effects in film that he has a journal named in his honor *(FXRH)*.

35. Richard Meyers, *The World of Fantasy Films* (Cranbury, N.J.: Barnes, 1980), 67.

36. Solomon, *The Ancient World in the Cinema*, 72.

37. Wilson, *Puppets and People*, 65. For comparison we might add that, as Adam Eisenberg notes, Ken Ralston's effects in *Return of the Jedi* "included a complex shot composed of more than sixty elements which took four weeks to compose and appears on the screen for about two seconds." "Jedi's Extra Special Effects," *American Film* 8 (1983): 36–39.

38. See Servius' comment on *Aeneid* 1.177; he explains that "Ceres" is simply *metonymia* for "grain." To R. G. Austin the ravaged Ceres is simply "soggy grain" and the weapons used on her *(Cerealia arma)* "the grinding outfit." *P. Vergili Maronis Aeneidos Liber Primus* (Oxford: Clarendon Press, 1971), 77.

39. For further discussion see my *Metaformations*, 236–70.

40. On the classical hero and the Western see Martin M. Winkler, "Classical Mythology and the Western Film," *Comparative Literature Studies* 22 (1985): 516–40.

41. Thus Solomon, *The Ancient World in the Cinema*, 72.

42. See Gilbert Lawall, "Jason as Anti-Hero," *Yale Classical Studies* 19 (1966): 119–69.

43. The ancient epicist often writes with the confidence, either real or feigned, that he will live through his work. Even the revolutionary Lucan, writing in protest against Caesarism and in praise of liberty lost, declares that he and his *Pharsalia* will live, although he was perhaps aware, even as he wrote these words, that his conspiracy to overthrow Nero had failed and that he would have to take his own life. See my *Lucan: An Introduction* (Ithaca: Cornell University Press, 1976), esp. 62–81.

The *katabasis* Theme
in Modern Cinema

Erling B. Holtsmark

University of Iowa

T O the extent that this paper falls into a genre of film criticism, it comes closest to the tenets of Russian formalism.[1] It
is true that the material examined assumes a vaguely Proppian
shape in that its analysis has its basis in the study of iterated motifs
and themes, but it will shortly become evident that the concern
here is not with a mere cataloguing of such repetitions in order to
construct an idealized "*katabasis* film." The films to be discussed
below are all formulaic in the sense that they fit, and draw on,
patterns of narrative expectation that are of great antiquity. Yet,
their very formalism need in no way detract from their originality,
which in fact lies precisely in the capacity of their creators to
manipulate audience expectation. As one author has noted:

> A successful formulaic work is unique when, in addition to the plea-
> sure inherent in the conventional structure, it brings a new element
> into the formula, or embodies the personal vision of the creator. If
> such new elements also became wildly popular, they may in turn
> become widely imitated stereotypes and the basis of a new version of
> the formula or even of a new formula altogether.[2]

And in connection with the Vietnam genre (which will be taken
up in detail later in this paper), the following truism has been
observed:

> The Vietnam film has not yet settled into the ripe generic dotage of
> the private eye or western genre, but it has reached the point where
> previous Vietnam films as much as Vietnam memory determine its
> rough outlines. As with any genre, a recurrent set of visual motifs,
> narrative patterns, and thematic concerns has emerged.[3]

The broadly classificatory approach at the start of my discussion is
meant to serve as a convenient template of the conventional
formulas of which the reader (and, in the future, viewer) should

be aware in thinking about and looking at the kinds of cinematic narratives treated here.

Although it may well be possible to investigate this or that corpus of *katabasis* films through an *auteur* approach, this has not been my choice here. The reason is quite obvious: the underpinning pattern which I am concerned with elucidating is so widely dispersed—vastly more so than is suggested by the necessarily selective group of films considered in this paper—and so common a literary property since the time of earliest antiquity that it is simply inappropriate to think of it in the more restrictive terms that an *auteur* critique would demand.

Because myth is so central a feature of ancient Greek literature—for reasons of plot, character, and allusion, among others—it has appeared tacitly axiomatic from the time of antiquity that myth largely informs literature. To call attention to this truism one may point further to the ubiquitous and wholesale adaptation of Greek myth by Roman and early medieval writers. The literatures of the High Middle Ages and the Renaissance, not to mention that of European classicism and romanticism, continue to bear eloquent testimony to the durability through time of myth as vehicle for shaping verbal and painterly versions and visions of reality.

What is perhaps not so generally observed, or at least consciously recognized, is the astonishing extent to which the mythic patterns of classical antiquity have worked themselves into the very marrow of the cinematic skeletons which support plot, action, and characterization. Film may historically be seen as a development of theater, which of course has ancient and classical foundations in its own right. And since, prior to the emergence of film, legitimate theater was essentially a literary mode, it is not too surprising that much of the thematic and narrative patterning of literature, including that deriving from myth, should have made itself felt in the cinema.[4] In this connection I am not concerned with such obviously mythic heirs as the cinematic versions of Homer's story of Odysseus (*Ulysses* [1955]), the heroic exploits of Heracles (*Hercules* [1959]), or adaptations of Greek tragedy (e.g., *Oedipus Rex* [1968]), but with films that have no overt relationship to the mythic background that does in fact inform them.

Although the *katabasis* films are not restricted to any one type, they do tend to fall into certain genres: Westerns, detective thrillers, war stories, and science fiction. (It may be noted in passing that these are also the literary genres that frequently map mythic patterns on their story lines.) This is not to say, however, that other genres fail entirely to offer examples of mythically conceived plots.[5] More specifically for the purposes of this essay, I am interested in the narrative, ancient even by the time of the archaic Greeks of Homer's world, that portrays the hero's descent into, and ascent from, the underworld, the journey to hell.

The Greek word *katabasis* literally means "a going down, a descent," capturing the imagined physical orientation of the "other" world relative to this one. Very briefly, the following generalizations can be made about the *katabasis*.[6] The entryway to the other world is often conceived as lying in caves or grottos or other openings in the earth's crust into the nether regions such as chasms or clefts. Further, since the "other" world lies beyond a boundary that separates it from this realm, such natural topographical delimiters as rivers, bodies of water, or even mountain ranges may figure as the physical tokens of demarcation. It is well known, for instance, that the underworld of classical mythology is penetrated by a number of rivers, most notably Styx and Acheron (the river of woe), which have to be crossed in a skiff punted along by the old ferryman Charon. The lower world is generally imagined as dank and darkish, and the journey usually takes place at dusk or during the night. The realm itself is inhabited by the wealthy king and queen of the dead, as well as the innumerable spirits of the dead, monsters (e.g., Cerberus) and traditional evildoers (e.g., Tantalus). The purpose of the journey is usually to obtain spiritual or material wealth (wisdom, gold, flocks, or some other form of treasure), or to rescue a friend or friends, often a woman or wife. The katabatic hero is often accompanied and helped by a companion (who may be female) or loyal retinue of retainers, some or all of whom may be lost in the course of the journey so that the protagonist returns alone. After his return, the hero sometimes assumes roles of increased responsibility and leadership (e.g., becoming a teacher or ruler) on the basis of the experiences undergone during his harrowing in hell.[7]

A critical point to appreciate for our purposes is the protean nature of the displacements to which the underlying paradigm is subject, as well as this paradigm's sometimes tenuous association with the cinematic product in question. Thus, for example, without too much imagination one can appreciate how the underlying "reality" of the cavernous entrance to the underworld may manifest itself associatively in any given narrative, whether literary or cinematic, as claustrophobic defiles or narrow mountain passes, or how the underlying motif of the demarcating body of water may, given the geographical exigencies of a particular narrative, appear inversely as a scorching desert.[8] And just as the paradigmatic elements undergo these transformations, so do the objectives. Thus, the journey is no longer a literal descent into the actual underworld, as in book 11 of the Homeric *Odyssey* or book 6 of Vergil's *Aeneid*, but becomes a displaced trek into such emblematic hells as enemy terrain (e.g., the Vietnam of *The Deer Hunter* [1979] or the hostile Mexico of *The Professionals* [1966]), prison (as in *Brubaker* [1980]), the sleazy world of the Times Square area (as in *Midnight Cowboy* [1969]), the urban universe of drugs and crime (as in *Lethal Weapon* [1987]), or the futuristic outworlds of science fiction (as in *The Empire Strikes Back* [1980]).

Any hero who, like Odysseus, literally descends into hell, in a sense dies, and is then reborn when he ascends once more into the upper world. This theme of the katabatic hero as "dying" before being "reborn" gives rise to numerous shifted variations, all displacements, to a greater or lesser degree, of the underlying idea. In the detective or police thriller, for example, the protagonist goes "under cover," that is, he is no longer the real he but some concoction dreamed up by his superior or control.[9] Thus, in *Raw Deal* (1986) a discredited FBI agent seeks to reinstate himself with the bureau by undertaking an undercover mission that requires him first to "burn himself" to death in a refinery explosion.

It is time now to turn to a more detailed consideration of some specific films in order to note how this ancient and pervasive concept of the katabatic hero is worked out.

The 1986 film titled *Cherry 2000* offers a flashy variation on the basic *katabasis* pattern. Sam Treadwell owns a robot, a model Cherry 2000 that is his beautiful live-in mistress. She is actually an android, externally indistinguishable from a real human being (an evocation of *West World* [1973] and *Blade Runner* [1982]). After she shorts out during a love session on the floor and water clogs her circuits beyond repair, Sam realizes he loves her. When she cannot be fixed at the repair shop, Sam is given her miniaturized "personality" disk and told that a replacement husk is in all probability stored at a "Graveyard" in Zone 7, a dangerous land beyond civilization. His journey to the Graveyard to find a new Cherry-husk for his disk is thus a displaced form of the hero's search for a lost woman. His guide is one of the most famous "trappers" of Zone 7, a woman, as it turns out, called E. Johnson. A large part of the film is given over to the katabatic journey proper, which they make in this sexy Sybil's souped-up Thunderbird.

This journey is replete with and remarkably faithful to the

ancestral themes we have come to expect for this part of the
descent tale. They travel mainly at night, thus avoiding the various marauding outlaw bands that dot the barren landscape
through which they move. The Nevada desert scenery spec-
tacularly embodies the theme of barrier separating this world
from the one below. In a striking scene, Johnson and Sam cross a
vast chasm at whose bottom lies a great river. Plunging down
through a cavernous hole into the "underworld," they are met by
an old man fittingly attired as a spelunker, Six-Fingered Jake, a
friend of Johnson's and the archtrapper reputedly killed by the
outlaws but still alive. This character, with his emblematic attire of
the underworld and knowledge of the underground caverns, is
clearly a guide figure of the sort often encountered by the katabatic hero: Jake is an incarnation of Charon. Jake then trans-
ports Sam and Johnson across the river on his spare barge,
powered by two outboards in place of the traditional punting pole
that Charon employs.

Johnson reconditions an old plane and flies Sam to the Graveyard ahead of the pursuing outlaws. Arrived at the repository, the
guide leads the hero in a final descent through a skylight into the
ghostly pale chamber where countless husks hang etiolated and
lifeless in the eerie gloom. In seeing them one cannot help but
think of Anticleia's description of the *psychai* (spirits) to her son
Odysseus:

> The flesh and bones are no longer possessed of strength,
> but the powerful might of blazing fire overpowers them
> as soon as the personality has abandoned the white bones.
> And the spirit goes flying, flitting off like a dream.
> [*Odyssey* 11.219–22; my translation]

It is perhaps relevant to this ancient passage to note that when
the original Cherry shorted out electrically, she was enveloped in
crackling flashes and fiery sparks, and that her miniaturized laser
disk containing the complex program for all her emotions and
feelings ultimately traces its ancestry back to Homer's *thumos* (personality, life-force). Sam has removed the disk from the original,
the whole point of his journey being to find another husk in which
to insert it.

As soon as he does, she pops alive. But Sam soon recognizes
that all her emotions are mere programs. In a climax fraught with
shoot-outs against the outlaws and narrow escapes from disaster,
Sam jettisons the newly activated Cherry and makes it back to

earth with Johnson, with whom a romantic relationship has been developing as they proceed deeper into the "underworld."

Needless to say, this particular twist on the typical ending, in which the hero abandons the woman he came in search of and takes up with the Sybil, has no counterpart in Greek and Roman myth. In this film, however, it emerges naturally out of the paradigm and will strike the viewer as an ingenious and organically motivated innovation on a design now some five thousand years old.

Finally, the hero, Sam, who was at first a moping and rather helpless individual, undergoes a transformation as a result of the journey and, typologically speaking, returns with enhanced wisdom. For he learns, largely through the agency of his Sybil, Johnson, to fend for himself and to improvise daringly as circumstances require. He comes to recognize what love is all about (at least in the American cinema of the eighties).

Although this is not a well-known film, it should be. It adheres believably to the type and yet allows for some clever adaptations. Played with a gentle humor, primarily thanks to Melanie Griffith's excellent and laid-back portrayal of the psychopompic Sybil, it succeeds admirably as an example of the genre. A katabatic sleeper, as it were!

The Western undoubtedly has the most readily available material for transformation and remapping: unbroken deserts and delimiting mountain ranges stretching ceaselessly westward, filled with hostile Indians, Mexican bandits, and greedy outlaws bent on rape, pillage, and murder.[10] The film *100 Rifles* (1969) contains some good elements of the type as well as an interesting inversion at the end.

A black lawman, Lyedecker, comes from Arizona into Mexico, to bring back a bank robber, a half-breed named Yaqui Joe. As in *The Professionals* (see below), Mexico here functions as the displaced underworld. The point is underscored by the visual emphasis throughout on the stark landscapes of looming mountains and sere deserts, as well as the graphic hanging and displays of suspended corpses at the beginning of the film. The sheriff, a kind of combination Hermes and hero, has entered this realm in order to return the thief to Phoenix, an antithetical variant on the search for a friend. One is tempted to see the choice of town as intentional, evoking, as the name does, the notion of rebirth. This quest in turn undergoes mutation within the *katabasis* proper, and the focus comes to rest on the rifles Joe had purchased for the Yaquis with the stolen money. Thus, typologically speaking, both treasure and "friend" are the motives for this particular journey into hell.

Joe and Lyedecker get on the wrong side of a savage Mexican general, Verdugo (Spanish for executioner), and are almost killed by him on several occasions, most dramatically in front of a firing squad before the brutalized Yaqui Indians come to their rescue. These near-deaths, like unconsciousness, sickness, or sleep, are thematic displacements of death itself, and as such they are emblematic of the larger realm of death in which the protagonists move.

A katabatic inset occurs in this film, as such thematically recapitulating the larger *katabasis* of the cinematic narrative and foreshadowing a successful resolution of the latter. After some Yaqui children are taken hostage by Verdugo's men, Joe and Lyedecker organize the Indians for a raiding party into the outpost to which the general is moving. They kill the men and stage an ambush on the column escorting the children. The action is set in nocturnal darkness, and after the enemy are slain, the post is turned into a fiery inferno from which the Indians escape with their children. This use of the parallel, even embedded, mininarrative that reflects or somehow comments on the core tale is a familiar literary device; from classical literature, for example, one thinks most prominently and immediately of the strategies encountered in Homeric poetry and in Ovid's *Metamorphoses,* not to mention the ancient romances. In the *Odyssey,* for example, the journey of Telemachus is played off against the journey of Odysseus, and the banqueting scenes at Ithaca, Pylus, and Scheria are set off against the banquet in the Cyclops' cave. And in Vergil's *Aeneid,* the hero's journey into the underworld is a culmination of his other journeys in the preceding books for information about his future.

In the final scenes Lyedecker is transformed into the unwilling leader of the Indians in their final conflict with Verdugo and his militia. The katabatic hero has in effect become a leader in the nether realm, and leads his companions into a successful defense against Verdugo. In the end the hero relinquishes this role as unbecoming to himself, and turns it over to the half-breed, Yaqui Joe. And contrary to typological expectation, the hero does not bring back the "friend" he was sent for, but decides to return alone to Phoenix and bequeathes to Joe the leadership of the Yaqui Indians.

The film *100 Rifles* is an interesting variation on the *katabasis*. Among its more unusual aspects are its defiance of thematic expectation and the repeated suggestion that Joe and Lyedecker are split aspects of one persona, each of which, as a result of this particular harrowing of hell, finds himself at the end.[11]

Set in the same general time and place as *100 Rifles*, southern Texas and northern Mexico at the beginning of the century, *The Wild Bunch* (1969) likewise lends itself to analysis as an extended *katabasis*. The "underworld" becomes an unusually fluid concept in this film. Initially it is represented by the south Texas town Pike's marauders enter in order to steal railroad funds. After mutual slaughter among the townsfolk and Pike's band, they pick up an old man named Sykes, who functions typologically as a kind of Charon-Hermes figure. He knows the terrain and has had a lot of experience in it, and he is good with horses and wagon. He is also the only member of the gang who does not die at the end. When the Bunch cross a demarcating river into Mexico, a kind of topographical reversal takes place. The United States subsequently becomes the place to which they must journey in order to secure their particular version of treasure, a trainload of rifles for the Mexican general, Mapache. In a dramatic return from this displaced hell they cross desert and a bridge spanning the riverine boundary between the realms, making it back safely to Mexico with the weapons for which Mapache pays them $10,000 in gold. One of their group, the Mexican Angel, is taken prisoner by Mapache after the delivery of the rifles. In a fashion predictable from the type, Pike and Dutch, who fills a subordinate leadership role, decide to ignore the lethal dangers of confronting Mapache and his 200 soldiers in their stronghold, and the Bunch enter it to rescue their companion. Thus the locus of hell shifts once more, although the mapping conforms to the type: they ride down from the mountains, cross the desert, and enter through the portals, offering to buy Angel back from the drunken and darkly dressed Mapache. When the latter slits Angel's throat, a fierce gun battle erupts in which most of the townspeople and Mapache's soldiers, as well as all of the Bunch, are killed.

It is also to be noted that "enclosing" these *katabases* is a larger one, in which an unwilling agent of the railroad and former member of the group, Thornton, has been pursuing Pike's gang and, after the train robbery, is trying to intercept the rifles and capture the thieves. From Thornton's point of view, Mexico is the underworld which he is forced to enter with a useless crew of miscreants, a group reminiscent of Odysseus' often less than helpful companions who, like Thornton's, are killed because of their greed long before they make it back to *their* "upper" world. Typologically speaking, it is the hero who survives the journey through hell, and therefore Thornton emerges as the protagonist: he alone survives the "descent" and in fact will assume some kind of leadership role in helping to rebuild Angel's village after the film's narrative has concluded.

Why this unusual shift in the locus of hell, and the different points of view about hell? As abbreviated *katabasis* narratives in their own right, they provide parallel accounts, a multiplication of the informing pattern. Conceptually, however, the viewer is left with the sense that hell is where you make it, and for the likes of Pike's gang hell is wherever they are, as Mexico certainly proved to be for them. Lest there be any doubt about this point, the camera, after its nightmarish panning and crosscutting among the combatants' dances of death, lingers suggestively over the strewn corpses and waiting buzzards.[12]

The katabatic subtheme of the rescued woman occurs in *The Professionals* (1966). A wealthy older man, Grant, hires four individuals to cross the desert into Mexico to recover Mrs. Grant, kidnapped by the Mexican revolutionary Raza. The four adventurers each have an area of expertise: Rico is an arms expert with leadership ability; Dolworth is an explosives man with considerable inventiveness; Ehrengard is a natural horse-handler; and Sharp is a tracker par excellence.

In terms of the ancient prototypes, these four men distributively represent the typological constants familiar from the *katabasis* narrative: the hero is of course a fighter, is clever as well as strong, and frequently has special abilities or associations with animals. The black man, Sharp in this film, as often in modern cinematic incarnations, is clearly a Hermes figure, the *psychopompos* (or, escorter of the dead), who not only guides the hero into hell but also helps him return to the upper world.[13] In the ancient tales, sometimes the hero is alone (Heracles rescuing Alcestis), and at other times he is accompanied by companions who may be especially helpful (e.g., Peirithous has the help of Theseus in trying to get Persephone back from the lower world) or not (e.g., Odysseus' journey to the Cyclops' cave). Thus, from a typological point of view it matters little whether we are dealing with many capabilities condensed into a single hero, or several heroes who have split among themselves the varied abilities of a single personality. In any event, at the end of the story of *The Professionals* our thematic expectations (as well as Grant's hopes) are foiled in that the "rescued" woman was originally a willing victim who wanted out of Grant's clutches and is finally returned to Mexico. The suggestion emerges, then, that Grant is in effect the real Hades from whom she had to be rescued.

Although certain film genres such as Westerns and detective narratives seem to lend themselves more intuitively to patterning on the *katabasis* theme than others, even such films do not, of course, all fall into the general type. Yet, even where the overarching design is lacking, it may manifest itself in smaller segments entering into the makeup of the composite whole.

A good example is *The Long Riders* (1976). The story of the James-Younger gang in post-Civil War Missouri, the film is structured essentially as a series of parallel episodes based on bank robbery followed by celebration and involvement with women, the first and last bank robbery of the film creating a ring-compositional frame. It is the last robbery that is relevant to the current discussion. For once the gang decides to leave the familiar territory of Missouri and do their robbing in distant Minnesota: the band leaves home for a place far from home which is reached by train (shown traveling at night). They are going to this distant place in search of treasure, as one of the band has learned that the bank in Northfield, Minnesota, is full of money. Appropriately the bank is located next to the town mortuary, a point emphasized not only in dialogue but also visually, for a shot of Cole Younger waiting outside the bank places him prominently and lingeringly against the mortuary in the background. As it turns out, the town knows that the gang is on its way, and the latter are unable to get any money from the bank. In addition they are ambushed as they try to escape. All but Jesse are wounded or killed, and Jesse, along with his brother Frank, abandons the rest of the men. He is himself later betrayed and shot.

The interest in this minor instance of the theme is that it is played off against the expectations we have of the standard tale. It is a kind of anti-*katabasis*, fully understandable as such only against the backdrop of familiarity with the general tale. For here the hero neither gains treasure nor, certainly, any wisdom (Jesse returns to Missouri and wants to start a better gang to rob banks). Rather than bringing back friends from the dead he leaves them dying or destined for long prison terms. Thematically, then, it seems appropriate that Jesse is shot at the end, since he never escaped from the harrowing journey to hell in Northfield where the rest of gang came to their end.

The classic Western *Shane* (1953) has a memorable *katabasis* narrative at the ending of the film. In a resolution of the fierce range war that has polarized the film's world, Shane rides into town during night, crossing the river that separates the settled, civilized homestead, on whose behalf he is fighting, from the corrupted town. Little Joey, his friend, follows him and is shown crossing a graveyard on the way. We assume that Shane did also, although this is not specifically shown. For the final showdown with the land-hungry Ryker and his hired gun, Wilson, Shane enters a tavern through swinging doors. These saloon doors have appeared numerous times throughout the film, and have become a kind of iconic shorthand for entering a zone of danger, that is, a katabatic realm. One may note that a common euphemism in classical myth for the underworld was *Pylae* (gates, entryway).[14] The classical hero not infrequently is associated with cattle, or is involved in a confrontation with an owner of cattle, as in the case of Odysseus and the cattle of the Sun, Heracles and the cattle of Geryon, or Amphitryon and the stolen cattle of the Taphians.[15] Ryker is a ruthless cattle baron, and typologically speaking Shane, in overcoming him and his henchmen, embodies the role of the hero as master of cattle. As if to underscore the contrast between the hero and the murderous agent of this lethal cattle owner, Shane is dressed in light clothing, Wilson in black.[16] Shane shoots both Ryker and Wilson, and as he begins to walk out of the saloon, Joey, who has been watching, alerts him to a man with a rifle aiming at him from the upper story. One should recall that it is not unknown for the hero to receive help at some point in his journey from a woman, child, animal, or other kind of escort, and the aid Joey gives Shane may be seen as a form of this element of the narrative. Although Shane is ostensibly helping Joey's father and the homesteaders in the valley, his confrontation with the Thanatos-like Wilson reinforces in himself the self-knowledge to which he has come, and now carries out of the gunfight. As he tells Joey: "A man has to be what he is, Joey. You can't break the mold. I tried it, and it didn't work for me." A man of violence is a man of violence, just as a man of peace is a man of peace. And Shane knows, finally, what he is.

Katabasis aside, this sentiment, is in itself strongly classical. Its underlying meaning is captured in the Delphic injunction, *gnōthi sauton* (know thyself), and is repeated in countless guises throughout Greek literature. Dress plays an important part in orchestrating this shifting of roles by Shane. When we first meet him, he wears his "armor," that is his gunfighter outfit complete with pistol and gunbelt; as he tries to fit into the civilized society represented by the homesteaders, he buys farmer's clothing and a new belt, which he wears until he starts on his trip into town to deal with Ryker and Wilson; at that point he once more dons his "armor."[17]

Another Western, *Ulzana's Raid* (1972), dealing with the pursuit of renegade Apaches into the Arizona territory, is structured as a typical *katabasis* but accommodates certain shifts toward the end. A young lieutenant, Garnett, full of peaceful Christian pieties that are quite inappropriate to the infernal desert where the Indians live, leads an army party in pursuit of Chief Ulzana and his band of horse raiders. Garnett's commanding officer sets the tone at the film's start by recalling General Sheridan's observation that if he owned hell and Arizona, he would live in hell and rent out Arizona.

Into this harsh and uncompromising land goes the naive lieutenant, escorted by a scout named MacIntosh and an Apache in the service of the army, Ke-Ni-Tay. The searing desert and the mountainous defiles through which they pass conjure up the Western version of the katabatic landscape filled with pillage, burning, and rape by the Apaches.[18] For the lieutenant this campaign proves to be as much the emblematic journey for practical knowledge of the world as it is the ostensible pursuit of horses and thieves. Throughout he questions MacIntosh and Ke-Ni-Tay about the land, the Apaches, their customs, and the reasons for their cruelty. As scout, MacIntosh is the Hermes figure who at the start conducts the lieutenant and his men into the wilderness, but it is the native scout Ke-Ni-Tay who, gradually, has come to assume that role. Indeed, since MacIntosh is dying at the end, Ke-Ni-Tay escorts the corpse of Ulzana, whom he has killed, to burial. Both the white and the Indian scout teach the lieutenant about the land as much as they teach him about his need to learn that Christian charity, while laudable in the fort, is a dangerous delusion in the desert. By letting Ke-Ni-Tay have his way, Garnett symbolically lays aside his Christian arrogance and, it is implied, begins to learn how to accept the land on its own terms as he sets out for the "real" world of the fort.

We come finally to a consideration of the *katabasis* in films based on the collective American descent into the hell of Vietnam. The graphic portrayal of a displaced underworld in *Platoon* (1986), for example, is striking. Here the topography of hell is etched by the Vietnamese landscape of a clinging, claustrophobic jungle, crawling, like any katabatic terrain, with impeding monsters, here shown as preying insects and leeches, venomous snakes, and murderous Viet Cong. The notion of rebirth after the ascent, which is an underlying assumption of the whole *katabasis* narrative, is emphasized both verbally and visually in this film by the frames that ring the narrative. Thus, at the start of the film, new infantry are seen disembarking through dust and smoke from a transport plane, the new recruit, Taylor, muttering that it feels like hell here. At the very end, as he ascends in a helicopter from the jungle charnel house created by the great fire fight he has just survived, he observes sotto voce that he feels like a child who has been born of two fathers, Barnes the psychopathic sergeant, and Elias the crusading sergeant. These two have condensed into his personal *psychopompos*, guiding him through hell; in order for him to become his own self, both are killed. For the child must be freed of paternal influences before he can grow up to be an adult in his own right.

Elias, who is consistently portrayed as a thoughtful and caring soldier and comes to represent a model of good soldiering for Taylor, is shot in cold blood and left for dead by Barnes. When Taylor realizes what Barnes has done, he gets into a fight with the sergeant and is almost killed by him in the "underworld," an underground bunker some of the soldiers have built for relaxing and indulging in drugs. Shortly thereafter, as if to cancel the potentially evil influence of Barnes that he might bring back from Vietnam, Taylor kills him. Because this film has strong overtones of the classic *Bildungsroman,* it seems appropriate that the hero should be seen as liberated from the continuing intrusion of the spiritual ancestry of Elias and Barnes on his life after he returns to America.

Though it is perhaps fortuitous, Taylor's first name is Chris. While he is no more a saint in this film than anyone else, the name of this katabatic protagonist nevertheless evokes the name of Christ, the katabatic protagonist of Christianity's central myth of death, descent, and resurrection. Further, it is perhaps worth noting that the major engagement that leads to Taylor's "rebirth" begins on New Year's Day, a symbolic day of renewals and beginnings, when, in Taylor's words, they are all marching through the jungle like "ghosts in a landscape" (a phrase recalling the "ghosts" who inhabit the Homeric underworld).

At the start of the film Taylor was an inexperienced grunt. Indeed, he makes an issue of this point in a letter he is writing to his grandmother: like the other soldiers, most of whom he sees as American society's underclass and therefore forced to fight in Vietnam, he thinks of himself as a loser at the bottom of the barrel; since he is so far down in the mud, he can only go up (this metaphorical direction has of course immediate relevance to the katabatic themes of "going down" and "going up" again). And he emerges from his journey through hell as a person who has learned to refashion himself and his values out of the meaninglessness of war, and will live with this awareness in the world of America to which he returns.

There are, moreover, a number of incidents throughout the film that function as katabatic insets that comment by way of parallelism or antithesis on the overarching *katabasis* informing the film as a whole. An early parallel is the minor inset when Taylor thinks he has been shot and is dying from what is only a slight head wound; another soldier is in fact killed, however, and Barnes takes the opportunity to make of him a memento mori for the rest of the soldiers who did not die this time. Shortly after this first baptism of fire, Taylor is introduced by a black soldier (who should be understood as a psychopompic figure here) into the "underworld"; his introduction of Taylor to the others is significant, for he calls him not Taylor, but Chris. This abbreviated evocation of the Christian archetype of death and resurrection, then, parallels the larger theme of the *katabasis* and foreshadows the ultimate return of the hero from the harrowing experience of Vietnam. For in both this small "underworld" and in Vietnam as a whole he enters an innocent, passes certain ritualized initiation ceremonies, and emerges a different character: from the "underworld," as accepted by the other grunts, and from Vietnam, accepted by himself.

In parallel stands the incident in which Elias at one point descends into the cavernous, riverine tunnels of a Viet Cong underground bunker where he confronts and kills the enemy deep in their lair; his safe ascent again signals the emergence of the katabatic hero from the underground enemy entrenched in this part of the countryside. In antithetical fashion, in one inset the soldiers cross a river and climb *up* a hill to invade a village, brutalize some peasants, almost rape some of the children, torch the entire compound, and drive off the still living as though they were cattle. This invasion of a microcosm of Vietnam can also be seen as an inverted katabatic episode in that the directions are reversed, enemies rather than friends are led back, and the hero, along with Elias, opposes rather than promotes the operations undertaken. As in most such films about Vietnam, much of the action takes place either in nocturnal darkness or the tenebrous passageways beneath the covering jungle canopy, and fires burn everywhere in a land scored by rivers large and small.

The shape of Stanley Kubrick's *Full Metal Jacket* (1987) owes a diffused but unmistakable allegiance to the *katabasis* type. Indeed, though less schematic than *Platoon* in its overt deployment of the specific details characterizing the pattern, the film involves two *katabases:* the sojourn of the young men at Parris Island, and Joker's campaign in Vietnam. Each complements and comments on the other.

Being an island, the boot camp is a world unto itself, separated from the mainland by a body of water. It proves to be a harrowing hell for the raw recruits who, during the opening sequence, are emblematically shorn of their connections to "this world" by the barbers trimming their hair down to the skull. The sadistic drill sergeant, Hartman, who runs their "other world," has set himself up as a minor deity empowered to remold them into killing-machine Marines, and they must do constant obeisance to him and his torturous training regimen. One of them finally snaps, and, at night in a communal toilet room while the protagonist and narrator, Joker, looks on helplessly, takes a kind of communal vengeance on Hartman by killing him (and himself) with his rifle.[19] Cut to Saigon.

This world, ten thousand miles from the United States, is steeped in deceit, corruption, and death. On several occasions the men characterize it implicitly as the "other world" when they speak of eventually "rotating back to the world" if they are not first killed in Vietnam. Joker works for the army newspaper, *Stars and Stripes,* and is sent upcountry to join the platoon of his boot-camp buddy, Cowboy. The topography of his journey is consistently infernal: dark billowing smoke, flames, bombed-out buildings, death, killing, a demarcating Perfume River, corpses, a mass grave, and a virtually invisible enemy. Entering an urban shell of concrete rubble the men are pinned down by sniper fire and some of them are killed. A rescue party is sent to "take out the gooks" and recover the corpses of the dead, a resonatingly Homeric motif, as is seen in the mutilation of Sarpedon's corpse (*Iliad* 16.545–46) or the fight over the body of Patroclus (*Iliad* 17.700–

736).[20] In the final confrontation with the enemy, Joker enters a cavernous edifice of twisted girders and pitted foundations eerily lit by dancing fires only to discover that what appeared as a large concentration of hostile troops who have been decimating their ranks turns out in reality to be a single woman, really not much more than a girl. Joker, acting for the men, kills her after she has been seriously wounded.

The narrative is unified by the ending of the boot camp sequence, during which emphasis was repeatedly placed on equating rifles with girlfriends and even valuing weapons over penises, and this final Vietnam scene of the killing of the woman sniper.[21] The men have already had a number of debasing encounters with Vietnamese prostitutes, and whether it is literally with a military weapon or symbolically with a bodily tool, they end up raping and destroying the country. And herein lies the chilling irony of the film, for in reversing the normal katabatic pattern in which heroes rescue a woman abducted into hell, Kubrick has the men prove themselves by killing a woman who is an inhabitant of hell (which is her real home). The deeply ironic parallel with Pyle's shooting of Hartman is unmistakable: like Pyle, Joker now becomes a liberator in that he, too, destroys a communal nemesis, but in so doing invalidates the whole point of the traditional journey down, the *saving* of the woman. The frightening inversion of values in *Full Metal Jacket* is clearly seen in his being the one who *kills* the woman. If one "reads" Joker as a Pyle and the sniper as a Hartman, there is little if any difference between the Vietnamese and the American persecutor, and apparently little difference between the deadly actions of Pyle and Joker. In Joker's case the murder is to be seen as justified by the murderous behavior of the Oriental woman, but in Pyle's case the murder of the white man who had turned them all into state-sanctioned killers is not to be countenanced. When, within the larger narrative perspective of the *katabasis*, the killing of a woman is "right," something is very much "wrong." What does America stand for? Where is hell?

Like *The Professionals*, Francis Ford Coppola's *Apocalypse Now* (1979) is a classic *katabasis* tale, although inverted. Here the protagonist, Willard, is sent upriver Vietnam not to rescue a friend but rather to kill an officer who has now come to be seen as an enemy of American interests. He is to cross over into Cambodia and "terminate with extreme prejudice" a renegade American field commander, Kurtz, a highly decorated hero and once brilliant leader of the Special Forces. The man has carved out a little empire for himself deep in the jungle, and his native troops worship him like a god. The film is steeped in such typical emblems of the *katabasis* as enclosing jungles, nocturnal patrols, and bridges and borders typically demarcating this world from that.

Most striking, however, is the centrality of the patrol boat that takes Willard on a perilous passage up a broad river snaking through the dense and enclosing Vietnamese jungle. The vessel takes Willard both geographically and symbolically farther and farther away from the civilized security of Saigon into an increasingly dangerous landscape. Passing the "last American outpost," itself a bombed-out encampment of lost and leaderless GIs, he continues across the border into Cambodia. The black chief who skillfully guides the patrol boat past one danger after another is a mix between Charon and Hermes, being both the helmsman of the infernal skiff and the conductor into the underworld. The fact that he is killed before Willard and his men reach their destination seems to underscore the inverted nature of this narrative.

The film is based on Joseph Conrad's *Heart of Darkness* and is also influenced by T. S. Eliot's *The Waste Land;* and a brief but highly significant camera pan of a copy of Sir James Frazer's *The Golden Bough* in Kurtz's corpse-filled precinct is crucial for an appreciation of the film's conclusion. This, then, is a mythic tale of sacrificial death and ritual resurrection appropriately melded with the *katabasis* of a dying-and-rising god, Willard. A famous scene at the end intercuts the ritual hacking to death of a sacrificial steer by the Montangnards with Willard's cutting up of Kurtz, and thus serves to point out the latter's death as a sacrifice on the barbaric altar of American political and military expediency. The pattern deployed here relies heavily on the theories of Frazer: *rex est mortuus, vivat rex* (the king is dead, long live the king). No sooner has Willard completed his "mission" and killed Kurtz than the natives bow down to him and offer precisely the kind of religious obeisance that, we had been told at the start of the film by the general briefing Willard, they once did to the now dead Kurtz.

In a manner of speaking Willard has been resurrected: at the start of the film he was lost to home and family and half-crazy as well, but now he is a god. Yet, in the very last scene, as he starts off downriver on the patrol boat in the utter black of night, his grotesquely camouflaged face fills the screen—dark eyes staring, the last words of Kurtz echoing in his mind: "The horror! The horror!" This is a katabatic protagonist who will never return to "this world" a psychically whole individual ready to assume roles of responsibility and leadership.

Platoon and *Full Metal Jacket*, though both treating the stories of given individuals, seem more concerned with looking at the "underworld" of Vietnam from the vantage of its ultimate effect on the protagonists. In short, they stick to the fundamental *katabasis* theme of death and rebirth of the hero. But *Apocalypse Now* takes a grimmer view and examines the effect of the descent on an individual man who, as noted, is not likely, in any wholesome sense of the word, to "return" (as did Odysseus, for example). The other two films show us protagonists who seem to have been able to internalize and appropriate their harrowing other-world experiences without being overwhelmed by them, but *Apocalypse Now* elaborates a much bleaker vision of the hero's future, leaving him seemingly stuck forever in his own private inferno.

I have looked at only a few cases of what must by now be evident to be a rather common informing vision, the mapping of the *katabasis* typology onto essentially nonunderworld enterprises set in modern times and even in the future. It remains to consider briefly why the notion is so widespread in a medium so hugely popular and culturally international.

As indicated at the outset, a consideration of the genealogy of modern film suggests that the thematic as much as the narrative devices of drama and literature in general are built into the new medium. And since these elements in literature go back largely to ancient sources, it is not surprising that some of the strictly mechanical patterns are embedded in numerous films. Since there appears to be a tacit (and, in my view, erroneous) assumption that ancient literature, the "classics," is inaccessible to all but those with an extensive knowledge of ancient Greek and Latin, how can it be that such a prevalent aspect of an "inaccessible" corpus is so prevalent in the most popular of popular media? Obviously the pattern speaks to something deeply human, for whether it is consciously recognized as such or not by the mass audience or the filmmakers, the cinematic *katabasis* continues to entertain viewers not only brought up in the Western tradition, but in practically any other culture as well. This may simply be a less than compendious way of saying that what is at heart mythic, e.g., the *katabasis*, is at heart universal. The whole concept of Jung's *Tiefenpsychologie* and its archetypes is of course a complex elaboration on such a view, and if one accepts (as many do not) his articulation of the innateness of these psychic operators, then the appeal of the *katabasis* type is freed from any kind of anchoring in specific cultural traditions.

Whatever one's larger attitude adopted on this question, I

would offer, on a less theoretical scale, that the thematic "displace-
ment" of *katabasis* themes discussed shifts onto the narrative the
power of a death tale, or part of a death tale, and hence lends to it
a certain urgency, an import beyond the surface structure of the
presentation. Thus, for example, when Heracles takes the cattle
of Geryon, although there is no reference to a physical descent
into a lower world, the adventure clearly takes him beyond the
normative world and forces him to confront, in Geryon, a Death
demon (in triplicate at that!) whom he must overpower before
being able to abscond with his new-found wealth.[22] Of the films
examined above, this associative connection is most evident in the
ones about Vietnam, and thus tends to lift them out of the particular to a more universal application. Not everyone may have
been a Willard in Vietnam, but everyone has journeyed into the
dark and perilous Cambodia of the self or the heart of his or her
own darkness—some not as deeply, some more so, and some with
less success, others with more. The protagonists of the Western as
well as of the science fiction tale and the detective thriller likewise
make their descents into the varied katabatic landscapes to which
their quests bring them. The pattern endures because it has been
our own since Gilgamesh first went in search of immortality in the
fourth or third millenium B.C.; extrapolating from the last five
thousand years, we may assume that it will in all likelihood continue to be central to our vision of ourselves.

NOTES

1. On its relevance to film criticism, see Peter Wollen, *Signs and Meaning in the Cinema*
(Bloomington: Indiana University Press, 1972), 46, 93–94. See also Vladimir Propp,
Morphology of the Folktale (Bloomington: Publication of the Indiana University Research
Center in Anthropology, Folklore, and Linguistics 10, 1958). Although my paper is an
analysis of a cross-generic (e.g., Westerns, war films, sci-fi, etc.) "template" derived from
classical myth (i.e., the *katabasis*), it is not, strictly speaking, "genre" criticism as such; it
does, however, clearly skirt this approach, and readers are well advised to consult the
stimulating and contentious essays in Barry Keith Grant, ed., *Film Genre Reader* (Austin:
University of Texas Press, 1986).

2. John G. Cawelti, *Adventure, Mystery, and Romance: Formula Stories as Art and Popular
Culture* (Chicago: University of Chicago Press, 1976), 12. Although this work is not
oriented toward film, it contains much insightful information relevant to the kind of study
here undertaken, and the first chapter in particular is strongly recommended ("The Study
of Literary Formulas").

3. Thomas Doherty, "Full Metal Genre: Stanley Kubrick's Vietnam Combat Movie,"
Film Quarterly 42 (1988–89):24.

4. Such obvious links between film and literature as the screenwriting careers of
William Faulkner, F. Scott Fitzgerald, and many lesser luminaries (e.g., Erich Segal, Joseph

Wambaugh et al.) underscore the overt relationship. For a more theoretical exploration of this connection see Gerald Peary and Roger Shatzkin, *The Classical American Novel and the Movies* (New York: Ungar, 1977), 1–9; Joy Gould Boyum, *Double Exposure: Fiction into Film* (New York: Universe Books, 1985), 3–20; and Kenneth MacKinnon, *Greek Tragedy into Film* (London: Croom Helm, 1986), 4–21.

5. A good instance is *10* (1979), whose middle-aged protagonist undertakes his own odyssey in search of a meaningful relationship.

6. For a more detailed analysis than the one that follows of the typology of the hero's descent, see my *Tarzan and Tradition: Classical Myth in Popular Literature* (Westport, Conn.: Greenwood Press, 1981), 97–99, 137, and *Edgar Rice Burroughs* (Boston: Twayne, 1986), 18–20.

7. Further discussions may be found in Raymond J. Clark, *Catabasis: Vergil and the Wisdom-Tradition* (Amsterdam: Grüner, 1976), and in Anton D. Leeman, "Aeneas' Abstieg in das Totenreich: Eine Läuterungsreise durch Vergangenheit und Zukunft," in *Form und Sinn: Studien zur römischen Literatur (1954–1984)* (Frankfurt: Lang, 1985), 187–202.

8. Consider the informative paper by Jarold Ramsey, "From 'Mythic' to 'Fictive' in a Nez Percé Orpheus Myth," *Western American Literature* 13 (1978): 119–31. In general, on such suggestive associations or antitheses in myth, see Joseph Fontenrose, *Python: A Study of Delphic Myth and Its Origins* (Berkeley: University of California Press, 1959), 6–9.

9. Some of the terminology for such heroes is highly suggestive, such as naming him a "mole" (an animal that literally burrows down and lives under the earth, the standard location of the underworld) or a "sleeper" (sleep readily being understandable as a displaced form of death—interestingly, *Thanatos* [Death] and *Hypnos* [Sleep] are brothers in Greek mythology).

10. On the mythic in general in Westerns, see Martin M. Winkler, "Classical Mythology and the Western Film," *Comparative Literature Studies* 22 (1985): 516–40.

11. For example, both are nonwhite, the one black and the other half Yaqui Indian; both are leaders (indeed, Joe steps right into Lyedecker's role at the end); and, most dramatically, for a portion of the film they are handcuffed to each other, at one point engaging in a ferocious fight while attached to each other, as if, meatphorically speaking, components of the persona were at odds with its entirety. Lyedecker several times comments gnomically on knowing who he is and doing the kind of job he is best suited for, while Joe, at the end, is made to realize what it is he is best suited for—leading his people.

12. Although the film's structure (aside from its iterations of the *katabasis*) has little to do with the main thesis of this essay, it is worth noting that the film is organized in classical ring composition, with the winning of treasure (the rifles) at its center and the slaughter of the two towns (in Texas at the start and in Mexico at the end) framing the whole. Minor thematic moments enhance this sense of conservative, almost paradigmatic, structure: Pike helps (after being bumped by) an old woman at the start and shoots (after being shot by) a young one at the end; the innocent and mindless cruelty of children at the start is picked up by the consequential and deliberate cruelty of a child at the end; the *Iliad*-like despoiling (albeit by definite anti-heroes) of the corpses of the slain at the start involves only clothing and personal effects, but at the end the stakes have been raised to gold-filled teeth; and the blood-spurting slaughter of innocents is portrayed in graphic slow motion at both ends.

13. As such, blacks typically have roles as escorts or to point the way, like that of tracker (as here); of pilot of the boat running up the Mekong Delta in *Apocalypse Now* (1979); of bringing the hero back to his world, as the black drummer does by driving into the desert to find the hero in *The Jazz Singer* (1980); of mentor to instruct the protagonist in the arts and attitudes of championship soccer in *Hotshot*. Consistent with this "color" semiology of the modern "underworlds" is the inverted use of albinos as monster types. Thus, in *Lethal Weapon*, the freaky albino, Mr. Joshua, is a transcendent Death monster with whom the

hero wrestles at the end. And the equally "crazy" albino, Moke, in the film *Stick* (1985), a Death demon suitably dressed completely in black, is another twist on the same inversion. The etiolated death figures are evil incarnate, while the black ones embody the instructive psychopompic function of the Hermes figure.

14. See Fontenrose, *Python,* 329f.

15. For this cattle owner as a Death demon, see Fontenrose, *Python,* 335f., 346; see also G. S. Kirk, *The Nature of Greek Myths* (New York: Penguin Books, 1974), 189f.

16. On this use of imagery, see Andrew Tudor, "Genre," in Grant, *Film Genre Reader,* 5.

17. This emblematic use of clothing is common in film; another excellent deployment of it in a katabatic setting is the opening of *Midnight Cowboy,* where a country hick from Texas gets himself outfitted for his descent into the dark netherworld of male prostitution in the urban hell of New York City.

18. It is worth noting that the topography in fact does assume such a role in native American *katabasis* narratives. See above, n. 8.

19. A persistent metaphor for the "other world" of boot camp and Vietnam in this film is the word *shit,* and to be enduring the horrors of being in either hell is, with an appropriate awareness of direction, "to be in deep shit." Doherty, "Full Metal Genre," comments sensibly on this use of langauge and speaks of "a veritable fecal obsession" (27). One is reminded of the Aristophanic use of the same metaphor in *Pax,* where the "world without peace . . . is visualized in images of excrement." See Jeffrey Henderson, *The Maculate Muse: Obscene Language in Attic Comedy* (New Haven: Yale University Press, 1975), 63. See also K. J. Reckford, " 'Let Them Eat Cakes'—Three Food Notes to Aristophanes' *Peace,*" in Glen W. Bowersock, Walter Burkert, and Michael C. J. Putnam, eds., *Arktouros: Hellenic Studies presented to Bernard M. W. Knox on the occasion of his 65th birthday* (Berlin: De Gruyter, 1979), 192–93; and C. H. Whitman, *Aristophanes and the Comic Hero* (Cambridge: Harvard University Press, 1964), 110.

20. In general, see Charles Segal, *The Theme of the Mutilation of the Corpse in the "Iliad"* (Leiden: Brill, 1971).

21. Throughout the story there is much talk about "cocks," "queers," "jerking off," and "pussy." Though this use of language is only peripherally related to the *katabasis* theme, the terminology of nonnormative sexual behavior as metaphor for nonnormative behavior in general is developed to a remarkable degree in this film. Similarly, war as nonnormative behavior is the topic of Joker's discussion with a superior who objects to his wearing a symbol of peace, a normative form of human interaction. The language as such is typical of soldiers, and hence consistent with their realistic portrayal. In general, sex and talk about sex in the film seem to function as subtext for male initiation into manhood, which is also an important result of the hero's return from his *katabasis.*

22. See G. S. Kirk, *Myth: Its Meaning and Functions in Ancient and Other Cultures* (Berkeley: University of California Press), 185–86.

The Classical Amazon in Contemporary Cinema

Kristina M. Passman
University of Maine

T HE figure of the Amazon has been the subject of many and varying interpretations, from mythological to psychological to historical and feminist.[1] In this paper, I wish to contribute to the discussion of the nature of the Amazon by investigating the influence of the Amazon from classical antiquity upon the portrayal of Amazon figures in contemporary cinema. In the first section of the paper, I outline the development of the myth of the Amazon during the classical period, in conjunction with the Homeric heroic code and with Greek and Roman ideologies. In addition, I briefly note the major modifications of the figure during the Middle Ages. Following this historical overview, I discuss the figure of the Amazon in four contemporary films. The Amazon continues to represent the ideology of the heroic code, in that she either willingly or unwillingly trains to be a fighter and resorts to violence in support of a male hero or to save the world. Yet she retains the basic feminine characteristics of nurturance, maternity, and loyalty to men. In conclusion, I offer suggestions as to the "significance" of the Amazon today. As she did historically, the Amazon today signifies the many ambiguities surrounding women who fight; these ambiguities reflect the changing economic and social situation, where women are often single parents and face life without a male "protector."

Contemporary cinema more and more acknowledges the quest of the woman for knowledge and understanding of her place in the world, indicative of a move beyond the rigid categories of gender which have heretofore constrained male and female spheres of activity and permissible aspirations; these societal changes are reflected even in the traditionally male-oriented genres of fantasy and science fiction films.

Although it is beyond the scope of this paper to discuss the process of mythopoesis, it is important to state the theoretical attitude toward myth and the part that myth plays in film which

informs my analysis. Myth is a product of culture and has historical significance; in many cases, it is possible to trace the origin and
development of a given mythos, or mythological narrative pattern, within a culture. Thus, although a myth may appear to be
atemporal and ahistorical, it is actually grounded in the intersec-
tion of cultural and historical data and ideology. Indeed, with
Barthes, Jung, and others, it is my contention that myth both
carries ideology and gives an indication of the major psychic
issues of a given period. Study of the variations of a particular
myth can therefore provide important information pertaining to
a given culture both synchronically and diachronically.[2]

It is the same with film. In his pioneering study of media,
popular culture, and mythology, Roland Barthes emphasizes that
everything which can be translated into speech can be a myth; it is
the *social usage* of material which determines whether or not it is a
myth:

> some objects become the prey of mythical speech for a while, then
> they disappear, others take their place and attain the status of myth.
> Are there objects which are *inevitably* a source of suggestiveness, as
> Baudelaire suggested about Woman? Certainly not: one can conceive
> of very ancient myths, but there are no eternal ones; for it is human
> history which converts reality into speech, and it alone rules the life
> and death of mythical language. Ancient or not, mythology can only
> have an historical foundation, for myth is a type of speech chosen by
> history: it cannot possibly evolve from the "nature" of things.[3]

Film is one of the primary conveyers of modern mythology.[4] We
should therefore expect to find cinematic representations of the
old myths, including the myth of the Amazon, and also variations
on versions from the past which reflect contemporary issues.

Finally, myth is, by its very nature, conservative and usually
serves the status quo. Thus, although variations upon ancient
myths may reflect certain changes in the reality of contemporary
culture, such as single women parenting children, the myths will
also reinforce basic conceptualizations of "the feminine": the
"good" Amazon, although often alone and fighting for her survival, is still a mother, is still loyal to a man, and is still motivated to
preserve the world for future children. Her essential nature as
woman remains.[5]

THE AMAZON FIGURE IN ANTIQUITY

The development of the Amazon myth in classical Athens provides an excellent illustration of the manner in which myth re-

flects history and ideological change. The following description of the mutations in the Amazon figure in the course of its development in antiquity is meant both to provide the reader with a background in the various "natures" of the Amazon and to demonstrate the close relation between mythology, ideology, and sociopolitical concerns.

Amazons were known from the time of Homer and were closely connected with the ancient heroic code. The heroic tradition consisted of a set of conventions which held that the hero was usually isolated, even within the group of his companions, that he did everything he could to harm his enemies and his allies' enemies and help his friends. He gained immortality for deeds of great valor; thus the hero would remain in the memory of his people. Individual combat against other great heroes as well as an *aristeia*, a great battle scene, was the usual source of this glory. Thus the heroic code was a code of great individualism, and gave rise to the deeds celebrated in the great epics of antiquity.[6]

In Athens the Amazon mythos came into its own. Amazons first appeared in Athenian art, as far as can be determined, in 575 B.C. They appear, without discernible antecedents and in great numbers, on vases.[7] Heracles' Ninth Labor, his quest for the girdle of the Amazon queen, Hippolyte or Antiope, is the earliest Amazon scene depicted.[8]

Amazons and Athenian Political Ideology

Tyrrell has suggested a political explanation for the sudden appearance of the Amazon:

> Pisistratus, the tyrant of Athens from 545 to 527 B.C., sought to identify himself with Heracles as the protégé of the city's goddess, Athena. The evidence is circumstantial, but Pisistratus' return from his second exile (546 B.C.) in a chariot driven by a tall woman dressed as Athena might have been intended to strike a parallel with Athena's introduction of Heracles into Olympus.[9]

A new hero, Theseus, replaced Heracles at the end of the Pisistratean tyranny in 510 B.C., and with him came new stories involving Amazons.[10] Theseus was popular as local hero and champion of Athenian ideals. There was a close identification of Theseus with Heracles, upon whom several of his mythical exploits are modeled. The variation of the Amazon story associated with Theseus is significantly different from stories associated with Heracles, for Theseus' Amazon story is about war and marriage.[11]

Theseus, his good friend Peirithous, and a charioteer raid Themiscyra, home of the Amazons. Theseus rapes an Amazon (called Hippolyte or Antiope) and takes her back to Athens with him. In turn, the Amazons invade Attica, and lay siege to Athens, surrounding the Acropolis. Finally, they are defeated, and the Amazon abducted by Theseus helps conclude a treaty.[12] Theseus has a son, Hippolytus, by this Amazon, and later abandons her to marry Phaedra, considered more suitable for a king because she is Greek. In an interesting twist, the Amazon is killed by Heracles when she disrupts the wedding party.[13]

The myth of the rape, abduction, and abandonment of the Amazon was soon superseded on vases and reliefs by a more pointedly different, "public" use of the Amazon figure. The Athenians utilized the Amazons' siege of the Acropolis to identify Amazons not as women to be tamed but as a lethal threat to national security:

> The myth of the rape appeared on the Temple of Apollo Daphnephorus in Eretria about 510 B.C. and on vases, all dating before the Persian Wars (490, 480 / 79 B.C.). It disappeared after the wars, when the invading Persians from the East were equated with Amazons. In postwar myths, the Amazon is killed fighting with Theseus or against him, and the Amazons themselves are annihilated.[14]

There is much additional evidence for the propaganda use of the Amazon myth as a justification for Athenian imperial practices.[15] In the course of this development, Amazons became more and more represented as "others," strangers and barbarians who would destroy Athenian democracy. The reason for this increasing vilification as well as fascination with the Amazon arises doubly from the xenophobia and the gender ideology of the Athenians, an ideology which declared that women were "others" and that only Athenian men were "truly human."

Amazons and Athenian Gender Ideology

Athenian culture of the classical period was one of the most misogynistic patriarchal cultures to arise in western Europe. The Amazon myth as developed in Athens is a perfect representation of Attic political ideology and the ideology of male supremacy.[16]

Before discussing this ideology, I shall briefly describe the basic features of Amazon society.[17] The Amazons were a race of warrior women. They lived apart from men, somewhere in the East.

When they wished to have daughters to keep their race and society alive, they captured and enslaved men. They kept any resulting girl-children and either killed or mutilated their boy-children or simply gave them back to their fathers, whom they returned to their home villages once pregnancy was established— a strong denial of stereotypical views of the romantic and emotional nature of women. Amazons were eager for military campaigns and conquests and were unbeatable in battle, fighting from horseback. They were called the "daughters of Ares."[18] Amazons were also closely connected with Artemis, the goddess of hunting and protectress of young girls, who lived separately from the civilized world of cities and Greek social customs.[19]

Naturally, it is unlikely that Amazons, as described, ever existed, but this is not to say that there were not cultures wherein women fought. This particular "society," however, is created from oppositions inherent in Athenian cultural and gender ideology; the question is not, Were there Amazons? but, Why create Amazons?

The Greek language frequently deals in dualities, containing special constructions which invite and imply polar opposition.[20] The Amazon myth expresses opposites to patriarchal reality: for a society which did not recognize women as independent and autonomous and, indeed, did not permit them to be independent and autonomous, Amazons *were* independent and autonomous. In contrast to a society which exalted boy-children and openly practiced female infanticide through exposure, Amazons treasured their girl-children and gave away, mutilated, or killed their male offspring. Unlike a society where "good" women were secluded and could not leave the house without permission of their male guardians, Amazons were free and rode horses across the land. In Athenian society the women were weak, housebound, and often ill-nourished. Amazons on the other hand had weapons, were strong, and hunted. According to the Homeric heroic code, a model for centuries, the only true immortality was found on the field of battle, where heroes met, fought, and died in great struggles. Amazons met and fought with the greatest heroes, such as Heracles, Theseus, and Achilles, and were killed by them.[21]

The Athenian myth of the foundation of marriage provides a clue to the extreme constraints placed upon Athenian women:

At Athens Cecrops first yoked one woman to one man. Before then mating was at random and promiscuous. . . . Cecrops laid down laws so that men had intercourse with [women] openly and were contented with one wife. *He also discovered the two natures of the father and the mother.* . . . Cecrops legislated that women, who before mated like beasts, be given in marriage to one man.[22]

From this account, two imperatives of patriarchy are established: heterosexual monogamy (the restriction of women's sexuality to intercourse with men, and to one man in particular) and patriliny (the idea that the male has rights over the child and a guarantee that he is the father).[23]

In considering the rule of the household and the state, Greek polar thinking allowed only two alternatives, rule by men or rule by women. On the private level, rule by women translated into the death of the husband and destruction of the household, as detailed in Aeschylus' *Oresteia*.[24] On the public level it meant matriarchy, a situation considered equivalent to chaos and regression.[25]

In her heroism on the field of battle, however, the Amazon is depicted with all those "noble" qualities which warfare and the call to glory elicited in men under the heroic code. In those vase paintings where she is depicted in battle, she is killed in hand-to-hand combat with a spear-thrust or sword-thrust through the breast.[26] This indicates her worthiness as an opponent to the greatest Greek heroes, for the highest honor in battle was to face a great hero in individual combat. The tale of the marriage of Theseus and Antiope/Hippolytè brings the private and the public spheres together, mingling the Amazon's heroism with the barbarism the Athenians projected upon her. It illustrates a point of transition in the development of the myth from the idea that rape and abduction might assimilate the Amazon, the "other," to Athenian ways up to the thought that "blood will out" and that she will revert to savagery; this would leave only one option: to kill the barbarian.

The ambivalence the woman warrior elicited in Greek men is further illustrated by the goddess Athena. Athena is most often depicted in art and literature as a warrior. She was the product of Zeus' ingestion of her mother, Metis (Wisdom), for Metis' son would prove greater than his father. Athena emerged into the world in full battle dress and giving a war cry. Athena bargained with her father to remain unwed in return for perpetual virginity and loyalty to her father. She became an advisor to great heroes, appearing in the *Iliad* to stop Achilles from the rash action of publicly killing Agamemnon, and playing a prominent part in the *Odyssey* as advisor to Odysseus.[27]

Athena is a skilled fighter and capable of planning strategies which are cunning and full of forethought. As the patron deity of Athens, she represents a beneficient Amazon: closely allied to Zeus, she upholds his law, protects heroes from danger, and counsels them when they are in difficulty. Rather than withdrawing from Athenian culture she maintains it; the Amazons as developed by the Athenians would be her deadly enemies.

The Romano-Celtic Tradition and After

As Roman cultural ideology was different from that of Athens, the development of the Amazon myth was also different in the hands of the Romans. They used the Amazon for propagandist purposes, chiefly as part of their justification of empire.

The writer to establish the Roman idea of the Amazon was Vergil, who created Camilla, the Volscian warrior dedicated to Diana, the Roman counterpart to Greek Artemis. Vergil's concerns in the *Aeneid* center around, among other things, the cost of empire, which included the sacrifice of individual customs and cultures.

Vergil had many different traditions to draw from in his portrayal of ancient Italy at the time of the Trojans' arrival, but Celtic tradition was of particular interest to the Romans. They never forgot the Gallic invasion and conquest of Rome about 400 B.C.; the province of Cisalpine Gaul was a reminder that the Celts had never really left the Italian peninsula.

The Romans knew it was not unusual for a Celtic queen to lead her people in battle. The most famous examples come from Tacitus, writing of the Icenian rebellion in Celtic Britain. In his account of the events of the year A.D. 59, Tacitus reports that the greater warrior queen Boudicca, outraged at her public flogging and the rape of her two daughters by the Roman occupational forces, incited the tribes to rise against their oppressors.[28] Cassius Dio gives a physical description of Boudicca:

> She was huge of frame, terrifying of aspect, and with a harsh voice. A great mass of bright red hair fell to her knees; she wore a great twisted golden necklace, and a tunic of many colours, over which she had a thick mantle, fastened by a brooch. Now she grasped a spear, to strike fear into the hearts of all who watched her, and spoke as follows.[29]

These warrior women did not live separately from men in order to retain their autonomy. They were often, if not always, portrayed as women loyal to their tribes, fighting side by side with men to protect mutual interests. Some, such as Boudicca, were mothers as well and fought to protect their children.

Let us return now to Vergil and his depiction of Camilla. In the *Aeneid*, Camilla fights on the side of the Latin people against the Trojans, whom they perceive as invaders. She was raised in the wilderness by her father Metabus. The child was nursed by a wild mare, which gave her a special affinity to horses. Her father brought about her transformation into a warrior at an early age, teaching her to hunt and dressing her in tiger skins instead of girl's clothing. She could have married when she came of age, but instead devoted herself to Diana as a virgin and hunter.[30]

Like other Celtic women fighters, Camilla does not hate men and does not hide in glades and forests. Camilla is reminiscent of the warrior queen from the Celtic tradition in that she plans the strategy for the entire Italian defensive; until her death, the Latin commanders follow this strategy.[31] It is her delight in and enthusiasm for martial glory which eventually lead to her death; before she dies, however, she has a glorious *aristeia*, a battle in which she faces foe after foe and kills them without mercy and with great skill. Vergil makes it clear that the man who killed her, Arruns, did not gain glory, for he tracks Camilla like an animal rather than facing her as a hero in individual combat, and kills her from ambush.[32] Camilla becomes the perfect symbol of a noble but doomed population.

The Roman Amazon functions in a way that illustrates the political ideology of Roman imperialism, just as the Greek Amazon illustrates the political ideology of Athenian Greece. The Romans were destined by the gods to wage war upon their enemies and create a great empire which would last for all time.[33] In their great national epic, the *Aeneid*, Aeneas, the father of the new race which would accomplish this, learns not only to do this duty but also to act with the expediency necessary to conquer Italy so that the new race can come into being and fulfill its destiny. Camilla, with her attributes of independence and autonomy, ought not to be understood as a woman who did not "know her place" and so had to be killed, a view far more in line with the sexual ideology of Greece than of Rome; rather, she should be understood as representative of cultures such as the Celtic as well as of other indigenous cultures of Italy and Western Europe. Romans viewed these cultures with respect, but for the stability of the empire these people had to be brought under control.

After Camilla, there is a final major Roman literary example of the Amazon figure, that of Penthesilea in Quintus of Smyrna's work, the *Posthomerica*. Written in the fourth century A.D., it brings together the earlier characterizations of Amazons to create a romantic, tragic heroine in Penthesilea. Here are his descriptions of Penthesilea's arrival at Troy and of her death:

> As when Dawn comes down from weariless Olympus with the lovely-haired Seasons, glorying in her shining steeds, amid all she is conspicuous, so beautiful as though the others are blameless, thus did Penthesilea come to Troy pre-eminent among the Amazons. The Trojans rush from all sides and wonder greatly when they see the high-greaved daughter of the weariless Ares alike to the blessed mortals. The beauty of her face was awesome and radiant. Her smile was lovely, and beneath her brows her eyes, sparkling like rays, aroused desire. Modesty blushed her cheeks, and over them was a godlike grace clothed in war prowess. . . .

> Though she lay fallen in dirt and gore, beneath her lovely eyebrows shone her beautiful face, even in death. The Argives, crowding about, were amazed when they saw her: she seemed like the blessed immortals. She lay on the ground in her armor like tireless Artemis, daughter of Zeus, sleeping when weary from chasing swift lions in the lofty mountains. Aphrodite, beautiful garlanded wife of mighty Ares, made Penthesilea radiant even in death to cause the son of blameless Peleus to grieve. Many men prayed that when they came home they would sleep in the bed of a wife like her. Achilles suffered greatly in his heart, that he slew her and did not bring her to Phthia as his shining wife, since in height and beauty she was blameless and like the immortals.[34]

I have quoted this passage at length, for it serves as the final example of the figure of the Amazon in the classical period and illustrates her essential characteristics. The Amazon is by this time established as a literary figure. She is beautiful, tall, and graceful. She rides a horse, is often accompanied by a troop of other Amazons, and is closely associated with Artemis and Ares. Her erotic potential is indicated by her association with Aphrodite and by the fact that many heroes wish to take her to their beds. She dies in battle, fiercely fighting a great hero, and is mourned by all, including her killer and the gods. Penthesilea is a true hero in the sense that a hero was more than mortal but less than divine. The language used of her is much the same as the language used of the great heroes. This is the Amazon who continues through societal fluctuations, upon which I shall touch below, into contemporary cinema.

The development of organized Christianity and the consequent fear of carnality placed a new constraint upon the figure of the "good" Amazon: like a literary figure such as Camilla and unlike

historical warrior women, she must be a virgin. By the High
Middle Ages, the figure of the "manly woman" had become familiar through epic romance. Beautiful, courageous, virtuous, she
appears frequently in Continental literature as well as in the early
literature of the New World.[35] With the grave temperament the
Reformation brought to Europe, and the suspicion under which
pagan texts fell, the fountain of romance and the heroic code,
both of which had fed the Amazon myths, was stilled; only with
the reawakening of romantic sensibility did the Amazon return to
art and literature, where she has remained.

Contemporary Amazon Characteristics

In today's representations of the Amazon figure, there are two
kinds of Amazons, one ultimately derived from Greek culture, the
other from the less rigid Romano-Celtic tradition. These are
represented in the physical types of "good" and "bad" Amazons.
"Good" Amazons are tall and blond, or red-haired with fair skin,
following Cassius Dio's description of Boudicca. "Bad" Amazons
are shorter, darker, and have black or brown hair. "Good" Amazons look like Nordic Celts, and "bad" Amazons look if not Greek,
at least swarthy. Thus there is an opposition between darkness
and light, between northern Europe and the Mediterranean (including Africa). This stereotyping and its underlying racial-sexual
ideology continues in the depiction of Amazons in contemporary
cinema.

The motivations for the "good" Amazon are often presented as
justice or selfless love, while those of the "bad" Amazon are power
or lust. The character of the "good" Amazon is simple and child-
like, reflecting her virginal nature, whereas that of the "bad"
Amazon is complex and mature, dangerous through her knowledge of her sexuality and her desire to fulfill her desires. The
"good" Amazon is a "loner," following her own path and living by
her own standards, much like the isolated male hero in contemporary cinema and literature. However, when she joins forces with a
male hero, she is both loyal and lethal in her defense of him. Such
Amazon figures, like their classical counterparts, are skilled in the
use of weapons and strategy. In each film the Amazon has an
aristeia in which she faces the enemy and emerges triumphant. In
the one film where the Amazon is killed (*Conan the Barbarian*), she
is not killed in battle but by treachery.

In general, an Amazon may be defined as a woman who fights
with skill and, either initially or in the course of her exploits,

comes to derive satisfaction from fighting and killing. She comes to embody the heroic code, and like her male counterpart possesses or learns skills with a variety of different weapons. She is aggressive and not dependent upon others for physical survival in a violent world. She combines physical attractiveness to males with traditionally "masculine" characteristics of courage, endurance, action, decision-making, and heroism. True to the conservative nature of myth, she does not deviate from the social norm of the "good" woman, being clearly heterosexual and either celibate or monogamous.

The Amazon in Film

The first film to be discussed depicts an Amazon who conforms both to the stereotype of the "good" Amazon and also possesses many of the characteristics associated particularly with Athena.

Conan the Barbarian (1982)

"Do you want to live forever?" This is the taunt of Valeria, the young Amazon whom the hero Conan encounters in John Milius's *Conan the Barbarian*. Valeria makes her appearance about halfway through the film; up to this point, the audience has seen the boyhood and youth of Conan. True to the film's title, he is a barbarian, amoral and dedicated only to himself, working or stealing for subsistence. Lured by the promise of riches, he has made his way into the fortress of the evil Thulsa Doom, where he encounters Valeria, who is herself preparing to plunder Doom's temple. They join forces, steal a treasure, and fall in love. Against her advice, Conan agrees to rescue a princess who is in Doom's power. He makes his way alone, but is captured and left for dead. Valeria finds him and pledges her life in exchange for his. She is treacherously killed by an arrow shot by Doom. Conan defeats Doom and kills him; in the final scene, he is alone.

In the scenes in which they are together, Valeria and Conan are depicted as equals. Valeria is equally as brave, foolhardy, aggressive in bed, almost equally as drunk, and equally as barbaric in her costuming as Conan.[36] She is tall, blond, and fair, dressed in the usual thigh-revealing outfit common to these films, and armed with sword and dagger. Valeria has lived alone on the periphery of society, an accomplished thief and swordswoman. Her stance and boldness suggest a seasoned fighter, one who is quick on her feet and able to survive on her own. When Valeria goes into battle, her *aristeia* is deadly; she fights with the same violence, determination, and bloodlust as Conan himself.

Her bravery is unquestionable. When she cannot dissuade Conan from his quest to free the princess and avenge the death of his family, she rescues him from death. She battles with the spirits of the dead who seek to take her injured lover. Upon his return to consciousness, she says to him: "All the gods could not sever us. If I was dead and in the pit of darkness, I'd come back from hell to be at your side." In her loyalty and love for Conan she resembles Patroclus, the dear companion of Achilles, who, to uphold Achilles' honor, fought and died in his place.[37] Valeria feels that her death is payment for Conan's life, as her dying words to him indicate: "I [vowed] I would pay the cost." She is much like Camilla, who also thinks of others at the moment of her death: her final words are for Turnus and the Italian war effort.[38]

During the final battle between Conan and Thulsa Doom's forces, Valeria makes her last appearance. Conan is about to be killed, but a figure appears and strikes away his opponent's sword. Conan looks up and sees Valeria, dressed in silver armor. She seems to be a Valkyrie. She repeats the words she spoke to him earlier, "Do you want to live forever?" This is a reference to the heroic code, which held that heroism yielded undying fame; the price of this immortality was often death. His glimpse of her is only brief; Conan turns to retrieve his sword, and she is gone.

The emphasis placed on the sword is paramount in the film; it includes the religious notion that the god Crom will ask each man upon his death if he knows the secret of steel. If he does, he may enter Valhalla; if not, he is hurled into the pit of hell. When the film opens, we see a sword being forged: it is on the anvil, heated to a red-hot state, and tempered in snow. This scene acts as a metaphor for Conan's experiences up to the climax of the film, when his red-hot rage has finally been tempered by the decapitation of his enemy. Its abatement is symbolized by the dousing of thousands of torches, one by one, in a pool of water, until he is left alone, a huge, solitary figure, walking away from the destruction he himself has created.

What Conan does not learn is that "steel" is a metaphor, and that both love (Valeria) and persuasiveness (Doom) are stronger than steel (might). He continues to believe in a *literal* world, and thus his chances for growth are limited to the sword. The second film, *Conan the Destroyer* (1984), shows this very clearly. Its entire premise is that if Conan obeys the commands of an evil queen, she will bring Valeria back to physical life. That Conan believes this until the end of the film underlines the fact that he does not know that Valeria's transformation has occurred on a metaphysical, symbolic level, and that the only way he can "join" her is by changing himself.

Valeria is the perfect type of the "good" Amazon. As discussed earlier, she lives in isolation, much like the male hero, and is an adept fighter, taking joy in battle and killing. Physically, she fits the Amazon stereotype. Her character is represented as simple and loyal to Conan, much in the manner that Camilla and the Celtic warrior women were represented in the *Aeneid*. Also like Camilla, Valeria dies from an unseen assault, and in an even less heroic fashion: she is wounded in the back by Doom's magic arrow. The film also combines the tradition of Athena, the goddess who champions, intervenes for, and advises the ancient Greek heroes, with the ancient Norse tradition of the Valkyrie. In the manner of traditional hero tales, Conan's companion Valeria acts as his foil and comments upon the flaws in his character. Conan does not understand the true "secret" of steel, which is what Odysseus learns from Achilles in Hades: that values other than that of the sword, such as the relationship with a loving woman, are what gives meaning to life.[39] At the close of the film, Conan, like Achilles, has lost what gave meaning to his life, his dear companion, for the sake of the code of the sword and the need for vengeance.

Red Sonja (1985)

In Richard Fleischer's film *Red Sonja,* the main character is a warrior woman; the Amazon figure is no longer secondary to the male hero. Along with its emphasis upon the heroic code and deeds of valor, the film also concerns itself with justifying Sonja's actions as a woman who kills.

The film opens with a girl who has crawled free from a burning cottage. A voice calls her name, and an apparition forms—a female figure carrying a mystic sword. This goddess figure gives the audience the necessary background information: Sonja is suffering now, but vengeance will be hers. She tells Sonja that Queen Gedren, a power-hungry woman who sexually desired Sonja, has inflicted terrible punishment upon the girl for scarring the queen's face while resisting her advances. She ordered Sonja's family murdered before her eyes and had the girl raped by her soldiers and left for dead in her burning home. These events are shown in a series of quick shots set into the opening scene, the final one a close-up of Sonja shrieking as she is raped. The figure goes on to say that in her quest for justice Sonja will need a strong sword arm. She touches Sonja in a manner reminiscent of the bestowal of knighthood.[40]

Sonja's quest involves retrieving a sacred talisman from Queen Gedren, who has slain its priestesses and guardian Amazons. Only this sacred society of women can guard the talisman, which kills any male who touches it. The talisman will destroy the world in thirteen days unless it itself is destroyed; Gedren, however, disbelieving the danger, is using the talisman to gain control of the world.

On her quest, Sonja becomes involved with a surrogate child, a spoiled young prince whose kingdom Gedren has ravaged. Sonja is depicted as having the potential of being a good but strict mother, a match for the most unruly of boys. Sonja will not be a mother, though, if she cannot bring herself to permit men to touch her; her aversion to physical contact is illustrated during her training as a swordswoman. She will not even allow the embrace of a fellow student whom she has bested in friendly competition.

Whereas in *Conan the Barbarian* it was clear that Valeria did not "need a man" and that it was their equality as warriors which made the mutual attraction and love between Conan and Valeria possible, in *Red Sonja* the heroine cannot accomplish her tasks on her own. A mysterious warrior, Kalidor, appears at each stage of her quest to offer aid and, if necessary, to recue Sonja. When they are finally alone together, he reveals (in the best heroic fashion) that he is the Prince of Eterna, and that his hereditary duty is to see the talisman destroyed when it becomes evident that it is a danger to the safety of the world.

When he begins to kiss her, Sonja yields momentarily, then pulls away and tells him she has taken a vow that she can only give herself to a man who has bested her in a fair fight. They fight until exhausted, neither having bested the other. This scene takes the place of a love or sex scene. The implication is that love is a battle, a competition, a violent act. The scene contains traditional male assumptions about what women "really want" and about the manner in which women's minds work, an attitude consonant with the fundamentally reactionary nature of the science fiction and fantasy genres of film.[41]

As they make their way into Gedren's fortress, Kalidor is shown "helping" Sonja, but in the bloody battle scenes within the fortress each fights individually. Both Kalidor and Sonja are effective, accomplished, and violent fighters. When Sonja confronts Gedren in her throne room, the queen has captured Sonja's "son" and is threatening to kill him. The evil queen fights with the aid of magic, thus engaging in foul play, while Sonja fairly uses her skill and sword. The final battle between them takes place as the talisman begins to destroy the world. Sonja, stunned and bleeding, manages to break the queen's sword and stabs her through the breast. She then hurls her into the fiery pit beneath the Hall, and throws the talisman after her. In the closing scene of the film, Kalidor declares that he will never choose a woman who has not bested him in a fair fight. He and Sonja draw swords and spar for a moment, then kiss, swords interlocked.

In its treatment of the Amazon figure, *Red Sonja* is particularly interesting in several regards. Sonja physically conforms to the Amazon type, being tall and red-haired. As noted above, she is skilled in weapons of war and an accomplished fighter. Although not a virgin, she is not sexually active; her character is simple and straightforward, and she, too, is a "loner." She fulfills all of the characteristics of the "good" Amazon. In addition, in this film there is also a "bad" Amazon, Queen Gedren.

Gedren is ambitious for personal power and, if not stopped, will destroy the world. One major characteristic of the "bad" Amazon is the linking of her lust for power with lesbianism or with a voracious heterosexual appetite. Gedren has lesbian desires which she aggressively seeks to fulfill. She is very much like the Amazon created out of Greek misogyny, particularly in her contempt for men and her murderous intent toward the boy-child. Her disregard for the fate of the world is a modern reflection of the chaos the Greeks felt had to erupt when women were in power. Thus the filmmakers have brought together the "good" and "bad" Amazon in representations basically unchanged from antiquity. The problem of having for a protagonist a "good" woman who kills is addressed in several ways.

Because the main character is a woman, the ideology of the sword vies in this film with that of gender. Although Sonja is shown to be a confident and competent fighter, her character as a warrior woman is coupled with the subtext of "a proper woman's role" from the start. The facts that her role as a warrior is divinely sanctioned and that she ultimately fights not for vengeance (although she coincidentally accomplishes this) but to save the world, serve to justify her killings. Furthermore, she has a surrogate son and is shown interacting with that son in a properly maternal fashion. Her physical relations with Kalidor are hesitant, but her natural desire for him is clear. At the end we know that Sonja has completed her task and that she will be released by the goddess who gave her the extraordinary strength necessary for her quest to live happily with her prince. Unlike Valeria, this Amazon will now become a wife and mother, and will no doubt be effective in her role. In the ideology of the film, the part Sonja has played as an Amazon is a kind of deviation, but an important stage which has saved the world and has given her back to herself through the achievement of her quest.

The Terminator (1984)

Science fiction concerns itself with many of the same issues and uses many of the same formulas as fantasy films, such as the problem of good and evil, the quest (often disguised) for self-knowledge and identity, and the code of heroism.[42] The figure of the Amazon plays an important part in recent futuristic films. In the two films I discuss, the major characters are women who fight the alien invaders and destroy them. It is difficult at this early point to determine whether this new trend in a traditionally male-oriented genre is a reflection of the massive change in gender roles which has occurred recently in Western society, or whether it is merely a commercial twist of a popular formula.

James Cameron's film, The Terminator, is a variation of the Christ story, with emphasis upon the development of the potential mother of the savior from an "ordinary" young woman into a "legend."[43] The narrative details two worlds, the present and a post-holocaust world in the year 2029. The film presents us with a time traveler and intercuts, through the device of flashbacks, details of his future world as he recalls them.

In the future, defense computers have developed independent intelligence and have combined with other machines to exterminate humanity. Human beings are on the verge of extinction when a charismatic figure, John Connor, rises up and shows them how to fight back. The machines send a terminator, a machine made of human tissue, metal, and circuitry, back to the twentieth century to kill John Connor's mother, Sarah. This will prevent John Connor's birth and, subsequently, the rebellion. However, Connor has sent the man who will father him to the past in order to save Sarah and teach her how to survive.[44] This man, Kyle Reese, has fallen in love with Sarah after seeing a photograph John has given him. Reese protects Sarah and teaches her to fight, giving her lessons in guns, bomb-making, offensive driving, and increasingly ruthless defensive measures, until she is able to defeat the Terminator.

Blond, blue-eyed Sarah is not an Amazon at the start of the film. She is shown, however, to have Amazon potential: she rides a motorbike, a touch which indicates her individuality, reminiscent of the Amazon's horse. Her affinity to nature as well as her ability to embrace the unusual is indicated by a pet Gila monster. The requisite chastity is also present.

During Kyle's narrative, the audience receives glimpses of the post-holocaust world. There are no gender distinctions; men and women fight together as equals. When Sarah asks what the women in his time are like, Kyle simply says, "Good fighters." He does not understand Sarah's questions about love and romance, for these things do not exist in the future.

Sarah quickly learns to handle weapons, to move defensively, and to show great courage under fire. As Kyle becomes weaker due to exhaustion and injury, she becomes stronger and assumes more and more control over the situation, even saving him from several encounters with the Terminator. Eventually, she has become superior to the killing machine; to destroy it she utilizes both her own intelligence and another machine, a metal press, thus taking on characteristics of her enemy. At the end of the film Sarah, no longer a modern Amazon in jeans and sneakers, is the pregnant madonna of the future savior, dictating the story of the film into a tape recorder as she drives into the mountains.

This film is grittily realistic, presenting Kyle and Sarah as human beings with a wider variety of emotions and motivations than the mono-dimensional stereotypes found in *Conan the Barbarian* and *Red Sonja*. Kyle, the man from a future where humanity can no longer afford gender distinctions and survive, assumes that Sarah is untaught, not inept; when she dresses his wound he compliments her. There is no stereotypical notion of "woman as nurse," but rather the idea of one fighter helping another. He understands Sarah's terror at her danger from the Terminator, for he has felt it all his life. He tells her the truth about the Terminator: it will stop at nothing to kill her and might succeed. Sarah, in turn, offers Kyle love and comfort. It is she who initiates sex, out of compassion and empathy for Kyle's pain and love for her. In the film's obligatory sex scene, Sarah is in the superior position, choosing Kyle as the father of her son.

The Terminator utilizes many of the characteristics of the Amazon from antiquity, including Sarah's physical traits, her skill with weapons, loyalty to the man next to whom she is fighting, and the final battle, her *aristeia,* in which she triumphantly destroys her enemy. Similarly to the heroine in *Red Sonja,* Sarah Connor is responsible for saving the human race; she defeats the Terminator, thus surviving and giving birth to her son. The motifs of saving the race and of motherhood, as well as the fact that the Terminator is not human: all this mitigates ambivalences in modern culture regarding the woman who kills in that her actions are presented as justifiable. The fact that Sarah is a "reluctant" Amazon, someone forced to learn to fight, and this primarily for her own survival, further vindicates her violence.

The Terminator also reflects current issues regarding sexual equality by its emphasis upon the lack of gender distinctions in the world of the future. The fact that Sarah learns to be a fighter and will also give birth indicates a change from the fates of the Amazon figures in the two films examined previously: in *Conan the Barbarian,* Valeria, the most traditional Amazon character, dies; in *Red Sonja,* Sonja puts aside her life as an Amazon to become a wife. Sarah will not be a wife, but she will continue to fight and will also be a mother.

Aliens (1987)

The science fiction film *Aliens,* also directed by James Cameron, pits the reluctant survivor of an encounter with a single alien being against, ultimately, the mother of an alien race. The plot relies upon the fact that the viewer has seen Ridley Scott's previous film, *Alien* (1979), to which this production is the sequel.

Ripley, the only survivor of an attack by a deadly alien, has slept in suspended animation for fifty-seven years. Sinking more and more into nightmares and delusions of having been impregnated by this alien, she finds that no one believes her tale of the existence of alien beings. Shortly after her rescue the Company, which is colonizing the planet Ripley had fled, can no longer reach that planet by radio. The Company charters a group of Colonial Marines to investigate and asks Ripley to accompany the expedition. After much hesitation, she agrees to go along. In addition, a Company official, Burke, who has befriended Ripley, joins the group. They find the colony deserted, except for a seven-year-old girl, Newt. The aliens are indeed there; they have captured and used the colonists as incubators for baby aliens.[45] The aliens kill nearly all the marines; through Burke's treachery, Ripley finds that the Company intends to use the aliens for its own sinister purpose. The film then centers around Ripley, Newt, and two marines, Hicks and an android, and their attempts to escape the planet as well as to destroy the aliens before they can be imported by the Company and used against humanity. There is a subtext in the film about the military-industrial complex and its blatant disregard for consequences in the development of the aliens as "ultimate weapons." It cannot be chance that "the Company" is also a designation for the CIA.

When Ripley begins destroying baby aliens, the mother alien pursues her. At the final confrontation, all the male characters have been incapacitated, and Ripley must face the mother alien alone. She dons a fork-lift suit that functions as mechanized armor, and she and the mother alien battle for Newt's and Ripley's life. Ripley succeeds in dispatching the mother alien into space. The final scene shows Ripley putting the child to bed, in preparation for suspended animation, as they make their way back to earth.

Perhaps because Ripley's character could originally have been cast as either male or female, Ripley breaks the standard physical pattern of the Amazon in that she is brunette (although tall and fair-skinned).[46] As one would expect from an Amazon of the future, Ripley is competent with machines and quickly learns the use of defensive weapons. Having dealt with the aliens before, she is the others' source of wisdom in defeating them, much as Reese functioned in The Terminator. Her intelligence and refusal to rely upon the judgments of the marines allows her to assume control of the operation and make decisions which would have ensured the survival of the majority of the marines had it not been for Burke's treachery.

There are several other women in the film who qualify as Amazons; these are the women who are part of the Colonial Marines. It is "natural" for them to be in combat situations. These women have chosen to fight because it is a job. In their speech and mannerisms, they are easily recognizable as "hard-boiled" soldiers. They have short, male, military haircuts and bulging biceps. They are capable fighters and illustrate Kyle Reese's comment in The Terminator that in the world of the future women are "good fighters." Since James Cameron directed both films, this is not surprising. Although nothing is said explicitly about the sexuality of the women marines, the character of Vasquez is very much the stereotype of the male-identified lesbian. She is an almost tragic character in that she dies nobly, sacrificing herself to save her comrades.

In the earlier film, *Alien*, Ripley is a "good woman" due to a lack of sexual involvement and the love for her cat. She is clever and outwits the alien both through cunning and control of her terror rather than in battle. The second film, *Aliens*, finds her completely alone, trying to make sense of her survival fifty-seven years later. The film details her development into a "good Amazon." Her task, like Sarah's and Red Sonja's, is to save humanity; like them, Ripley acquires a child and exercises her maternal qualities. As did Sarah in *The Terminator*, Ripley takes on the qualities of her enemy to survive. Toward the end of the film, she becomes the visual equivalent of the alien mother by donning external armor. (The alien creature largely consists of a metallic substance, a natural armor.) In doing so, she is able to overcome the alien in a clever, ferocious, and highly suspenseful *aristeia*. There is the implication at the close of *Aliens* that Ripley and Newt have become a family without a father figure; the audience also realizes that Ripley will remain an independent woman.

CONCLUSION

In the standard mythological pattern, the hero struggles against terrible perils, culminating usually in a fight with a dragon. Upon its death, the hero finds a priceless, hidden treasure, wins glory, and marries the princess. In the past, no woman was a hero, not even an Amazon. In terms of both history and mythological tradition, however, the existence of the Amazon as a heroic figure is undeniable. With the exception of *Conan the Barbarian*, the films examined here heighten our awareness of the Amazon, previously only a foil to the hero in her loyalty and fighting ability. The films associate the "good" Amazon with the larger concerns of society (ultimately, with the survival of humanity) and emphasize her "essential" feminine nature by providing her with a child. At the same time the Amazon figure begins to point beyond traditional assumptions regarding women and takes on aspects of the male hero.

The Amazon figures in these films, with the exception of Valeria, must learn to be Amazons and thus to integrate characteristics of the masculine into their personalities. Yet they are still women and as such, once again with the exception of Valeria, concern themselves with the survival of children. Thus the Amazon's quest is different from that of the male hero. She is not seeking the glory of social affirmation which accompanies marriage; instead, her quest deals with the biologically appropriate issue of the continuance of the race.

This is the significance of the child given to Red Sonja, Sarah, and Ripley: it is the symbol of the potential for the future and a sign of female maturity and motherhood. In turn, Valeria's transcendent state in *Conan the Barbarian* indicates that through the sacrifice of her earthly existence she has attained the highest degree of understanding and awareness in terms of the heroic code and, having done so, has become an Athena-like guardian for the male hero Conan.

In films of the fantasy and science fiction genres, the heroic code and the power of the blade have retained their fascination. The old mythological patterns remain; today, they speak to us through communications and entertainment media, especially film. The Amazon figure, closely connected with the heroic code, is increasingly represented in film and may well be a response to the increased participation of women in the public sphere. More and more women have entered arenas which are traditionally male, and we now require myths which account for women's experience as heroic women, as women who face the same challenges and dragons as their male counterparts.[47] Films such as the ones discussed reflect the needs of contemporary men and women to have stories which, on the mythological level, deal with this new type of woman. The characteristics of the Amazon have remained constant since they were established in antiquity, but with the modern addition of motherhood. Many women are raising their children alone today and face great economic and social challenges as they do so. Amazon films which emphasize motherhood and the future of the human race subliminally respond to this situation, in a sense valuing the heroic effort involved in motherhood under such circumstances. If myths act both as patterns of experience and reflections of the normative values of the society which produces them, the constancy, loyalty, bravery, and fierce maternity of the Amazon in contemporary cinema well illustrate the manner in which popular media may become the expression of popular mythology.[48]

NOTES

1. Mythology: Donald J. Sobol, *The Amazons of Greek Mythology* (New York: Barnes, 1973); history and myth: William Blake Tyrrell, *Amazons: A Study in Athenian Mythmaking* (Baltimore: Johns Hopkins University Press, 1984); feminism: Page DuBois, *Centaurs and*

Amazons: Women and the Prehistory of the Great Chain of Being (Ann Arbor: University of Michigan Press, 1982); psychoanalysis (Jungian): Jean Shinoda Bolen, *Goddesses in Everywoman: A New Psychology of Women* (San Francisco: Harper & Row, 1984).

2. Roland Barthes, *Mythologies*, trans. A. Lavers (New York: Hill & Wang, 1972). For the interplay of cultural ideologies and the visual media, see John Berger, *Ways of Seeing* (London: Penguin Books and BBC, 1972), and Bill Nichols, *Ideology and the Image* (Bloomington: Indiana University Press, 1981); also C. G. Jung, "Psychology and Literature," in *The Spirit in Man, Literature and Art*, trans. R. F. C. Hull, *Collected Works of C. G. Jung*, vol. 15 (Princeton: Princeton University Press, 1971).

3. Barthes, *Mythologies*, 110.

4. For a discussion of film and mythic thought see Yvette Biró, *Profane Mythology: The Savage Mind of the Cinema*, trans. I. Goldstein (Bloomington: Indiana University Press, 1982); for a discussion in terms of Jungian psychoanalysis see Don Fredericksen, "Jung/ Sign/Symbol/Film, Part One," *Quarterly Review of Film Studies* 4 (Spring 1979): 167–92; "Jung/Sign/Symbol/Film, Part Two," *Quarterly Review of Film Studies* 5 (Fall 1980): 459–79.

5. On the conservative nature of myth, see Barthes, *Mythologies*, 133–45 and 148–55.

6. For a description of the "rules" for heroic behavior derived from the epics of Homer see Cedric H. Whitman, *Homer and the Heroic Tradition* (Cambridge: Harvard University Press, 1958), 154–80. For references to Amazons in the *Iliad* see 2.811–14, 2.181–89, and 6.172–86.

7. Dietrich von Bothmer, *Amazons in Greek Art* (Oxford: Oxford University Press, 1957), 6.

8. Tyrrell, *Amazons*, 2.

9. Ibid., 3; also, John Boardman, "Herakles, Peisistratos and Sons," *Revista Archeologica* (1972):57–72.

10. Tyrrell, *Amazons*, 3–4; W. R. Connor, "Theseus in Classical Athens," in *The Quest for Theseus*, ed. Anne G. Ward et al. (New York: Praeger, 1970), 143–74.

11. Probably first recounted in the *Theseis*. This was an epic poem that recounted Theseus' adventures; although its date of composition is uncertain, evidence points to the sixth century B.C. On the evidence for the *Theseis* see W. S. Barrett, *Hippolytos* (Oxford: Clarendon Press, 1964), 2–10; and G. L. Huxley, *Greek Epic Poetry from Eumelos to Panyassis* (Cambridge: Harvard University Press, 1969), 116–18. See also Tyrrell, *Amazons*, 4–5.

12. The original name of the Amazon involved with Theseus was Antiope; see von Bothmer, *Amazons in Greek Art*, chap. 8; Barrett, *Hippolytos*, 8–9, n. 3, points out that the Amazon appears to have been named Hippolytae only after she became the mother of Hippolytus.

13. It is noteworthy that Heracles, whose labors Theseus duplicated, makes his appearance here. Most likely this is because Heracles belongs to an earlier, less civilized generation, and therefore is an appropriate figure to kill the barbarian interloper. The new, civilized Theseus, model for future generations through his repudiation of the foreign woman in favor of a Greek wife, is dissociated from the Amazon's death.

14. Tyrrell, *Amazons*, 5.

15. For a full discussion, see Tyrrell, *Amazons*, 9–22.

16. For the economic bases of male domination, see Stephanie Coontz and Peta Henderson, "Property Forms, Political Power and Female Labour in the Origins of Class and State Societies," and Monique Saliou, "The Processes of Women's Subordination in Primitive and Archaic Greece," both in *Women's Work, Men's Property: The Origins of Gender and Class*, ed. Stephanie Coontz and Peta Henderson (London: Verso, 1986), 108–55 and 169–206; for the social and legal bases of this attitude see Sarah B. Pomeroy, *Goddesses, Whores, Wives and Slaves: Women in Classical Antiquity* (New York: Schocken Books, 1975), 57–92.

17. A full discussion is in Sobol, *The Amazons of Greek Mythology*.

18. Amazons were said to be the daughters of Ares and the goddess Harmonia, who is considered the daughter of Aphrodite. Thus the ideas of love and war, often linked in the minds of the ancients, are part of the heritage of the Amazons. There is, of course, emphasis upon their warlike qualities in the designation, "daughters of Ares."

19. Artemis represented the Amazons' separation from more recent, civilized society and their closeness to nature. The ancient goddess was primarily an aspect of the Great Mother, an earth/fertility goddess of great power in the Mediterranean. For a general discussion see Marija Gimbutas, *The Goddesses and Gods of Old Europe 6500–3500 B.C.: Myths and Cult Images* (Berkeley: University of California Press, 1982). For the *Magna Mater* see E. O. James, *The Cult of the Mother-Goddess: An Archeological and Documentary Study* (New York: Praeger, 1959); for a summary of the influence upon and transformation of the ancient goddess by ascendant patriarchy see Heide Göttner-Abendroth, "Matriarchal Mythology in Former Times and Today," trans. by the author with Lisa Weil, in *Crossing Pamphlet* (Freedom, Calif.: Crossing Press, 1987). An excellent discussion of the nature of Artemis may be found in Christine Downing, *The Goddess: Mythological Images of the Feminine* (New York: Crossroad, 1987), 157–85.

20. On polarity in ancient Greek thought see G. E. R. Lloyd, *Polarity and Analogy* (Cambridge: Cambridge University Press, 1966), 15–171. See also Michelle Rosellini and Suzanne Saïd, "Usages de femmes et autres nomoi chez les 'sauvages' d'Hérodote: Essai de lecture structurale," *Annali della Scuolo Normale Superiore di Pisa* 8 (1978): 949–1005. A seminal article is that by Sherry Ortner, "Is Female to Male as Nature Is to Culture?" *Feminist Studies* 1 (1972): 5–32, reprinted in *Women, Culture and Society*, ed. Michelle Rosaldo and Louise Lamphere (Stanford: Stanford University Press, 1974), 67–87.

21. Tyrrell, *Amazons*, 44–63.

22. Ibid., 28; my emphasis.

23. For the importance of monogamy (for women) and patriliny in the development of patriarchy see Nichole Chevaillard and Sebastian Leconte, "The Dawn of Lineage Societies: The Origins of Women's Oppression," and Saliou, "The Process of Women's Subordination in Primitive and Archaic Greece," both in Coontz and Henderson, eds., *Women's Work, Men's Property*, 76–107 and 169–200; and Gerda Lerner, *The Creation of Patriarchy* (Oxford: Oxford University Press, 1986), 54–122. For Athenian marriage customs and the lives of Athenian women in general see Pomeroy, *Goddesses, Whores, Wives and Slaves*, 57–120.

24. On this see Froma I. Zeitlin, "The Dynamics of Misogyny: Myth and Mythmaking in the *Oresteia*," in *Women in the Ancient World: The Arethusa Papers*, ed. John Peradotto and J. P. Sullivan (Albany: State University of New York Press, 1984), 159–91.

25. See Tyrrell, *Amazons*, 28.

26. Ibid., *Amazons*, 113–28.

27. For a discussion of the role Athena plays in the heroic ethos see Walter F. Otto, *The Homeric Gods: The Spiritual Significance of Greek Religion*, trans. Moses Hadas (New York: Thames & Hudson, 1954), 43–60.

28. Tacitus, *Annals* 14.35; *Agricola* 16.

29. Cassius Dio, *Epitome of Book LXII* 2.3–4; quoted from Nora Chadwick, *The Celts* (Harmondsworth: Penguin Books, 1970), 50.

30. *Aeneid* 11.532–91.

31. *Aeneid* 11.498–519. Turnus, on the verge of ambushing Aeneas and winning the war for the Italians, deserts his post upon hearing of Camilla's death (11.897–912).

32. *Aeneid* 11.759–867.

33. For the major prophecies of Roman greatness see *Aeneid* 1.254–96, 6.798–886, and

12.830–42.

34. Quintus of Smyrna, *Posthomerica,* as quoted in Tyrrell, *Amazons,* 78–79.

35. A study of the popularity of women warriors in Medieval epic has yet to be done. Marina Warner, *Joan of Arc: The Image of Female Heroism* (New York: Vintage Books, 1981), provides a good beginning; see esp. 198–217. Spanish literature of the Colonial period used the Amazon figure extensively; see Irving A. Leonard, "Conquerors and Amazons in Mexico," *Hispanic American Historical Review* 24 (1944):561–79; and Julie Greer Johnson, *Women in Colonial Spanish American Literature: Literary Images* (London: Greenwood, 1983), 9–59 and 142–46.

36. Their equality is established shortly after the two meet, in the sex scene obligatory in this kind of popular fantasy. They engage in mutual caresses, exchange of positions (neither is featured as being "superior"), and we see them lying side by side. The scene ends with Valeria cradling Conan to her breast in a fiercely maternal gesture which expresses her protective love toward him and foreshadows both her vigil over him when he is severely injured and her agreement to exchange her life for his.

37. Whitman, *Homer and the Heroic Tradition,* 136, notes that Patroclus represents the human side of Achilles. In *Conan the Barbarian,* Valeria represents the possibilities of human happiness for Conan. Heroes are often paired with companions who have this function, a further extension of the idea of the foil. Perhaps the best-known representation of this kind of friendship in epic is in the Sumerian/Babylonian *Epic of Gilgamesh,* where the motivation of Gilgamesh to find immortality is supplied by his beloved friend Enkidu's death.

38. *Aeneid* 11.823–26.

39. *Odyssey* 11.473–91.

40. An Italian film based upon Ariosto's *Orlando Furioso,* released in this country as *Hearts in Armor* (1983), contains a similar scene. A mysterious figure who has just rescued Bradamante from rape gives her a magical sword and an armor of invincibility. This film adaptation of Ariosto's epic is an example of the Amazon figure as used in medieval epic and illustrates the connection these fantasy films have with the medieval epic cycles.

41. John Baxter, as quoted in John Brosnan, *Future Tense: The Cinema of Science Fiction* (New York: St. Martin's Press, 1978), 13–14, notes that "SF film offers simple plots and one-dimensional characters in settings so familiar as to have the quality of ritual. It relies on a set of visual conventions and a symbolic language, bypassing intellect to make a direct appeal to the sense. . . . sf cinema, like the comic strip, endorses the political and moral climate of its day."

42. Patrick Lucanio, *Them or Us: Archetypal Interpretations of Alien Invasion Films* (Bloomington: Indiana University Press, 1987), 82–130, discusses this.

43. Hugh Ruppersberg, "The Alien Messiah in Recent Science Fiction Films," *Journal of Popular Film and Television* 14 (1989):158–66, points out that the Terminator is a "negative messiah." He outlines the Christian mythology in this film and notes that the aliens in *Alien* and *Aliens* also function as negative messiahs (164).

44. John Connor sends his friend Kyle Reese back in time to engender him and to die; in other words, he chooses his own father and has full knowledge that his father will die. For a discussion of the Oedipal implications of *The Terminator,* see Constance Penley, "Time Travel, Primal Scene, and the Critical Dystopia (on *The Terminator* and *La Jetée*)," *The Future of an Illusion: Film, Feminism, and Psychoanalysis* (Minneapolis: University of Minnesota Press, 1989), 121–39.

45. The threat of dehumanization is the common terror that aliens represent in space invasion films; see Lucanio, *Them or Us,* 74–81.

46. On the casting of the part of Ripley see Danny Peary's interview with Sigourney Weaver, "Playing Ripley in *Alien,*" in *OMNI's Screen Flights/Screen Fantasies: The Future*

according to Science Fiction Cinema, ed. Peary (Garden City, N.Y.: Doubleday, 1986), 162.

47. For a discussion of this issue see Estelle Lauter, *Women as Mythmakers: Poetry and Visual Art by Twentieth-Century Women* (Bloomington: Indiana University Press, 1984), 1–20.

48. I wish to thank my colleague Kathryn Slott for lively conversations about feminism and cinema.

Greek Poetics and Eisenstein's Films

J. K. Newman

University of Illinois

I

AT the beginning of the *Iliad,* the priest Chryses asks for his daughter back from Agamemnon. The other Greeks agree enthusiastically. Agamemnon refuses, "enjoining on him a violent word":

> "Let me not find you, old man, by the ships, either lingering now or coming again later, lest the staff and garland of the god avail you nothing. Her I will not release: before that old age will come upon her in my palace at Argos, far from her native land, as she toils at the loom and tends my bed. Off with you, don't provoke me, so that your return may be safer."
> At this, the old man felt a stab of fear, and he did as he was told. And he went in silence along the shore of the gurgling sea. [*Iliad* 1.26–34][1]

It is hardly an exaggeration to say that the whole future of European narrative technique is contained in these famous lines. Nine points may be noted:

(a) The *Iliad* is an epic, but this is a *dramatic* confrontation. In a fashion typical of later Attic drama, two violently opposed characters face each other before what may be thought of as a chorus, in this case made up of the Achaean soldiers.

(b) The scene is filled with *irony.* As Homer's audience knew (*Odyssey* 1.36), Agamemnon was not in fact destined to enjoy the sexual favors of Chryseis or anyone else until her old age in Argos. Fearful and powerless in the presence of the mighty king though he seemed, Chryses was going to win this conflict, and on terms so crushing that they form the whole "tragedy" of the *Iliad* to come. Agamemnon's bluster would lead to Achilles' withdrawal from the fighting, to the deaths of Patroclus and Hector, to the eventual confrontation between Priam and Achilles, and to the realization of the mortal condition affecting us all.

(c) There is great use of *antithesis* (polarity). While the other

Greeks, for example, have only one word (*epeuphēmēsan*) to indicate their approval, Agamemnon speaks his disapproval at length.
Chryseis is young, but she will be old. She was free and a virgin—
here; she will be a slave and the king's mistress—there. The old
priest is silent, but nature ("the gurgling sea") takes up and mag-
nifies his indignation for him.

(d) The dramatic scene convinces by its use of concrete, *telling
detail*. Agamemnon does not say, "lest your sacred rank avail you
nothing" but "lest the staff and garland of the god. . . ." He does
not say, "your daughter will be my slave and mistress," but singles
out tasks vividly denoting the role of slave and mistress. The
silence of the old priest, contrasting with the noisy sea, particularizes what "the old man felt a stab of fear" means.

(e) *Characterization*, not spelled out in unassimilated authorial
generalizations but *emerging from the linguistic structure*, is important. Agamemnon is violent and crude. He twice uses *egō*. In a
more literal translation he says: "Off with you—don't go on
provoking me—so that you may return more safe." The word
order shows his agitation. "Don't go on provoking me" is inter-
jected, and he is projecting his own wrongdoing onto the priest.
He is the one who is "provoking," and if he is "provoked," it is by
the erethism of his own lust. "Safer" (*saōteros*) is an idiom of the
type found elsewhere in the Homeric phrase "more female
women" (*Il.* 8.520), where women are not being contrasted with
other women, but with men. The affix *-ter* implies a contrast
(more antithesis), not between two types of safety but between
safety and what could happen (what Agamemnon would like to
do) to Chryses.

(f) Pathos is developed by a peculiar technique in which *the
listener is required to collaborate with the verbal construct*. Homer is
evidently aware of what it is for the old man to lose his daughter
in defiance of all morality, because afterwards (v.36) he makes
Apollo, "*son* of fair-tressed Leto" (aware therefore himself of
family ties) quick to answer his priest's call. The priest will say in
his later prayer (v.41): "May the Greeks pay for my tears with
your arrows." But what we do not hear is that the priest weeps
here and now, only that he feels afraid and that he is silent. We
have to read his distress over and beyond this fear and silence
retroactively into the scene—until we learn how to get the most
out of poetry on first reading.

(g) The phrase "the gurgling sea" offers a hint of the priest's
inner storms. But on the other side this *powerful image* symbolizes
the world as it is given by the gods, greater than our concerns, not

to be disturbed by human wilfulness. "There is the sea, and who shall quench it?"[2]

(h) *Repetition*. Homer says that Agamemnon "enjoined on him a violent *word*" at the start, and this is the "word" which the old man obeys at the end. This is the so-called ring composition, perhaps essential in an oral technique, but later developed to extraordinary and effective lengths. It is a device prevalent in all Greek literature, including the prose of Herodotus and Thucydides.

(i) There is musicality (*sound gesture*). This cannot be divorced from repetition, since repetition is one of the most characteristic procedures in music.[3] This implies more than euphony and assonance. If we examine the lengths of the individual segments making up the narrative (*Il.* 1.17–52), we find:

I.	Chryses asks for his daughter back:	5 lines
II.	The other Greeks agree:	2 lines
III.	Agamemnon disagrees:	2 lines
IV.	He speaks threateningly:	$(3+4=)$ 7 lines
V.	Chryses goes off in fear:	4 lines
VI.	He prays:	6 lines
VII.	Apollo responds by assailing the Greeks:	10 lines

The departure, the prayer, and the response (V, VI, and VII) are in perfect balance (10, 10; cf. the first prayer [I] of 5 lines). Agamemnon's jarring isolation from the other Greeks is suggested by his anomalous 7 lines (IV). But even this antithetically (antiphonally) echoes I + II, where by contrast the prayer meets with enthusiastic acceptance.

We may be skeptical about this kind of analysis because we divorce music from poetry and both from mathematics. But the ancients did not: "I remember the numbers: if only I could think of the words!"[4]

Normative as it was for later Greek poets, the Homeric technique could still admit refinement. Homer's epics had presumed the existence of other types of poetry;[5] in particular the choral lyric as developed by Stesichorus seems to have had an epic dimension and have acted as a bridge between the two styles. The fragmentary state of so much Greek choral poetry prevents us from tracing post-Homeric development in any detail, but Simonides, Pindar's older contemporary, is credited with the saying that painting is silent poetry, and poetry painting that speaks.[6] He is also cited in a passage of the anonymous treatise *On the Sublime*

(15.7) in which the author is discussing special effects of imagination (*phantasiai*). He declares:

In general, imagination may be defined as any thought which in its occurrence produces speech. In this context the term is most common nowadays when, under the influence of enthusiasm and emotion (*pathos*), you seem to see what you are saying, and then communicate that vision to your hearers. [15.1]

Euripides, we go on to learn, is a good example of this argument. But there are also cases in Homer, Aeschylus, Sophocles— and Simonides. In both these last authors, when the Greek fleet was leaving Troy for the last time, the shade of the dead Achilles appeared to the departing army above his tomb, "a scene (*opsis*) which nobody perhaps has depicted as vividly as Simonides" (15.7).

In Pindar we find both a polemic against Homer and a modification—in essence a concentration and intensification—of his narrative techniques. Scholars single out, for example, the myth of the first *Nemean Ode*.[7] The miraculous deed by which baby Heracles signaled his more-than-human birth is related essentially in a series of dramatic, colorful, painterly scenes. In the following translation, an effort has been made to preserve some of the affective word order of the original:

how, when from his mother's womb immediately into the marvelous light the son of Zeus fleeing the birth pang with his twin brother came—how not escaping golden-throned Hera the saffron swaddling clothes he entered. But the queen of the gods, angry at heart, sent serpents forthwith. They, as the doors flew open, into the broad recess of the chamber entered, around the children their swift jaws to wrap eager. But he raised his head and made his first trial of combat, the twin—with his two—serpents by the necks seizing—ineluctable hands.[8] And as they were strangled, time breathed out the lives from their unspeakable limbs. Unbearable fear struck the women who were in attendance at Alcmena's bed. She herself got to her feet unrobed as she was and rushed from the couch in spite of all and tried to ward off the insolence of those monsters. And swiftly the Theban chiefs with bronze weapons ran up all together, and in his hand Amphitryon brandishing a sword naked from its scabbard arrived, by sharp distresses stricken.

At this point, the poet breaks off to remark:

For what is close to home oppresses every man alike, but straightway the heart feels no pain for another's care.

The story resumes:

> There he stood, by astonishment, both unbearable and yet happy, confused. For he witnessed the unwonted spirit and power of a son. Backward-tongued the immortals made for him the news of the messengers, and he summoned his neighbor, the eminent spokesman of most high Zeus, right-prophesying Teiresias. . . . [*Nem.* 1.35–61]

Teiresias then delivers a prophecy, muffled in the circumlocutions of "reported speech," of the victorious career of Heracles to come, culminating in his fight on the side of the gods against the (snake-limbed) Giants. Evidently Heracles' own life comes full circle in an existential ring composition.[9]

This story proceeds in a series of pictures: the birth, the sending of the serpents, the mysteriously opening doors, the response of the baby son of Zeus, the strangulation of the two serpents, where the interlocking word order cuts from the baby's grasp to what he is grasping until finally we realize with relief that around their necks he has his hands! But this high point is anticipation. The story cuts back to the serving women, and then particularizes the reaction of the mother, struggling in her weakened state to get out of bed, not even bothering to seize a robe. Negative adjectives ("ineluctable," "unspeakable," "unbearable," "unrobed") force us to do a great deal of the poet's work for him by suppling their positive counterparts, since in themselves negatives make no appeal to the imagination. Now the Theban chiefs arrive, armed in bronze, and again someone is particularized among them, father Amphitryon, his bare sword flashing.

Verbs of movement have so far predominated: "fleeing," "came," "entered," "sent," "entered," "eager,"[10] "rushing," "ran," "arrived," but here the narrative halts, as the poet reflects on his version of the old adage that blood is thicker than water. This has been thought of as merely a holding remark, unimportant in itself, and intended to allow the listener to savor the vivid picture so far presented. But it is more, as the sequel shows.

Amphitryon reacts ambiguously, with mixed feelings. "Wonderment" is the appropriate reaction to a divine epiphany, and the unity of opposites illustrated by pain and pleasure together is also part of this extraordinary mystical etiquette. His intervention, as it turns out, is not needed. His son is quite able to look after himself, and the alarming news brought by the messengers is reversed. But what did these messengers say? Perhaps, "Your sons are in mortal danger." The reversal would be: "Your sons are not in mortal danger." But suppose both parts of the original message were negated: "Not only are your sons not in mortal danger, but this miracle shows that the bolder of them is not in fact your son." No wonder the erstwhile father's feelings were mixed, as he struggled to assimilate this conclusion, simultaneously flattering and devastating. It was perhaps some inkling of it that caused him to send for the spokesman of Zeus most high, because, as we were told at the beginning, the father of the child is precisely—Zeus.

But this sheds another light on the gnomic reflections just alluded to. In cold logic, Amphitryon has been quite literally bothered about "another's care" since Heracles is now shown to be no child of his. His trouble was wasted, his assumption of responsibility premature, his weapons were unneeded, and, in the fashion of all cuckolds, he is left looking rather a fool. Like Homer's Agamemnon in his middle-aged lust, the hero is caught in a less than heroic moment. All he can really do is—stand there.

The fourth *Pythian Ode,* the most elaborate of Pindar's odes, contains a long narrative of the seizure of the Golden Fleece.[11] It strikingly illustrates a technique by which Pindar, following Homeric example, seeks his listener's cooperation in the fashioning of the work of art. Jason has just completed his plowing with the brazen bulls commanded by Aeetes:

> And at once the wondrous child of the Sun (Aeetes) told of the shining Fleece, and where the sword blows of Phrixus had stretched it out. He was hoping that this toil at least Jason would not fulfill. For it lay in a thicket and clung to the savage jaws of a serpent that in bulk and length outdid a fifty-oared ship finished by the blows of the iron. It is long for me to travel the cart road. Time presses, and I know a certain short cut. To many others I am a leader in the poet's craft. He slew the fierce-eyed, spangle-backed serpent with arts, Arcesilas, and stole Medea with herself, the murderess of Pelias. And they plunged into the expanses of Ocean and the Red Sea, into the tribe of Lemnian women that slew their husbands. . . . [*Py.* 4.241–52]

At the height of the action, the poet simply abandons his story. Instead, he breaks off to congratulate himself complacently on his own prowess.

But this is part of his prowess, for, in our impatience, and drawing on our familiarity with longer narrative poetry, we reconstruct the combat in our own imagination while we are waiting. Since we do this, presumably we are satisfied with our own work. The poet's thesis and claim of mastery have been triumphantly vindicated.

Pindar has offered hints about what he wants done: "blows of iron" in his narrative, although at first sound blows of shipwrights' hammer and mallet, could just as well in another application be sword blows. What has happened is that the Argo has metamorphosed into and itself subsumed this final confrontation, just as the serpents blended into the Giants in the first *Nemean Ode*. This is why in that ode it was precisely Time (the word is repeated a little later at v.69) that "breathed out the life from their unspeakable limbs." So here, although we do not hear a great deal about what will happen to Medea and Jason, we are told that she will be the death of Pelias: and the first stop on the voyage home is to be the isle of women who murdered their own menfolk. The *phon-* root (= "murder") is repeated twice in three lines.

Pindar, who congratulates himself here on his virtuosity as a narrator, both develops and implies a theory of narratology.[12] He opens the second *Dithyramb*, for example, by remarking:

> Earlier there crawled the *schoenus*-length song of the dithyrambs, and the false *san* from men's lips.

The *schoenus* is an ancient unit of measurement, and so this is an objection to irrelevant length in poetry. There may be an allusion in *san* (an old name for *sigma*) to some experiment perhaps by the poet's teacher Lasus of Hermione in avoiding the use of the consonant *s*.[13] But, in any case, the language of the *schoenus* is certainly picked up in Alexandria by Callimachus (*Preface to the Aetia* 18, *schoenoi*).

In Pindar's *Paean* 7b (v.11), we read a reference to Homer's "cart track," a term already familiar from his fourth *Pythian* (v.247) and again later to be borrowed by Callimachus (*Preface to the Aetia* 25). In a now fragmentary passage, the chorus was perhaps advised not to travel along it and not to ride on other people's horses.

This polemic must not be exaggerated. Every poet needs to stake out his own terrain by sharply distinguishing himself from his immediate predecessors. Paradoxically, the long-dead Homer was an immediate predecessor for the Greeks, partly because of his lasting prestige, particularly in Greek education, and partly because he was the nominal patron of a great mass of "cyclic" poetry loosely associated with his tradition. But we can see that Pindar has reinforced certain features already noted in our extract from the *Iliad*. Selectivity and compression have been carried even further. In the first *Nemean Ode*, the emotional element has been heightened, the interplay between human and divine veers toward the tragicomic. The lighting effects have been carefully studied ("light," 35; "golden-throned," 37; "saffron," 37; "bronze," 51; "brandishing a naked sword," 52). Everything moves from divine to human and toward a still of the kind familiar from Japanese kabuki theater, as at the climactic moment the armed father standing in the doorway, his chiefs behind him, stares with a mixture of awestruck emotions into the bedroom at his (or not his?) triumphant baby son, and ponders what it can all mean.

Simonides had said that poetry is "painting that speaks," a phrase that in an essay about film may perhaps be paraphrased as "painting with a sound track." We do not know how soon painting caught up with poetry and what indeed poetry had previously borrowed. But the sophisticated technique of narration by omission, already familiar in the poets, had been made famous in the classical period of Greece by the painter Timanthes of Sicyon. Cicero related how, in depicting the sacrifice of Iphigenia, Timanthes indicated varying degrees of sorrow among the spectators waiting at the altar.[14] It is permissible to interpret his remarks. The priest Calchas stood there, sorry, of course, though for him perhaps this was the almost routine fulfillment of a religious duty. Next was Odysseus, hardened, shrewd, but perhaps less impervious to human feeling than his clerical colleague. Then Menelaus: with what eyes could he watch his virginal niece being cut down in the flower of her youthful beauty, for the sake of his honor and desire to recover his adulterous wife? Finally, the girl's father stood by the altar—Agamemnon. What were his feelings? His daughter, his own flesh and blood, was to die in order to preserve his position and prestige as commander in chief. Did he weep? Did he try to seem resolute? How would he look? The painter showed him turned away, muffled in his robe. It was for the spectator to supply the father's feelings from his own heart and to his own satisfaction.

This leap into another dimension, from showing to not showing, made Timanthes' picture famous throughout antiquity. And these techniques of antithesis were perfectly familiar to the Athenian stage. The *hypothesis* to Euripides' *Medea* notes that some critics blamed the author for inconsistencies in his heroine's character:

He is blamed for not sustaining Medea's role and for her resort to tears when plotting against Jason and his wife.[15]

Horace later seems to echo this critical blame when he urges that characters should remain true to one guiding emotion (*Ars Poetica*

119, "in agreement with themselves"). But the Greek writers knew
differently, as did the painter Parrhasius when he depicted the
Athenian people as a mass of contradictory emotions:

> His painting of the Athenian "Demos" also shows great talent. He
> portrayed it as fickle, passionate, unjust, changeable, yet flexible,
> compassionate and lenient, boastful, proud and humble, bold and
> cowardly, in a word, everything alike.[16]

The route by which this complex legacy was transmitted to the
later world has not always been accurately traced. Greek civilization did not pass directly from Athens to Rome. The role of
Egyptian Alexandria in the mediation of Greek antiquity even to
Byzantium, and therefore ultimately to Russia, is too easily forgotten. The duty of the Greek Alexandrian poets, led by Callimachus, in the third century B.C. was to assess the legacy of the
past at a time when they were beset on two fronts: by the achievements of fourth-century prose; and by the monopolization of the
epic manner by writers like Choerilus of Iasos, who, following a
pattern set by his earlier namesake Choerilus of Samos, supposed
that unthinking imitation of Homer's mannerisms could do to
serve the propaganda needs of modern conquerors. Alexander
the Great had been fastidious enough to remark that he would
sooner be Homer's Thersites than Choerilus' Achilles.[17] But the
bitter polemic that eventually developed between the Calli-
macheans and the anti-Callimacheans over the question of epic
shows that not all Hellenistic grandees were as fastidious as Alexander.

It seems very clear that Callimachus, in rethinking the task of
narrative poetry, was much influenced by the example of Pindar.
In particular, he takes over some of Pindar's terms and, very
interestingly, in one place (but precisely in an imitation of Pindar)
appears from our perspective to think ahead to a filmmaker's
verb:

> Let [the reader] add his own thought and so *cut* length off the song.[18]

In fact, although Callimachus is often thought of as a great
innovator, here he simply repeats an idea already attributed to
Pindar's contemporary, Aeschylus, reputed to have said that his
plays were slices ("cuts") from Homer's banquets (Athenaeus,
Doctors at Dinner 8.347e). Callimachus' verb (*tamoi*) and Aeschylus'
noun (*temakhē*) share the same root. Closer inspection of Callimachus' implied poetic reveals a number of principles: the analogy with music; selection of detail; vivid presentation,

concentrating especially on emotion; balance and recurrence in language and overall set up, seriocomedy (irony) of tone. It is a measure of the importance of his poetic that it illumines not only him but also Vergil.

Between Callimachus and Vergil came Apollonius of Rhodes. The subtle unifying of his new epic by the repetition of key images has only recently begun to be understood. In particular, the red-gold of the Fleece occurs throughout the poem in many guises; in the blushing cheek of love, and in the red stain spreading over a sister's silvery dress as her unarmed and unsuspecting brother is foully done to death in the shrine of Artemis by Jason.[19]

II

Behind all the surface variations of emphasis in ancient and modern works lies common human nature, reacting with equal pathos to common conditions. More than this, there is for the classicist a common tradition without understanding which we are bound to miss what individual works of art mean. This is the supreme justification for the kind of investigation undertaken here as an essential development of classical studies.

Because of this shared tradition, a terminology dependent on both Aristotelian and filmic principles has already appeared to illuminate some parts of ancient poetic technique. We spoke, for example, of drama, selectivity, and characterization in Homer (Aristotelian insights), and of the unity of opposites and a Kabuki-like "still" (filmic principles) in Pindar's first Nemean Ode. Aristotle, the greatest of the ancient critics and also a poet, had immeasurably more of Greek literature than now survives on which to base his conclusions. Suppose we compare his reflections with those of the greatest of the modern theoreticians of film, Sergei Eisenstein.[20] If the theories of the two can be drawn together, it will be striking proof that the cinematic analysis of Greek poetry of which we have offered some examples here is not intrusive, but corresponds to the deepest insights of an ancient critic whose mind played over the whole range of classical Greek literature.

Things begin ominously enough. Lenin had said that in the class struggle the cinema was the most important of all arts. Eisenstein was the propagandist of revolution, and his task was essentially to expose the corruption of the old system and the compelling common sense of the new order, not in need of any hypocritical pretenses and disguises. It might have been thought then that it would have been enough for him merely to picture some sort of "scientific," objective truth.

What is extraordinary is Eisenstein's frank admission that the artist, even the Communist artist, is engaged in systematic distortion. He points out, for example, how much in his agricultural film *The Old and the New* (1926–29) he made use of "lens 28," rejected by other filmmakers because of its wide-angled deformation of the image. In his case, lens 28 was aimed at making objects go out of themselves, beyond the dimensions of the scope and forms prescribed for them by nature. This deformation, as Eisenstein goes on to explain, was also marked by the intentional use of irony. The hulk of the sleeping *kulak* (wealthy peasant), for example, from whom the activist member of the village cooperative, Martha Lapkina, hoped in vain to borrow horses for her plowing, was shot to look like the body of the dead Christ in a painting of Mantegna. The horses themselves were over-large, and poor Martha ends by using her old cow. The *kulak*'s bull was monumentalized until it looked like the bull that raped Europa. In comparable fashion, during the shooting of *Battleship Potemkin* (1925), Eisenstein's cameraman Eduard Tissé had actually hung netting or tulle over the lens in order to muffle his shots. This distortion is not, however, at the service of any narrowly personal feeling, even though Eisenstein declares that there is need of an artist who writes his works with the blood of his own heart. The artist is only interested in the personal so far as it can be universalized, as El Greco, to use Eisenstein's examples, may (or may not) have subsumed personal feelings in his *Storm over Toledo,* or Leonardo in his drawings of machines. This recalls the Aristotelian interest (*Poetics* 1449b8) in what is *katholou* (catholic, universal).

The artist, continues Eisenstein, may have a twofold relationship to his material. He may wish to reflect it simply: sad sadness, jolly jollity, and so on. But he may also have a comment to make. At this point irony enters in, the deliberate transgression of the bounds of normality and expectation. As this transgression becomes more marked, there may occur the unity of opposites, the blending of felt norm and felt transgression in order to secure a single artistic effect. Here is where Pindar's "unbearable and yet happy" (*Nem.* 1.55–56) and before that Homer's "laughing through her tears" (*Il.* 6.484) secure their rationale. Eisenstein believes with Heraclitus in the essential flux of phenomena, not in order to argue with Plato that they are therefore unknowable or contemptible, but to urge that they are growing and that there are mathematically determinable laws of this growth. It is why he strongly defends, for example, the use of the Golden Section and is pleased to note its occurrence in his own films.[21]

Although the cinema in the twenties was a new art, Eisenstein makes use of a great many terms of classical rhetoric. "Amplification," for example, was one of his basic concepts. By this, he meant the reshaping of reality to larger-than-life dimensions in order to serve an artistic purpose. He analyzes the novels of Zola to point out how that particular master of realism had already distorted reality. He notes that in a letter of 24 October 1894, Zola had compared his own use of repetition, for example, with Wagner's use of the leitmotif, and argued that in this way he secured greater unity for his works. Similarly, adds Eisenstein, in the preface to *Pierre et Jean,* Maupassant had claimed that critics often fail to discover all the most subtle threads, hidden and often invisible, used by certain modern writers in place of the previous single thread known as intrigue. Eisenstein claimed that he was the heir of the past.[22] It is already evident what different principles of appreciation for the classics he would advance from the untutored "common sense" usually thought adequate even for the chirurgic editor who proposes to heal an ancient text by emendation and so often leaves on our desks a bleeding corpse. These features of the Eisensteinian poetic deserve note. To each point he makes I attach a reference to a passage of Aristotle's *Poetics,* where a similar argument is advanced. I will then discuss each point in greater detail.

1. *The primacy of the theatrical.* The real heir to ancient epic is found in modern drama. Eisenstein thought that his art was the culmination and encapsulation of the art of the past. But *mutatis mutandis* this is the thesis of chapter 26 of the *Poetics.* In the same vein, Aristotle perhaps coined for Homer's artistry precisely the adjective *dramatikos* (*Poetics* 1448b35).

2. *The actor's art is paradigmatic also for the creative artist,* but this does not mean that the actor matters more than the story. The Russian cinema rejected the Hollywood system of "stars." Compare *Poetics* 1450a38 (the myth is the "soul" of tragedy) and 1455a29 ("helping to complete it [the script of the drama] with the [writer's] gestures").

3. *Metaphor is the chief and unteachable poetic gift* (*Poetics* 1459a6: "much the most important thing is to be metaphorical").

4. *Clarity is essential* and, to aid this, *the selection of detail.* The director's brilliance is chiefly shown in his ability to cut effectively,

a point also crucial to Eisenstein's contemporary, the director and theorist of film, V. Pudovkin. Consider especially the emphasis on *sapheneia* (clarity) in language at *Poetics* 1458a34 and praise of Homer at 1451a22.

5. *Factual (historical) truth is irrelevant to the artist's need for figurative truth* (cf. *Poetics*, chapter 9: "poetry is something more philosophical and serious than history").

6. *The work of art must have a controlling rhythm*, and this must be derived from the director's overall concept of what his work wants to say (cf. *Poetics* 1451a30–35).

7. *The artist must make use of pathetic structure.* By this, the recipient of the artistic experience is continually moved between opposite poles, until eventually this movement becomes so violent that there is a breakthrough or leap into another dimension. This may occur on the small scale, but also on the large scale, when it may have climactic and shattering emotional effect. With this we may provisionally compare Aristotelian *katharsis* (*Poetics* 1449b28).

These points made by the Russian film director may be taken up in order and applied to Greek poetry. This discussion amplifies without contradicting the analyses with which this essay began.

1. The theatrical has priority because all great art tends toward drama. Plato had condemned Homer for being "the leader of tragedy" (*Republic* 595b–c). When Aristotle developed and reversed this, especially at the end of the *Poetics*, he was thinking of the Attic tragedians. Shakespeare would have been a supreme illustration of his thesis and, because we take Shakespeare for granted, we cannot see what an amazing argument (for a conservative Greek) in defense of "modern" poetry Aristotle advanced. But he was with this one stroke both able to dismiss all flaccid epic writing that passed itself off as Homeric because it aped the external mannerisms of the grand style, and to seize upon the real merit of the *Iliad*, in particular that it was "dramatic" and "tragic." The dramatic scenes and their speeches that fill the poem are the proof of the correctness of Aristotle's insight.

Stesichorus early turned the choral lyric toward dramatic themes, and the tenth-century Byzantine Suda lexicon oddly attributes dramas even to Pindar. Whatever these may have been, the dramatic confrontations and character painting, for example, of the fourth *Pythian Ode* are clear.[23] Pelias is a crude, cunning, and bombastic liar, Jason, the soul of honor. As he raised tragedy to new heights, while—in Eisenstein's words—"visibly preserving the features of its line of inheritance from earlier (lower) stages of intensity,"[24] Euripides would be acutely conscious of the lyric drama, and in him it would reach its climax precisely on so traditional a theme (whatever the novelty of certain details) as *The Bacchae*.

2. Eisenstein admired the Russian stage directors Stanislavsky and Meyerhold and, although he does not mention him, was in his way a disciple of Duns Scotus's theory of *haecceitas* (thisness). You cannot depict grief, Eisenstein says in a famous passage,[25] you can only depict this grief in this person in this context, because only by visualizing and feeling your way into the specifics of the pathetic situation can you recreate them convincingly for the spectator. Horace, depending on Aristotelian tradition, says exactly the same thing:

> If you want me to weep, you have to weep yourself first of all. Then your misfortunes will bruise me, Telephus or Peleus. [*Ars Poetica* 102–3]

Aristotle himself said something broader. He urged that the playwright, if he hopes to persuade, should act out each part to himself. Commentators have found this very odd, though parallels are noted with Ibsen or Dickens. But, if it is so odd, why does the comic poet Aristophanes depict the tragedians Euripides and Agathon as wearing their characters' clothes while writing their plays?[26] Agathon in fact explains his behavior in quite intelligible terms. He says he changes his attitude according to what he has on:

> I wear clothing to suit my frame of mind. For a poet must suit his character to the plays he has to write. For example, when he writes about women, he must physically share in their character.[27]

Both writer and stage or film director then will need to be imaginatively inside their characters' minds if they are going to present them persuasively. Only then will they be able to recreate the desired emotion in the spectator's mind.

3. *The Old and the New* has already been mentioned. After noting certain individual features in this film, Eisenstein remarks that there was also need of an overall metaphor. In the case of this agricultural piece of propaganda in favor of the collective farm, the metaphor was that of a fountain of milk (recalling peasant proverbs about "rivers of milk"). But Eisenstein also argues for the importance of metaphor in general, of the feel by the author for an image that controls all individual representations of the

action. The content of Homer's and Mayakovsky's metaphors is different, he remarks, but the principle of metaphor is the same in both.[28] Just so, music may change, but rhythm is essential in all of it. Without metaphor, the details of the composition will tend to fall to pieces. This already implies the principle of selectivity since what is irrelevant to the reinforcement of the metaphor must be cut out. But, if this had been grasped by classicists, would not the appreciation of Apollonius' *Argonautica* by modern critics, and the role in it of the Fleece, have been immeasurably deeper? And what about those odes of Pindar in which a governing image is metamorphosed time and again to lend by its reappearances a musical unity to the whole? How much ink has been spilt on denying the existence of the "basic thought" or *Grundgedanke*, when in fact Eisenstein and Stanislavsky agree that without some such overarching aim or organizational principle (*sverkhzadacha*) the artistic production simply disintegrates?

4. Selectivity is obvious in Pindar and the Alexandrians. But Homer, for example, already chooses one particular episode from all the ten-year siege of Troy—and not a very thrilling episode to start with at that—to encapsulate the entire experience of men at war. In the passage already cited, the scene is set: brutal, irreligious self-gratification has taken over in Agamemnon's mind from any larger purpose. As he defends his action in his dramatic confrontation with Achilles later in the first book, it is clear that the war will not be finished by any sacrifice of his, since he has no imagination and no new method, but only the persistence with the old and failed. Achilles will break out of the stereotype, and in so doing become the first tragic hero of European literature. In books 20–22 of the poem, we will not hear the name of Agamemnon at all. The commander in chief becomes irrelevant. This is also why Homer, who knew about the Trojan Horse (*Od.* 4.272), says nothing about it in the poem where it might have made a difference. It is not clever tactics but the sacrifice of flesh and blood in mortal combat that changes history, and the profound meditation on what that means that changes poetry.

How much then Homer illustrates these remarks of Eisenstein:

> Composition takes the structural elements of the phenomenon represented, and from them creates the law of the thing's structure. Moreover, in the first instance, it takes these elements from the structure of the emotional behavior of the human being connected with the experience of the content of this or another represented phenomenon. . . . Precisely for this reason, genuine composition is necessarily deeply human.[29]

5. Eisenstein handled the events of the Potemkin mutiny with great freedom, and in general is opposed to the literalness which cripples the poetic imagination. But the war between historical poetry and imaginative larger-scale writing is already ancient. The preface to Callimachus' *Aetia* gives us some inkling of the bitter intensity with which it was pursued, for example, in Alexandria. Why this clash of opinion matters so much can only be fully understood outside the Greek world, since the principal protagonists in the battle are probably the Roman epic poets Ennius and Vergil, and the inability to understand this irreconcilable division no doubt resulted in the failure of Petrarch's *Africa*.[30] In the last analysis, the imaginative writer is asking for freedom to develop a larger truth, and that truth may not always be flattering to its heroes.

6. Eisenstein (like the Roman elegist Gallus) was trained as an engineer, and so was not afraid of the slide rule. He believed that pathos can only be present when there is an almost biological relation between the work of art and the laws of life and growth. He sees this relation in the spiral graph of the Golden Section. His film *Potemkin* he considered a five-act tragedy, and tragedy he says has five acts because of the Golden Section. It is this that allows a transition into a sharp opposition, in which the organic growth of the work of art breaks through into new levels of development without losing its coherence and structure.

To suggest that ancient epics or dramas must have a controlling rhythm seems like fantasy. It opens the door to speculations about numerical composition in whose labyrinthine complexities the too-often innumerate critic becomes quickly and irritably lost. But in arguing that a work of art must be *eusunopton* (easily viewable as one) and in rejecting the notion of a hypothetical creature of ten thousand stades, is not Aristotle already suggesting that there must be some degree of measure? Not to measure is to lose control.[31] As Attic tragedy recapitulates its development in Euripides, we see symmetry reclaiming its place, for example, in *The Troades*.[32]

7. "Pathetic structure," like the Aristotelian *katharsis*, is a difficult concept. Perhaps in the first instance it is best to let Eisenstein speak for himself:

> Pathetic composition in essence is nothing else but a degree of the formation of expressive methods in correspondence with a degree of the pathetic apprehension by the author of his theme, that degree at which this very composition indeed acquires the tokens of a new quality, but together with that visibly preserves the features of its line

of inheritance from earlier (lower) stages of intensity, which it is
possible to feel and detect through the lines of this new quality.[33]

And again:

Pathos is what causes someone to go out of himself. It is the same as
ecstasy. And ecstasy is the transition into another quality.[34]

Again:

Pathos is the unity of opposites within the actual principle of composition. The unity of the later and the simultaneous.[35]

But is not part of this the restatement in other terms of the
argument of the treatise *On the Sublime* already discussed, where
phantasia was praised as the power of vivid imagination, so vivid
that the emotion (*pathos*) of the artist was communicated to his
auditors? In this passage, the ancient author is moving in traditional areas, as his kinship with Greek Stoic thinkers and, on the
Latin side, with Horace and Quintilian shows. The technique was
familiar to the Renaissance. Erasmus remarks:

We use this (*evidentia*) whenever, for the sake of *amplifying*, adorning
or pleasing, we do not state a thing simply, but set it forth to be viewed
as though portrayed in color on a panel, so that it may seem that we
have painted, not narrated, and that the reader has seen, not read. We
will be able to do this well if we first conceive a mental picture of the
subject with all its attendant circumstances. Then we should so portray it in words and fitting figures that it is as clear and graphic as
possible to the reader.[36]

"Amplification" was already noted as one of Eisenstein's favorite
terms. In essence, the artist recreates the original process in himself, and the spectator recreates it with him. The visualization of
the work of art is determined by imaginative feeling, in which the
artist/actor projects himself into the character he is portraying.
This leads him to select those details for portrayal which will most
effectively convey the feelings of the character. These details will
also be juxtaposed in such a way as to throw the observer off
balance. When this happens often enough, a breakthrough occurs
to a new dimension of feeling, what the author of *On the Sublime*
calls *ekplēxis* (knock-out, astonishment). This term, although not
quite so exclusive or drastic in scope as it later became, is already
Aristotelian (*Poetics* 1455b17). Another part of what Eisenstein is
saying has to do with Aristotle's interest in the origin of the
classical Greek genres, with his assertion, for example, that classi-

cal tragedy grows out of the satyr play (*Poetics* 1449a20). The truth and relevance of this etiology is more and more evident.

The telling detail is selected by Greek poet and Russian film-maker for more than its vividness. If the artist narrates every-thing, not only will he bore his audience to death (cf. the *Thebaid* of Antimachus!), but he will leave nothing for it to do. If on the other hand he offers a few significant details by the principle of *pars pro toto*, the viewer or listener will be drawn into working these details into a total picture. Because he will be engaged in the artistic process, he will be more susceptible to its effect. This is why the old priest's tears in Homer were not mentioned at the time of the original insult. We deduced his grief by the contrast between his silence and the noise of the surging ocean. It is necessary to think into the text. This became so marked a feature of the Greco-Roman theater in its later "pantomimic" period that "eloquent silence" was already then, as now, a cliché.[37]

The power of a repeated image was understood even by the Greek scholiasts.[38] There is a plasticity of imagination in great artists by which they see the similarity in difference. This is why Aristotle thought that metaphor was the chief and unteachable poetic gift, as I mentioned earlier.

Eisenstein transforms his images time and again.[39] In *Potemkin* mutinous sailors are to be executed on the quarterdeck by a firing squad drawn from their own comrades. A rolled canvas is brought in, carried so that it already looks like a shrouded corpse. In real life, this canvas would no doubt have been spread on the deck to catch the blood of the victims. Eisenstein had the idea—although later, as he wryly reports, even the survivors of the mutiny recast their memories of the event to suit his artistic reconstruction[40]—of draping it instead over their heads, so that they are both dehumanized and buried while still alive (vertical time). A com-mand is barked and the firing squad raises its rifles. There is an agonizing wait, ended by the muffled cry, "Brothers!" The cry is heeded, the entire crew joins the mutiny, but one sailor, Vakulinchuk, is actually killed. The ship now sails for Odessa harbor, which is wrapped in grey mist, symbolic of mourning. Slowly the grey polarizes into black and white, culminating in the laying of Vakulinchuk's white-shrouded body on the black stones of the quayside. A tiny candle is placed between the corpse's fingers. This element of fire, added to the air, earth, and water we have had so far, grows into the townspeople's fiery anger and into the raising over the ship of the fiery red flag of socialist revolu-tion. It grows and reverses into the fire of the black and white uniformed militia of the Czar, who ruthlessly charge the unarmed protesting civilians on the steps leading down to the harbor. A woman is cut down. Her white blouse echoes the white canvas. The battleship fires back its defiance, shaking the theater where (symbolically out of view, because they are only irrelevant and posturing extras on life's stage) the Czar's generals are discussing their plans. The linkage of all these scenes by recurring images is the rediscovery of an ancient technique. Did not Eisenstein himself remark: "Let us begin, as always, from our ancestors," and did not those ancestors for him include the Greeks?[41]

If the principle of pathetic style appears to explain too much— Greek, Russian, whatever—the explanation lies in the shared humanity of the artist's psychology, which may be engaged either consciously or in some inspirational way, and here yet again there is agreement with Aristotle (*Poeticcs* 1451a24, "either through art or natural gift"). Eisenstein shares with Aristotle the belief that the actor's art is that of the author; that the true test of poetic genius is the use of metaphor; that music is the "sweetest" of the embellishments on which tragedy can call (*Poetics* 1450b16);[42] that epic finds its natural culmination in drama; that in drama not the hero but the action is of primary importance. He also shares something else, and that is the belief that the ultimate aim of pathetic structure is the leap into another dimension of consciousness which raises the spectator beyond himself, projects him perhaps into that *katharsis tōn pathēmatōn* (purging of the passions) which has been found so puzzling in Aristotle's *Poetics*. Eisenstein does not think that this leap into another dimension occurs only once or that it is the mechanical discharge of ugly and unwanted humors. The multiplying of pathetic details leads to a sharp transition into another level of apprehension. Pathetic structure, moving between antithetical polarities all the time, eventually pushes its patient into an ecstasy of pathos.

So it was that in *Potemkin* a revolutionary flag filmed in black and white suddenly looked red under pressure of the imagery of fire which pervades the entire film. So it was in Homer that the cheers of the applauding Greeks who were quite willing for Chryses to get his daughter back passed into Agamemnon's angry words, into silence, into the noise of the elemental sea, and thence into prayer and the supernatural sound of Apollo's bow (1.49):

And terrible was the clang of his silver bow.

NOTES

1. All translations throughout are by me, unless specifically stated otherwise.

2. Aeschylus, *Agamemnon*, 958. Shakespeare's "multitudinous seas" are familiar. To anticipate the argument, one may compare Eisenstein's remarks about the function of the vast, cathedral spaces of his film *Ivan the Terrible*. See *Izbrannye Proizvedeniya v shesti tomakh* (Moscow: Izdatel'stvo Iskusstvo, 1964), 3:353.

3. See *Harvard Dictionary of Music*, ed. Willi Apel (Cambridge: Harvard University Press, 1944), article on "Repetition," 636.

4. Vergil, *Eclogues* 9. 45.

5. For example, the wedding song on the shield of Achilles (*Iliad* 18. 493–95).

6. Plutarch, *Glory of the Athenians* 3.

7. Leonhard Illig, *Zur Form der pindarischen Erzählung* (Berlin: Junker & Dünnhaupt, 1932), 20–25.

8. I.e., in more normal English, "seizing the twin serpents by their necks with his two ineluctable hands." But the poet presents his picture in the abnormal order given.

9. Following the Athenian tradition described by Karl Schefold, *Götter- und Heldensagen der Griechen in der spätarchaischen Kunst* (Munich: Hirmer, 1978), 279, Pindar passes straight from the battle against the Giants to the final apotheosis. He ignores within the economy of his poem the details we find, for example, in Sophocles' *Women of Trachis*.

10. The adjective translates a Greek verbal participle (*memaotes*).

11. See my *The Classical Epic Tradition* (Madison: University of Wisconsin Press, 1986), 96–99. Individual studies are dedicated to the ode by Charles Segal, *Pindar's Mythmaking: The Fourth Pythian Ode* (Princeton: Princeton University Press, 1986), and Bruce K. Braswell, *A Commentary on the Fourth Pythian Ode of Pindar* (New York: De Gruyter, 1988).

12. This does not mean that Pindar was anti-Homeric, any more than Callimachus, but he was far more reflective about his art than Homer, and it is to Pindar, for example, that the controversial Callimachus looks back; see my *Augustus and the New Poetry* (Brussels: Collection Latomus 88, 1967), 45–48, and "Pindar and Callimachus," *Illinois Classical Studies* 10 (1985):169–89.

13. Dionysius of Halicarnassus, *On the Arrangement of Words* 14. Asigmatic poetry was written later in Byzantium, and so Lasus would certainly have been a highly conscious craftsman. Perhaps Pindar, however, was simply objecting to sigmatism in his predecessors of the kind later criticized in Euripides, for example, by Plato comicus (frag. 30, Kock).

14. Cicero, *Orator* 22.74: "The painter saw, when at the sacrifice of Iphigenia Calchas was sad, Ulysses more sad, Menelaus in mourning, that Agamemnon's head had to be muffled, since he could not depict with the brush that supreme degree of grief"; cf. Pliny, *Natural History* 35.73: "He veiled the face of her actual father, unable to depict it satisfactorily." A version of Timanthes' painting from the House of the Tragic Poet at Pompeii is preserved in the Museo Nazionale, Naples. See also the relief on the circular marble altar signed by Cleomenes (latter half of first century A.D.), now in the Uffizi Gallery, Florence.

15. In a similar vein, Eisenstein remarks: "In ancient tragedy one is frequently struck not so much by a double, divided nature but at times and above all by the unmotivated breakdown of a character into another extreme incommensurate and irreconcilable with the first, into another contradiction" (*Izbr. Proizv.* 3:137). The difference is that he approves of this method of composition.

16. Pliny, *Natural History* 35.69, trans. Katherine Jex-Blake (Chicago: Ares, 1982).

17. Porphyrio on Horace, *Ars Poetica* 357.

18. Frag. 57, Pfeiffer. See Peter J. Parsons, "Callimachus: Victoria Berenices," *Zeitschrift für Papyrologie und Epigraphik* 25 (1977):1–50.

19. More on the use of connected images in this poem in my *The Classical Epic Tradition*, 74–88.

20. Eisenstein's theories as they are relevant to this essay are available to the English-speaking reader in *Nonindifferent Nature*, trans. Herbert Marshall (Cambridge: Cambridge University Press, 1987). They are summarized here, however, directly from the Russian of S. M. Eisenstein, *Izbrannye Proizvedeniya*, 2:329–483, and 3:33–432. See also S. M. Eisenstein, *Selected Works, Volume I, Writings, 1922–34*, ed. and trans. Richard Taylor (Bloomington: Indiana University Press, 1988). Taylor speaks of Eisenstein as "by general consent the single most important figure in the history of cinema" ("General Editor's Preface," ix).

21. On the concept of the Golden Section in the Renaissance see Luca Pacioli, *Divina proportione* (Venice, 1509; reprint, Como, 1967); N. E. Huntley, *The Divine Proportion* (New York: Dover, 1970).

22. *Izbr. Proizv.* 3:238.

23. The analysis of the myth of the fourth *Pythian Ode* in the preface to Ludolph Dissen's edition of Pindar (Gotha: Hennings, 1830), liv–lviii, is still worthy of attention.

24. The quotation is taken from the remarks of Eisenstein cited at greater length below.

25. *Izbr. Proizv.*, 3:37.

26. *Acharnians*, 412; *Thesmophoriazusae*, 148–52.

27. This is an insight brilliantly exploited by Bertolt Brecht in his *Galileo*, where the originally liberal Cardinal Maffeo Barberini, dressing on stage in his papal robes after his election, becomes more and more illiberal as he assumes the garb appropriate to his new office as Urban VIII.

28. *Izbr. Proizv.*, 3:200.

29. *Izbr. Proizv.*, 3:38.

30. Petrarch wanted to be a second Ennius, i.e., a writer of historical epic, but his genius was too Ovidian, and in the fight between ambition and inclination the poem died. This thesis is developed more extensively in my *The Classical Epic Tradition*, 282–92.

31. This is the point of the later polemic against the turgid Antimachus, admired by Plato: "The *Lyde* is a crass piece of writing, and not clear" (Callimachus, frag. 398, Pfeiffer); "but let the common herd take pleasure in swollen Antimachus" (Catullus 95. 10).

32. Werner Biehl, "Quantitative Formgestaltung bei Euripides: Die Trimeterszenen der *Troades*," *Philologus* 126 (1982):19–43.

33. *Izbr. Proizv.*, 3:139.

34. *Izbr. Proizv.*, 3:60–61.

35. *Izbr. Proizv.*, 3:381.

36. Modified from Erasmus, *On Copia of Words and Ideas*, trans. Donald B. King and H. David Rix (Milwaukee: Marquette University Press, 1963), 47. *Ut pictura poesis* (Horace, *Ars Poetica* 361) is already an Aristotelian insight (see D. W. Lucas's note on *Poetics* 1447a18 in his edition of the *Poetics* [Oxford: Oxford University Press, 1968], 56). For what became of it in post-Aristotelian critical theory see P. Scheller, *De hellenistica historiae conscribendae arte* (Leipzig: Noske, 1911), 57–61, and Marie-Luise von Franz, *Die aesthetischen Anschauungen der Iliasscholien* (Zürich: Hummel, 1943), 23.

37. See Otto Weinreich, *Epigramm und Pantomimus* (Heidelberg: Winter, 1948), 144–45.

38. See Robin R. Schlunk, *The Homeric Scholia and the "Aeneid"* (Ann Arbor: University of Michigan Press, 1974), 41.

39. The following remarks on *The Battleship Potemkin* are paraphrased from Eisenstein, *Izbr. Proizv.*, 3:264, and show what he wished to emphasize rather than what may be valid in a total description of his film.

40. *Izbr. Proizv.*, 2:370.

41. *Izbr. Proizv.*, 2:393. On the Greeks, see, for example, *Izbr. Proizv.*, 3:136.

42. This traditional translation, however, is too mawkish. The connection of the adjective *hēdys* (sweet) with *hēdonē* (pleasure) must not be forgotten.

Cacoyannis's and Euripides' *Iphigenia:*
The Dialectic of Power

Marianne McDonald

University of California, San Diego

WAR has been a timeless concern for man; one questions its
goals and the price paid for them. War and its consequences
intrigued Cacoyannis, particularly from the point of view of
power: who holds it over whom, and what are its abuses. What is a
noble war (the Persian Wars), or what is an ignoble one (Greece's
civil wars)? Is a noble war even possible? These are Cacoyannis's
questions, as they were Euripides.'[1]

Euripides is a prime source of material for Cacoyannis, as war is
a predominant physical and philosophical landscape in his plays.
In *The Suppliants* (ll. 481–85), Euripides has a herald say that
when it comes to voting for war, no one thinks of his own death
but of the death of the "other," because if each saw his own death
before his eyes at voting time, "never would spear-mad Greece
perish." In *Iphigenia at Aulis* we see the death of the "other," and
"spear-mad Greece" rushing to its destruction. Destruction is the
price paid by oppressors, as Poseidon says at the beginning of
Euripides' *Trojan Women:* "He's a fool who sacks a city . . . he who
makes waste is later wasted" (ll. 95–97). Cacoyannis joins with
Euripides to let us see the "others" as ourselves.

Both Euripides and Cacoyannis make political statements in
their works. With their experience of war and exile, they wish to
show war's implications and consequences. Homer may extol the
glories of battle and the honor of heroes, but Euripides shows the
heroism of the victim which, more often than not, is futile. The
wages of war are earned by blood, and in this case the honor
gained by Iphigenia as victim is honor lost by Agamemnon.

In Euripides, *aretē* (excellence), is constantly betrayed by conventional male "heroes"; instead, true *aretē* is often found in
women, slaves, and children. The only valid construct in a morally
unstructured universe is *philia* (friendship), the tie linking one
person to another, as expressed by Euripides' Heracles:
"Whoever prefers wealth or power over good friends thinks

127

poorly" (*Heracles,* 1425–26).[2] Agamemnon violates the bonds of *philia* and consequently pays a fatal price for power.

Cacoyannis has made a film of Euripides' play and varied it in ways consistent with his vision of cinema, as both a political and artistic vehicle, meant to communicate to all people, not simply an elite. His approach is both naturalistic and symbolic: he presents us with a complete picture of man, both his physical existence and psychological drives. Cacoyannis uses the expanded spatial and temporal capability of the film over the theater, as well as the symbolic use of space, icon, and music.[3]

It is perhaps wrong to consider Cacoyannis an outsider in Greek cinema, but this is in its own way a compliment.[4] He escaped the commercial and often platitudinous films of the 1960s produced by the Greek film industry and gave Greece an international reputation with the popular *Zorba the Greek* (1964) and with his *Trojan Trilogy: Electra* (1961), *The Trojan Women* (1971), and *Iphigenia* (1976).[5] Many Greek directors have turned to the ancient classics for their films, but it is primarily Cacoyannis who has struck an effective balance between reproducing the play and fully exploiting its cinematic potential.

Peter Wollen, Christian Metz, Ian Jarvie, and others have demonstrated that film has its own semiology; cinema can be regarded as a language which sends complex messages.[6] Cacoyannis's semiology has a clear historical basis, and although we could analyze his work simply in cinematic contexts, we would lose much of the communicative interplay intended. Like Eisenstein and others, he uses historical models to provide ideological commentary on contemporary situations.[7]

There are many different approaches to making a film based on a play.[8] One can simply film a play (Tyrone Guthrie's *Oedipus*), put the drama into a theatrical setting (Philip Saville's *Oedipus*; Jules Dassin's *Dream of Passion,* based on *Medea*), put the drama simply into a contemporary "real" context (Dassin's *Phaedra*), or create a predominantly cinematic world by exploiting uniquely cinematic resources, e.g., montage. This Costas Ferris did in *Prometheus Second Person Singular*, Miklos Jancso in *Electreia*, and Pier Paolo Pasolini in both his *Edipo Re* and *Medea*, but these categories often overlap. The camera provides a viewpoint different from that in the theater. Close-ups allow intimate awareness of the players' reactions, far removed from the ancient mask seen at a distance in the Greek theater. Even when masks are used (e.g., by Guthrie and Pasolini), a sudden close-up can cause an emotional start which would be impossible in the theater.[9]

Cacoyannis has placed his trilogy in the Greek countryside. He becomes less and less stylized in each of his films in his dramatic use of characters, particularly in his deployment of the chorus. At the same time, he seems to have become more sophisticated in his use of the camera to provide symbolic commentary, coupled with a suggestive use of prologue and epilogue. His *Electra* deals with a personal drama in the family of the house of Atreus and with the consequences of the family curse. *The Trojan Women* is concerned with public disaster, the consequences of war. *Iphigenia* shows both the public and the private, and how a private sacrifice is made for what is said to be the public good.

Cacoyannis has softened Euripides' negative vision of a universe ruled by corrupt gods and an earth ruled by corrupt human beings. He altogether eliminates the gods, and in addition to a heroic Iphigenia shows us a heroic Achilles, a loving mother, and a concerned father who is trapped mainly by his own weakness. They are all confronted with Calchas and Odysseus, who are hopelessly corrupted by power and themselves depend on the whims of an unreliable mob, the army.

The lessons Cacoyannis himself learned from living through the days of an oppressive military government in Greece are conveyed in all his films, from his *Trojan Trilogy* through *Attila 1974* to his latest, *Sweet Country*. Cacoyannis dedicated his *Trojan Women* "to those who fearlessly oppose the oppression of man by man," and those words could well apply to each of these films and particularly to his *Iphigenia*. We see the price of war, paid for with the blood of children. The parallels to Euripides' own experience of the Peloponnesian War are obvious.

Both Cacoyannis and Euripides have political messages shaped by their own times. Euripides both accepted and subverted some of the traditions of Athens. He particularly showed their corruption, thus intending a process which might lead to change through an undermining of the corrupt powers. He questioned, even mocked, the gods by showing them as more depraved than human beings; political leaders often came close to the gods in their depravity.

Euripides had seen the Athenians, after they were victorious over the Persians, form an oppressive empire with the pretext of protecting Greece from the Persian threat. Various incidents led to the outbreak of the Peloponnesian War in 431 B.C., but the fundamental cause was, according to Thucydides, Sparta's fear in reaction to Athens accumulating power. In 416 B.C., when Melos refused to support Athens, the Athenians reacted by killing all adult men and selling the women and children into slavery. This episode and the *Machtpolitik* of the debates which led up to it are well described by Thucydides, and it seems likely that Euripides' *Trojan Women* was written in response and was performed in 415 B.C.. Sparta inflicted total defeat on Athens in 404 B.C., two years after Euripides' death and after the posthumous performance of his *Iphigenia at Aulis*.

Euripides' plays show a growing awareness of the realities of war and of the prevarications of the leaders who had to pander to a mob.[10] His later plays reflect Thucydides' evaluation of a general deterioration of moral values. Words acquired new meanings. Power and success were valued more than justice or truth. Euripides' Iphigenia, with her noble display of self-sacrifice for the sake of Greece, seems like a Homeric hero lost in a Thucydidean world, seeking honor when the people about her do not know the meaning of the word.[11]

From the very opening of his film, Cacoyannis makes us visually conscious of the power of the army. Euripides, with the limitations of ancient tragedy, could only suggest where Cacoyannis is visually explicit. Cacoyannis also makes Odysseus more prominent throughout than Euripides had done, and adds an obviously corrupt Calchas. He reproduces the corruption of the people and the political leaders he himself had known in Athens.

Cacoyannis in his youth saw Greece face a bloody civil war (1946–49) immediately following World War II and then witnessed the rise of a military junta and dictatorship under Colonel Papadopoulos (1967–74). The invasion of Cyprus by the Turks in 1974 is commemorated in Cacoyannis's documentary, *Attila 1974*, a kind of modern-day *Trojan Women*. Cacoyannis shows the weeping faces of the men, women, and children who mourn their dead and missing and are forced to leave their land in the wake of invasion. He knew the force and madness of an invading army and, like Euripides, understood mob passion and fickleness. When Iphigenia says that she is giving her life to free Greece from the barbarians, her words acquire a particular poignancy when we link them to Cacoyannis's documentary about the Turkish border in Cyprus, the Attila line. However, both *Attila 1974* and *Iphigenia* are films about betrayal and accommodation. As Iphigenia is sacrificed with the collusion of Calchas, Menelaus, Agamemnon, Odysseus, and the army, so in *Attila* Cacoyannis suggested that Cyprus had been betrayed by the junta in collusion with the CIA, the UN, and Turkey.

To Cacoyannis, all this carried overtones from his country's antiquity. The confrontation between the brothers Menelaus and Agamemnon showed the struggle for power among leaders which was familiar to Euripides. Conflicts and indecision such as theirs paved the way to an oligarchic takeover in Athens during the Peloponnesian War in 411–410 B.C. which led to arbitrary murders to consolidate the ruling power. The same thing happened many times in modern Athens when conflicts between various leaders allowed another to take advantage of the situation to seize power. For instance, when Papandreou made an alliance with the communists and opposed his father who was compromising with the royalists, these vacillations of leadership led to a general disillusionment with the government and to the military coup led by Papadopoulos in 1967.

Menelaus accuses Agamemnon of abandoning the people who helped him after he consolidated his power. This is parallel to Papadopoulos's gradual rise, followed by his abandonment of the constituency which had helped him obtain his leadership. Euripides and Cacoyannis show us that this is the lesson taught again and again by history: leaders make and break alliances with the people in accordance to expediency. Not surprisingly, the Greek Orthodox Church accommodated itself to the junta, and Cacoyannis's corrupt Calchas, who panders to military leaders like Odysseus, might well allude to this historical phenomenon. The church in Greece was known to have formed alliances with the military and conservative party. Cacoyannis humanizes Euripides by centering good and evil in human beings, with no divine element as either source or judge. With no supernatural framework or even suggested fatalism, man is wholly responsible for his actions. Euripides showed human alliances as a way of combating irrational but still controlling deities, but Cacoyannis sees man controlling his own fate.

In Cacoyannis's film there are other "humanizing" factors. The struggle is hardly simply for honor, vengeance, or some other abstract ideal; it is for gold. In *The Trojan Women* Cacoyannis has some of the soldiers discuss the war: they say that Helen is simply a figurehead and that the real motive for the war is gold. Now also in *Iphigenia*, Cacoyannis refers to his earlier film when Agamemnon says that Helen gave them an excuse to go to war but that Troy's gold was the real reason. The economic basis of power becomes clearer and clearer in the history of modern Greece; it was the major criticism leveled by Papandreou against the "palace, the junta, the economic oligarchy, and the American CIA."[12] This illustrates what seems confirmed by history again and again: an economically comfortable people are eminently governable.

Cacoyannis also varies Euripides by eliminating much of the text, such as many lines given to the chorus. A major change involves the ending of the play. How many viewers today would believe that a deer was substituted for Iphigenia at the last minute? Even Clytemnestra questioned it (*Iph.*, 1617).[13] Cacoyannis has eliminated this ending altogether. He presents us with the victim's perspective: thus, "the other" becomes us. We see what the victim sees when she dies. Her personal agony leads to Cacoyannis's political commentary and to our understanding. We think about the reasons which have led to this agony; Cacoyannis makes us think of modern parallels.

Back to the myth. How applicable to modern times is the idea of a son murdering his mother because an oracle has told him to in order to take vengeance for her killing his father who in turn had killed his daughter so that he could obtain favorable winds for a military expedition against a city whose prince had stolen his brother's wife? This is not likely to bring about much if any sympathy or emotional involvement from a modern audience. Yet Cacoyannis uses just enough from the ancient plot effectively to convey his modern message. He changed Euripides' plot particularly in rationalizing motivation. The chorus also has a more naturalistic role than usual in Euripides, and more so than in the other two films in Cacoyannis's *Trojan Trilogy*. There is hardly any stylized movement or recitation in unison. We see the ships in an opening pan of the camera, rather than hearing them listed in a choral catalogue. Cacoyannis replaces Euripides' Maidens from Chalcis, the original chorus who come to observe the fleet, with a group of friends who accompany Iphigenia, who share her horror and sorrow when they learn that they have not come to witness a marriage but a brutal sacrifice. Songs also take on a choric function: a lullaby by Clytemnestra, a rousing war song by the army, and, toward the end, Clytemnestra singing to Iphigenia, whom she holds in her arms, a song to ward off death.

Characterization has also been altered by elimination of parts of the Euripidean text. Cacoyannis presents an Achilles more sympathetic than Euripides', having cast a young, handsome actor in this role. In the play, Achilles may be seen as a self-satisfied prig who begins his first long speech to Clytemnestra by saying that he is well schooled in the virtue of self-restraint. Cacoyannis omits this, but retains Achilles' claim that all Agamemnon needed to do was to consult him personally if he wanted to use his name to lure Iphigenia to her death; after all, he would do anything for Greece. Euripides' Achilles concludes by telling Clytemnestra that it is she who should talk to Agamemnon, but also tells her not to shame her father by wandering distraught through the army, "for Tyndareus is not worthy of having a bad reputation, for he is great among the Greeks" (*Iph.*, 1028–32). Euripides emphasizes that all Achilles is concerned about is his own reputation and honor and how that of another Greek leader may be perceived. He is indifferent to justice or what he perceives as mere female whining.

On the other hand, Cacoyannis's Achilles seems to take both Clytemnestra and Iphigenia more seriously. He certainly seems more willing than Euripides' Achilles to risk his life for Iphigenia. Cacoyannis's Achilles is a hero capable of making her change her mind for his sake: this Achilles looks at her first with compassion, later with admiration. In the film, his first direct words to her are: "Don't be afraid, I'll defend you." In Euripides, he only addresses her directly after her decision to die willingly and begins by calling her "child of Agamemnon" (*Iph.*, 1404). In Cacoyannis's film we see him arguing with his men on her behalf and even being stoned for his effort. Euripides plays this down very much when Achilles says that the Argives almost stoned him for trying to defend Iphigenia (*Iph.*, 1349). Cacoyannis's Achilles acts heroically, and what was verbal in Euripides becomes visual in Cacoyannis.

Agamemnon also has been softened from his Euripidean model: Cacoyannis shows him as weak, but we never doubt that he is a loving father.[14] The weakness in Cacoyannis's Agamemnon is clearly visible as he wavers between sacrificing his child and giving up the expedition; he is finally resolved when the army hails him as leader and sings a song of victory at the instigation of Odysseus. He then takes a deep breath, one more nonverbal sign of defeat and acceptance. Another cinematic effect that conveys Agamemnon's weakness and hesitation is what we might call a visual and aural close-up: we see and hear Agamemnon scratching his nails across a clay jar (*pithos*) as he waits for his family; we hear his labored breathing and see his tortured eyes.

Cacoyannis makes it clear from his prologue and in Calchas' private interchanges with Odysseus that the seer has personally contrived the oracle, saying falsely that Artemis demanded Iphigenia's death. Odysseus tells Calchas to hurry the sacrifice because the winds are already rising. This is a radical change from

Euripides: after all, Artemis would send winds only *after* Iphigenia's death. But it is also clear that Cacoyannis's Agamemnon is fully aware of Calchas' corruption; he knows that Calchas has invented the oracle. Even when Iphigenia approaches him to ask him to spare her life, he does not counter with arguments that she is dying for Greece and to fulfill the will of the gods (as Euripides has him say); he says instead that it is too late: the army has been incited to frenzy and demands the sacrifice; to deny them means death, including his own and even his family's at home in Argos. At the end of the film when Agamemnon sees the wind rising and runs up the steps toward the altar and Calchas, he really is too late, and this also we see in his eyes. We see defeat in his eyes more effectively than words could convey. In this film there is no messenger speech; we read Iphigenia's death in her father's eyes. Eyes are the vehicle Cacoyannis uses to convey suffering, pity, love, hate, horror, defeat, and ultimately death. In his films they are true windows of the human soul. The camera is the director's eye with which we also see, observe, and understand. Similarly, Cacoyannis's verbal and visual text underlines differences between the sexes; sometimes the only recourse left to the female is to see and stare at the male.

Throughout this film we have references to eyes. Cacoyannis provides a visual text in addition to verbal allusions. Who sees and who does not see relates to the issue of power; more often than not seeing is the sole power of the female. There is a distinct difference between the way Cacoyannis visually presents males and females. Men are often static and seen from behind; they often avoid the eyes of the female. Women move and are seen from the front; female eyes stare, blaze, blame, and threaten. Iphigenia pierces her father with her eyes as she is crowned and sprinkled with water in preparation for death; Agamemnon avoids her gaze here as he did earlier when she first arrived in Aulis. He only stares at her after she is dead (cessation of movement). Clytemnestra's gaze is like the destructive gaze of the Gorgon, especially at the film's end.

Cacoyannis shows heroes (Iphigenia, Achilles), mixed characters (Agamemnon, Menelaus), and villains (Calchas, Odysseus, and the army). There are also those who are simply victims (Clytemnestra and the servant). This is in contrast to Euripides, who makes all except Iphigenia partially blameworthy. Some critics see even her as calculating; they interpret Achilles' words literally when he says that Iphigenia has aligned her will with what she sees as clear necessity (*Iph.*, 1409).[15]

Euripides has no heroes except Iphigenia and no out-and-out villains. Calchas and Odysseus are only mentioned in his play but never appear on stage. Even so, his Menelaus and Agamemnon are to some extent corrupt. Cacoyannis has made the brothers more sympathetic, particularly when after their argument he shows Menelaus swayed by family loyalty. (Iphigenia is, after all, his niece.) He takes Agamemnon's hand in a gesture of brotherly closeness. Calchas, Odysseus, the army, and eventually Menelaus call Iphigenia's sacrifice a "good," whereas its evil nature is clearly perceived by Agamemnon at times and by Clytemnestra always. Cacoyannis makes Agamemnon more sympathetic, showing more a weakling than a criminal.

Cacoyannis has also made Iphigenia's heroism more believable in the way he conveys her gradual realization that she has no choice about living or dying but that the manner of her death is crucial. He has eliminated Iphigenia's chilling comment to Achilles that "one man's life is worth more than 10,000 women's" (*Iph.*, 1394). Her dignity is unmistakable; it is the dignity of a brave child (the actress playing her is only twelve years old). Iphigenia wears bridal veils, but still has a dirty face. (We see it smudged, possibly from her attempt to escape, running and falling in the forest.) At the last minute, when she realizes the winds are rising, she tries to escape again, but is caught by Calchas as she screams. This is not a heroic final moment, but it does not diminish her earlier bravery. Her humanity intensifies her credibility for us and deepens our sympathy for her. She has much in common with Dreyer's heroine in *Jeanne d'Arc*. Both are young girls who are surrounded by either the corrupt or the weak. Unlike Jeanne, Iphigenia is not a leader of armies, but both women choose a heroic death. They are two young girls whose vulnerability, innocence, and moral choices contrast with the sordid nature of the people at whose hands they died.

Cacoyannis's nonverbal visual treatment, particularly in his prologue and ending and in the chase sequence in the middle of the film, resolves many of the ambiguities of interpreting Euripides' text, but it presents us with new ones. We have an open-ended drama, hardly the compact imitation of an action of a certain length, with a beginning and an end, as postulated by Aristotle in the *Poetics*.

Cacoyannis's prologue suggests the major themes of the entire film in nine minutes. He shows us the Greek fleet and the restless army, overcome with heat and impatient in its desire to sail to Troy. Agamemnon panders to his men by leading them on a slaughter of animals tended by Calchas and his followers (dressed, it may be said, rather like Zen monks, with flowing white robes and shaved heads). He tries to prevent the killing of a sacred deer, but is too late. We see the deer flee, trying to escape through the woods, and we see the woods through the deer's eyes, for the first time in the film sharing the victim's perspective. The animal's death proleptically suggests Iphigenia's; her life will be demanded by the army, and we shall share her point of view, literally and figuratively, as well.[16]

Over the dying deer, his sacred property, Calchas looks at Agamemnon. The close-up of his eyes suggests his future course of action and his vengeance, just as the close-up of Clytemnestra's eyes at the very end of the film suggests her vengeance upon Agamemnon after his return from Troy. Close-ups of eyes and shared perspectives convey the major issues of the film. After the death of the deer, Cacoyannis cuts to the fleet and then to a close-up of a mast which resembles a death's-head. The title *Iphigenia* appears over an almost blood-red sea. Close-ups and editing make for an ominous and immediately gripping opening of the film. The deadly game, a struggle for power in which the innocent will die, has begun. Later, when Iphigenia is hunted down, she runs through the forest chased by soldiers. We see the forest through her eyes just as we saw the forest through the deer's eyes earlier. The parallel is clear.

The film comes to an end at sunset when the ships are sailing, but the future is in Clytemnestra's eyes. Her face, in close-up, is superimposed on this long-shot and, smoldering with hatred, it is a promise of vengeance. The sunset colors the sea blood-red, and the wind, bought with her child's life, blows Clytemnestra's hair across her face. As we see the fleet sail away, the black strands of Clytemnestra's hair obscure our view: we, the spectators, have become Clytemnestra, just as earlier we had been the deer and Iphigenia. The film's final shot is of Clytemnestra waiting. We realize that the true end will occur not in Troy, but in Argos after Agamemnon's return: we anticipate the beginning of Cacoyannis's *Electra* and a sheer endless cycle of vengeance. Even a victim can become a perpetrator of violence. Iphigenia is dead, but her mother lives.

It is noteworthy that only after thirty-five minutes does Cacoyannis's film reach the beginning of Euripides' play. The opening dialogue between Agamemnon and his slave has been revised and cut to eliminate some of the textual difficulties which have plagued scholars.[17] The hunt described above is followed by

Calchas delivering his oracle. The camera then cuts between Mycenae and Aulis, showing us Clytemnestra telling Iphigenia about her intended marriage to Achilles and the start of their trip to Aulis. Menelaus observes Agamemnon as he roams about in his hut like a trapped animal. Here, too, a parallel is drawn between him and the deer; he is, in a sense, also trapped and our sympathy for him grows. His being trapped contrasts with the movement of his family to join him, but they are moving into a trap themselves.

This is an example of Cacoyannis's use of montage: the static vs. the moving by means of editing. The active heroic Iphigenia contrasts with Agamemnon, who is caught in numerous traps. Although she is brought by the soldiers to the camp, at the end she proudly walks by herself through the army to meet her death. Deep focus allows us to see Iphigenia against the army, dominating it by her forward movement yet encircled by it. Agamemnon falls deeper and deeper into the trap of leadership, a golden cage bought at high cost.

Cacoyannis's camera also creates perspectives. We see Calchas mainly from below, a perspective which suggests his dominance. He is initially a victim since he has lost his sacred deer, but we see his successful machinations toward vengeance accomplished in Iphigenia's sacrifice. This is hardly an equitable return, a child's life for a deer's, but for Calchas it is a question of power. Conversely, Cacoyannis's camera often shows us Iphigenia from above, making her a victim, small and helpless, easy spoil for Calchas and the army.

The camera gives us intimate close-ups, broad pans as of the army, rapid cutting as in the hunt sequences, and views from above and below. These perspectives create and underline the characters' importance. The camera assumes the commentator's function of the ancient chorus. Our view of the ancient palace of Mycenae, with Iphigenia running through the ruins, gives visual authority to Cacoyannis's reworking of the ancient myth. (The ruins also ironically comment on the eventual fall of the house of Atreus.) Through his camera Cacoyannis has escaped the limitations of theatrical space and those of time and text.

Costumes, sets, and colors also play their part. The brothers Menelaus and Agamemnon wear masklike helmets before the crowd of soldiers asking them for decisions about sailing: the mask/helmets are a sign both of authority and cowardice. They show rank, yet function as protection from both their own people and the enemy. The mask reduces the wearer's humanity and gives us Cacoyannis's visual commentary on the questionable character of Agamemnon and Menelaus. In the opening sequence Agamemnon and Odysseus wear their helmets as the army demands answers: the leaders are faceless; they command and yet are tools. In the final sequence Agamemnon at first does not wear a helmet, but puts it on after Iphigenia's death: he has given up his role as father and resumed his role as commander, but he has paid for it with his daughter's life. His hammered helmet resembles the well-known Mycenaean "death mask" of Agamemnon found by Schliemann. As do the ruins of Mycenae, this mask also makes an ironic proleptic commentary. The helmets vaguely resemble classical theatrical masks, which have been characterized as the constraint which allows the wearers to see the unseeable and speak the unspeakable.[18]

Concerning color, the splashes of red in sets and costumes recall the red of the deer's blood in the opening sequence: Menelaus' cloak, a red helmet, and a red rug in a white room on which Iphigenia, also dressed in virginal and bridal white, lies as her mother sings her a lullaby during their journey to Aulis, an innocent victim lying in her blood. Iphigenia is dressed in sacrificial white as she goes to her death at the hands of a Calchas who wears black. She wears a crown made of wheat sprays and is splashed with lustral water like an animal victim.[19] She says that death will be her marriage, her children, and her glory. Her father gives her not to the bridegroom who takes part in the ritual, but to a power-crazed priest as a victim in exchange for the gold of Troy which will be bought by countless other lives. We see here a perverted marriage ritual, and Clytemnestra screams at the army, "Unholy murder," as Iphigenia leaves to meet her death.[20]

Cacoyannis has Orestes play a symbolic role as well. He is a typical child and we see him run away as his parents are arguing. Then, as he waits in the courtyard for Iphigenia, he plays with armor, banging on it, just as earlier the army had banged on drums. He is being conditioned by violence and will play a violent man's part in the future as he is playing a child's game now. He will be the final link in this cycle of vengeance.

Cacoyannis has given us a Greek tragedy, with emphasis on "Greek." Here is Mediterranean fire, expressed in passionate embraces: brothers clasp hands as they renew their alliance, Agamemnon kisses and holds Iphigenia's hand and tousles her hair, Clytemnestra holds her daughter in her arms and rocks her as she sings a song as a charm against death. The language and the music intensify the warmth of the characters' emotions. Agamemnon calls Iphigenia his "sweet girl," words that are like an epithet of love in Greek *(glukeia mou kori)*, Iphigenia calls her mother *kali mou mana* (my beloved mother), and Clytemnestra calls Iphigenia *matia mou* (my eyes). These words convey the ultimate human value, the love of a parent for a child and of a child for a parent. These words are also used by weeping parents in Cacoyannis's documentary, *Attila 1974*. Emotion becomes visible as eyes flood with tears: we notice Agamemnon's tears when he first sees Iphigenia arrive, and Clytemnestra's tears when she realizes her daughter has chosen to die willingly. Cacoyannis lets us hear passion also: Clytemnestra's scream when she first learns of Agamemnon's intent is one of deepest anguish.

The music composed for this film by Mikis Theodorakis, with its military theme played by heavy brass and drums, and with an Iphigenia theme (a melody on a flute with light string background), which conveys her innocence as effectively as do her white veils, shows the contrast between the power and madness of the army and the innocent victim. Iphigenia's theme appears on the soundtrack when we first see her going to greet her father in the army camp; as she goes off to her death, it changes from minor to major and is presented with full orchestra, dominating the army's theme just as her noble act dwarfs their crime. But as the fleet sails away we again hear the army's theme which had begun the film. It now affirms the ultimate victory of the mob, but also ironically points to its moral defeat. Cacoyannis's choice of Theodorakis, an outspoken enemy of the Greek junta, provides additional political commentary. The modern music reinforces the use in the film of the modern Greek language; thus Iphigenia's cause becomes the cause of modern Greece.

Cacoyannis's *Iphigenia* is a film centered on power bought by betrayal. He shows us the army and makes us aware of its madness, its lust for a child's life which is a symbolic beginning of the subsequent ten-year slaughter at Troy. The oracle which Euripides had left ambiguous becomes an instrument to serve power in Cacoyannis's film.

Cacoyannis has varied Euripides in significant ways, adding villains and sentimentalizing family ties. There are more clear-cut black and white characters, and Cacoyannis sacrifices many of Euripides' ambiguities. But like Euripides, Cacoyannis conveys a topical political message, a warning that cannot be missed. He uses ancient myths in an unambiguous way for today's audience. Even television melodrama and public political rallies seem to have influenced his narrative technique as much as classical drama. Cacoyannis speaks to the people in a popular way. His message is still effective. Both Euripides and Cacoyannis have shown us the weakness of power and the power of the otherwise powerless. Iphigenia shows us that, in a world which limits our freedom, heroism is still possible. Freedom can still be a human creation.[21]

NOTES

1. I have dealt with Cacoyannis's and Euripides' *Iphigenia* earlier in "Cacoyannis' and Euripides' *Iphigenia at Aulis:* A New Heroism," in *Euripides in Cinema: The Heart Made Visible* (Philadelphia: Centrum, 1983), 129–91, and in "Kakojanisova i Euripidova 'Ifigenia': Moć Nemoćnih," *Pozorište* 56, no. 10 (1989): 54–57.

2. Much work has been done on *philia,* in particular in Euripides. See, e.g., Seth Schein, "Mythical Illusion and Historical Reality in Euripides' *Orestes,*" *Wiener Studen,* New Series, 9 (1975):55–66. See also David Konstan, *"Philia* in Euripides' *Electra,*" *Philologus* 129 (1985):176–85.

3. For the expanded spatial and temporal movement in cinema see Gilles Deleuze, *Cinema I: L'image-mouvement* (Paris: Minuit, 1983), and *Cinema II: L'image-temps* (Paris: Minuit, 1985).

4. He is called a "non-Greek" Greek and classified with Costa-Gavras and Jules Dassin by Mel Schuster, *The Contemporary Greek Cinema* (Metuchen, N.J.: Scarecrow Press, 1979), 202.

5. Three chapters in *Euripides in Cinema,* 129–319, deal with Cacoyannis's *Trojan Trilogy* in greater detail than is possible here. Kenneth MacKinnon, *Greek Tragedy into Film* (London: Croom Helm, 1986), reaches many of the same conclusions; e.g., he sees Cacoyannis's Electra as more favorably presented than she was by Euripides (77–78). I disagree with some of MacKinnon's conclusions, such as the "anti-tragic tendencies in Euripides which, by their ambiguity, render personal relationships 'cold' " (154); rather, I agree with Aristotle's assessment of Euripides as the most tragic of the tragedians, particularly through his use of human relationships which range from the most heated to the most frigid.

6. See, for instance, Peter Wollen, *Signs and Meaning in the Cinema,* rev. ed. (Bloomington: Indiana University Press, 1972); Christian Metz, *Film Language: A Semiotics of the Cinema* (New York: Oxford University Press, 1974); and Ian Jarvie, *The Philosophy of the Film* (New York: Routledge & Kegan Paul, 1987).

7. See, e.g., Eisenstein's *Battleship Potemkin* (1925), *Alexander Nevsky* (1938), and *Ivan the Terrible* (1944).

8. MacKinnon, *Greek Tragedy into Film,* classifies films based on Greek tragedy into four categories: those in Theatrical Mode, Realistic Mode, Filmic Mode, and Meta-Tragedy. His first three categories are based on Jack J. Jorgens, *Shakespeare on Film* (Bloomington: Indiana University Press, 1977). Cacoyannis's films are discussed as "Films in the Realistic Mode" (66–96).

9. See Béla Balázs, *Theory of the Film: Character and Growth of a New Art,* trans. Edith Bone (London: Dobson, 1952), 55: "The close-up can show us a quality in a gesture of a hand that we had never noticed before. . . . The close-up shows your shadow on the wall with which you have lived all your life and which you scarcely knew." See also Balázs, "Theory of the Film," in *Film: An Anthology,* ed. Daniel Talbot (1959; reprint, Berkeley: University of California Press, 1975), 212: "good close-ups are lyrical; it is the heart, not the eye, that has perceived them."

10. The word for "mob" (*ochlos*) occurs more often in his late plays, *Orestes* and *Iphigenia*, than in any others. He gradually realized the power of the mob and its demagogues. In regard to the Trojan War, it is clear that mob power is an anachronism: Euripides was speaking about his own time.

11. See Thomas Rosenmeyer, "Wahlakt und Entscheidungsprozess in der antiken Tragödie," *Poetica* 10 (1978): 14, who explains Iphigenia's change of mind, criticized by Aristotle, in terms of heroism: "Der Stimmungsumschlag erfolgt völlig unvermittelt, und das entspricht offensichtlich der heroischen Natur, die wohl klagen und sich fürchten mag, sich aber nicht auf eine Selbstbefragung einlassen darf." He sees Iphigenia as impelled by "Verlangen nach Ruhm," thus pursuing the Homeric ideal of *kleos aphthiton*, "immortal glory."

12. George Kousoulas, *Modern Greece: Profile of a Nation* (New York: Scribner's, 1974), 275.

13. This ending may very well be an interpolation in this very interpolated play. See Denys L. Page, *Actor's Interpolations in Greek Tragedy, Studied with Special Reference to Euripides' "Iphigenia in Aulis"* (Oxford: Clarendon Press, 1934).

14. There are many interpretations of Agamemnon, from the *Vater/Feldherr* theory (Agamemnon tries to be a father, but is forced into being a commander) to that which sees him as wholly corrupt. For a summary of the various theories about Agamemnon's motives see Herbert Siegel, "Agamemnon in Euripides' 'Iphigenia at Aulis,'" *Hermes* 109 (1981): 257–65, esp. nn. 1–3.

15. One of the earliest negative assessments of Iphigenia's actions was by Bruno Snell, "Euripides' Aulische Iphigenie," in *Aischylos und das Handeln im Drama*, Philologus supplement 20 (Leipzig: Dieterich, 1928), 148–60.

16. Cf. the rabbit hunt in Jean Renoir's *Rules of the Game* (1939), foreshadowing the brutality of World War II.

17. See Bernard Knox, "Euripides' *Iphigenia in Aulide* 1–163 (in that order)," *Yale Classical Studies* 22 (1972): 239–62.

18. See Tony Harrison, "The *Oresteia* in the Making," *Omnibus* 4; reprinted in Jubilee issue (July 1987): 52.

19. For humans as sacred victims see René Girard, *Violence and the Sacred*, trans. Patrick Gregory (Baltimore: Johns Hopkins University Press, 1977), and Walter Burkert, *Homo Necans*, trans. Peter Bing (Berkeley: University of California Press, 1983). See also *Violent Origins: Walter Burkert, René Girard, and Jonathan Z. Smith on Ritual Killing and Cultural Formation* (Stanford: Stanford University Press, 1987). For studies of human sacrifice in Greek drama see the chapter on "The Pure Blood of Virgins" in Nicole Loraux, *Tragic Ways of Killing a Woman*, trans. Anthony Forster (Cambridge: Harvard University Press, 1987), and E. A. M. E. O'Connor-Visser, *Aspects of Human Sacrifice in the Tragedies of Euripides* (Amsterdam: Grüner, 1987), 99–147.

20. See Helene Foley, "Marriage and Sacrifice in Euripides' *Iphigeneia in Aulis*," *Arethusa* 15 (1982): 159–80; reprinted in *Ritual Irony: Poetry and Sacrifice in Euripides* (Ithaca: Cornell University Press, 1985), 65–105. See also R. A. S. Seaford, "The Tragic Wedding," *Journal of Hellenic Studies* 107 (1987): 106–130, who treats Iphigenia in Euripides as an example of the subversion of the wedding ritual in tragedy.

21. I wish to thank Pelegrino d'Acierno, Dominick Addario, Athan Anagnostopoulos, George Anagnostopoulos, Nicholas Gage, Tony Harrison, Adrian Jaffer, David Konstan, Thomas MacCary, Bridget McDonald, Wanda Roach, Thomas Rosenmeyer, Avrum Stroll, Oliver Taplin, Melia Tatakis, and Zeno Vendler for their help in preparing this paper.

Photo Essay

Iphigenia

Michael Cacoyannis chose the following stills from his film as examples illustrating his approach to a modern cinematic "translation" of Euripides. He also provided the captions for these photographs.

After weeks of waiting on the beaches of Aulis, the Greek army riots.

Exposed to the sun, men faint, and the mood of the soldiers becomes even more threatening.

Wearing their war masks, Agamemnon and Menelaus face the other generals who accuse them of

At the generals' meeting, a priest hands Calchas, the High Priest and Agamemnon's enemy, a tablet containing the oracle.

In the presence of Odysseus, Calchas confronts Agamemnon with the oracle demanding

Against Agamemnon's wishes, Clytemnestra accompanies Iphigenia to Aulis, believing her husband's lies about Iphigenia's marriage to Achilles.

Clytemnestra arrives at the Greek army camp.

Clytemnestra, mystified by Agamemnon's evasiveness, discusses with him their daughter's wedding.

When Clytemnestra's confrontation with Achilles reveals Agamemnon's plot, an angry Achilles swears to avenge his honor by defending Iphigenia. Seeing her for the first time, Achilles is also

Clytemnestra, torn between fury towards Agamemnon and fear for Iphigenia, screams in anguish and defiance.

Abandoned by all, mother and daughter cling to each other.

The army is assembled for the sacrifice.

Interviews with Michael Cacoyannis
and Irene Papas

MICHAEL Cacoyannis has made Greek cinema interna-
tionally renowned. He was the first to star Melina Mercouri
(*Stella*, 1955), and his film of Nikos Kazantzakis's novel *Zorba the
Greek* (1964) has become a classic, making the title character's name a
household term. He is best known, however, for his three adaptations of tragedies by Euripides: *Electra* (1961), *The Trojan Women*
(1971), and *Iphigenia* (1976). These films were made in the order
in which Euripides wrote his plays, although the mythological
chronology is reversed. With his film and stage productions of
tragedy, Cacoyannis has given vivid new accounts of some of the
central Greek myths and demonstrated their timeless appeal.

Irene Papas, one of the leading actresses of our time, acquired
international fame for her starring role in Cacoyannis's film of
Euripides' *Electra*. She later played Helen in *The Trojan Women*
and Clytemnestra in *Iphigenia*. Irene Papas also acts on the stage;
she appeared, for instance, in Cacoyannis's production of Euripides' *Bacchae* in New York City. On television she was Penelope
for a European production of the *Odyssey* in the late 1960s.
Among numerous other films, both Greek and international, she
had memorable roles in Costa-Gavras's political thriller, *Z* (1968),
and in *Erendira* (1983), written by Gabriel García Márquez. Recently, she acted again for Cacoyannis in his film *Sweet Country*
(1986). She also gives concert performances.

The following interviews were conducted by Marianne
McDonald via telephone in November and December, 1988, from
a list of questions prepared by her and the editor of this volume.
The interviews were then edited and submitted to Mr. Cacoyannis
and Ms. Papas for final review.

INTERVIEW WITH MICHAEL CACOYANNIS

*Could you say something about your use of the ancient classics and of
history as a means of artistic expression in the medium of film? You are
actually dealing with two different things, mythology and history.*

159

Yes, except that Greek mythology is to a great extent based on history, so its characters are not necessarily mythological inventions. Take, for instance, Agamemnon and the whole family of the Atridae. One could certainly say these were historical figures elevated to mythical stature. They were used by poets, especially tragic poets, as dramatic characters and invariably elevated out of their true historical contexts. And that is what I find fascinating. The way they were presented, say, in the fifth century B.C., did not evoke any dim past, but powerfully reflected the cultural and philosophical climate of a civilization that transcended time. The mythical characters, in the way they are made to express themselves in the tragedies, do not come across as primitive people of the twelfth century B.C., the time in which their stories took place. They are not imprisoned in their age or in any age. And that's why they are still alive today and can speak basic truths. That's why they touch us.

Why do you think this would touch us more than a modern work which directly addresses current reality? For instance, your film Sweet Country *deals with contemporary history. What can the classics add to this?*

The Greek plays are among the greatest texts ever written. The characters are only the means for great minds like Aeschylus, Sophocles, and Euripides to express their attitude toward universal human problems. I am not interested in the "true" Agamemnon, Clytemnestra, or Oedipus. I know them through Sophocles and the others. I don't know what the "real" Oedipus was like. The Oedipus who means something to me is Sophocles' Oedipus.

Why did you choose Euripides rather than Aeschylus or Sophocles for the basis of your films?

It's because of the way Euripides explores the human condition. He attacked social evils of his time and shaped the historical legends to serve his ends. He was deeply concerned with the corrosion of human values in Athens during the Peloponnesian War. Parallels between the myths and his time easily spring to mind. I find the psychological makeup of his characters more multifaceted than in the other playwrights who were more bound by traditional forms, although, within these, Sophocles struck a perfect dramatic balance. The ritualistic aspect of Aeschylus' masterworks is very difficult to put on the screen, to transpose cinematically. I think there is a great film to be made of *Oedipus,* but not necessarily of *The Persians,* which is a great play for the theater.

Do you think Euripides is more concerned with psychology than with history?

Yes, he is concerned with our faults, with the fractured aspects of human nature. Man being mortal, being arrogant and selfish, imposing his will on others—these are all things that concern us to this day. That's why, in effect, Euripides is closer to modern audiences.

Why, out of the whole body of Euripides' works, did you choose Electra, The Trojan Women, *and* Iphigenia?

The idea of a trilogy wasn't there from the beginning. In fact, the whole concept started with *Iphigenia,* which reflected my feelings about war. Although it's the last of the three films, it was the first of the tragedies I had scripted. It had to wait quite a long time. But having made *Electra* I became convinced that the films could work as a unity. Unfortunately, we have lost their companions, the other plays in their individual trilogies, but here, although the films are drawn from different trilogies, there is an inexorable sequence of events within them. Euripides was a pacifist. He exposes the futility and folly of all wars, where there can be no clear-cut victor or defeated; he shows that everybody suffers. The idea that evil begets evil and revenge begets revenge is a predominant theme in all three plays. Also, I think that they may be his best works, alongside *The Bacchae,* which, to me, is a mind-boggling masterpiece.

The three plays, as well as The Bacchae, *also deal prominently with women. Are you particularly interested in the theme of suffering women? Do you have some feminist concerns with all this?*

Women in Greek tragedy have an important role to play. Feminist concerns predominate in Euripides, and this is why I never understood why some scholars have called him a misogynist. That is really outrageous.

What are your views about the situation of women in modern Greece? Do you see any connections to ancient Greece, and is there some kind of commentary on women's place in modern Greek society in your films of the tragedies?

I think there are connections between ancient and modern Greece. Women in Euripides are always raising their voices against oppression. And . . . well, who could be more liberated, from a modern point of view, than Helen or Clytemnestra, who rules with an iron will and a harsh tongue? Even though Clytemnestra paid the price for it, nobody would call her "poor Clytemnestra." There is, in fact, an interesting parallel between Medea and Clytemnestra: they both did a great deal to help Jason and Agamemnon. And they both paid their men back in blood for their betrayals.

Both men took up with another woman, Creusa and Cassandra. And Agamemnon had even been prepared to kill Iphigenia.

When confronting Agamemnon in Aulis, Clytemnestra reveals that she never loved him. But over the years she accepted her role and became a good wife and mother. As far as the people were concerned, she was a model wife, mother, and queen. She even warns Agamemnon about the monster he will release in her if he should kill Iphigenia. She had compromised because she had come to believe that he was worth it, in a sense. And then she finds out. . . . From her point of view he is a murderer, corrupted by power.

Did you find that working with Irene Papas made it easier to convey these aspects of Clytemnestra's character?

I had identified Clytemnestra with her before I made the film. She wasn't really cast, she was part of the decision to make the film. I'd had no other image of Clytemnestra in my head. It's that extraordinary physique of hers, and the power that goes with it. When Irene cracks, it's like a stone that cracks. There is no sentimental self-pity. Her cries are not hysterical; they are defiant cries against the order of things. When I was working in America, staging tragedies, I always found it very difficult to explain this to American actresses—that there is a kind of impersonal anger bottled up inside. It's not a narrow anger; it's like a challenge to the injustice of life. I think people who experienced centuries of oppression—I don't want to narrow it down to Greeks—know much more about this. Certainly Jewish people do. It's almost like a national trait handed down from generation to generation. It's not a question of having suffered personally; it's as if the voice of suffering echoes through time. You can hear it in Greek and Armenian laments, for instance.

Where did you find the actress who played Iphigenia?

That was luck. From the moment I decided that Iphigenia should be a very young girl, that narrowed down the field and made it an extremely difficult part to cast. I started searching for a young actress who wouldn't look older than sixteen, then I accidentally met a girl of twelve who had actually no acting experience but who happened to have that quality I mentioned before in regard to Irene, the looks, which are very important, the physical framework, shall we say. To go with this, she had a natural intelligence and poise beyond her years. Emotionally, she was immature. But I cast her anyway. I thought, if I can use that immaturity and push her to the level of subtle maturity that Iphigenia herself achieves through suffering, within a matter of hours practically . . . if I could work such a trick with the actress [*laughs*] . . . it would be a wonderful correspondence with the role. In a sense I had to violate, temperamentally and psychologically, a young girl to make her able to absorb and cope with the emotional demands of the part. In that I was very lucky; I could do it without hurting her.

Her interaction with Irene Papas as Clytemnestra was most interesting, the experienced actress and the inexperienced. It worked perfectly.

Yes, it did.

What do you think about stage plays being translated into films?

Obviously, I have nothing against that. Plays, after all, are based on dialogue and character, and very often they lend themselves even more to the screen than do novels. Novels often express philosophical states and attitudes which are very difficult to translate to the screen. As long as filmmakers are not absolutely tied down by a text, they are not making "film theater," which was never my intention.

You transformed the plays into something new, rather than merely illustrating a play on the screen.

I also took liberties. I edited or rearranged the text. I took liberties particularly with the chorus.

You added characters, too.

Yes, sure. In *Iphigenia* I added Calchas, I added Odysseus; I had to. In *Electra* I had peasants talking. I didn't add any characters unrelated to the plot, but visually I explored what on stage only happens in the wings.

In Iphigenia, *the viewer is very much aware of the army and of the power it possesses. You certainly have enough people there; it's an oppressive mass.*

Yes.

Why did you add Odysseus and Calchas and give them such large roles?

The way they come across to the audience is as Euripides evoked them via the characters who discuss them, especially Menelaus and Agamemnon. With film, I don't feel limited to the few actors of ancient theater. I can bring in the people who are being mentioned and make them real. If Euripides had written the script himself, I don't think he could have left those characters offscreen.

How do you see the character of Achilles in Iphigenia? *You have kept his self-involvement. But don't you see a change in him, in that mutual affection grows between him and Iphigenia, as when they look at each other in the courtyard at the end?*

That I preserved absolutely intact, the way it is in the play. When I staged the play in New York, this feeling came through the moment they looked at each other. There is no question that, once he has seen her, Achilles is willing to defend her to the death. And I think love is a strong motivation in her, too: not wanting him to risk his life for her sake conditions her acceptance of death. All that makes sense. Achilles is the only character in *Iphigenia* whose whole text I used. His arrogance and the reasons for it are in the original. Until he sets eyes on Iphigenia, his outrage is provoked not by pity but by the insult to his honor, to a hero's inflated ego.

His philotimo?

Yes, it's *philotimo,* but in the most negative sense. It's a narrow, arrogant pride. And I think that was one thing that came across about him on the screen. He tells Clytemnestra: "If only Agamemnon had asked me personally, I would not have hesitated . . . for the sake of Greece." That's his response to a mother's desperate pleas. Not a thought at the moment for the trapped girl. What also comes across is that Clytemnestra can't get back at him and has to accept his help, even if it is for the wrong motives. All that matters to her is her daughter's life.

Concerning Iphigenia's decision: weren't there several paths which you could have taken in interpreting Euripides? Do you think you took a positive one when she falls in love with Achilles?

What she does is crystal clear to me. What you could call negative in my approach is not to accept that Euripides can be interpreted in such a way that she becomes infused with sudden patriotism. Strength, yes—and defiance toward the army clamoring for her blood. She says, "I won't give them the pleasure of seeing me being dragged off and wailing. If I have to go, I shall go proudly, and of my own free will."

Do you see her as having a sense of loyalty to her father as well?

Yes, I do, but compassion even more than loyalty, stirred by his anguish and remorse. Once you are trapped and you know you are going to die, something happens inside you, something that gives you the armor to cope with that passage to nothingness, or to the other world.

In other words, if she has to die, she might as well die heroically?

Well, perhaps not heroically, but with dignity. She is aware that her refusal to die would plunge everybody into bloodshed. Not only would she herself be killed, but also her mother, her father, Achilles. In the film you feel this even more because of the power and danger which the surrounding army represents. I made a point of establishing the threat of a discontented mob in the opening sequence, just as I wanted to make clear Iphigenia's first instinct: fear and the desire to escape. So I had her run off into

the woods and be hounded down and dragged back. All this is not
in the play.

*The way you direct the hunt for her parallels the deer hunt at the
beginning of the film. A little girl being ruthlessly hunted down—this is
very powerful cinema which involves the audience emotionally, particularly if they remember the deer's frightened eyes when they see
Iphigenia's. And then her transformation, her change of mind, becomes all
the more effective. But this is contrary to Achilles saying that she made a
virtue of necessity: "You see there is no way out, so you are determined to be
heroic."*

At face value, certain parts of her last speech might be considered
patriotic: "They will teach the barbarians a lesson." But to anyone
who knows Euripides' views about the Greek motives for the
Trojan War—I touched upon this earlier in connection with the
Peloponnesian War—this kind of rhetoric lacks conviction.

Is she not simply repeating her father's words?

Yes, I think she is, but even his are spoken in desperation. He
says, "I would let you off if I could. . . ." And this is probably the
only thing Clytemnestra by that point cannot absorb: that he is a
broken man. If he could call off the expedition, he would, but by
that time Odysseus has told the army. There is no escape for
Agamemnon.

You bring out this ambiguity in him, and we even pity him.

Still, he does pay an altogether inhuman price for his ambition.
He was confronted with the choice of being the supreme general
or of refusing to sacrifice his daughter. It's a tormenting choice,
but he makes it. Not, I think, because he is swayed by an oracle
which, to him, reeks of political intrigue. He clings to the hope
that nature will prove the oracle wrong after all: "By the time I
send for her and she gets here, the winds are bound to blow and
we'll be off." He's playing for time.

*Why did you eliminate the gods? Did you try to convey the force of the
gods—anankē, nemesis, tychē—or any of these concepts?*

My aim was to interpret Euripides. Fate, which involves human
responsibility, is a recurring theme in his plays, but he does not

relegate it to the whims of the gods and is very critical about the way his characters behave in order to appease their conscience. He invariably uses the gods to diminish their stature and what they reflect about human nature. We know his philosophical position on religion very well. One doesn't have to resort to his satirical evocation of the gods, in whom he clearly did not believe, in order to get that across. To show them on the screen would be alienating to modern audiences who should identify with the characters and be as moved as Euripides intended his audiences to be. And they are—deeply moved, I know. It is not a question of any particular religious faith. That can keep changing. Euripides' faith transcended the concept of the gods and soared above and beyond them, not only with reverence but also with the humble awareness that human knowledge, whatever its achievements, can never fathom the supreme power, the divine justice, which shapes our mortal destiny. In *The Bacchae*, the message is clear: "Knowledge is not wisdom." No doubt Euripides would have something to say about the hubris of our scientific exploits today and about the violation of nature. Of course he understood the need for religion. People cannot cope with the unknown; for instance, their fear of death. What he warned against was using the gods as scapegoats for one's own evil deeds.

Do you have a political message in your films? Are they, for instance, anti-junta?

They are against any form of political oppression. I made *Electra* before the junta.

What about Iphigenia?

That it is antimilitaristic, antiwar, goes without saying, but dramatically, not didactically. It exposes the arrogance of rulers who, in their thirst for power, have no regard for the lives of others— they bring about death arbitrarily and senselessly. The depiction of such situations and of the suffering that results is what makes Euripides so uniquely powerful.

Do you see a parallel in Iphigenia *to the Cyprus situation, as* The Trojan Women *might have related to the Melian disaster as recounted by Thucydides?*

Every major crisis or conflict, every tragic situation that happens in the world can be related to Greek tragedy. It covers the whole range of the human condition—as does Shakespeare, of course. You can relate everything, at any time, to Shakespeare's plays. They and the Greek plays are like mirrors in which you can see all of life.

Do you think art can influence politics?

I wish I could say it does. If it were so, after *The Trojan Women*, there should have been no more wars. But the greatness of art is that it goes on raising its voice regardless, to quote Edith Hamilton.

Do you see a connection between your Euripides films and some more openly political films, such as Z?

No, because the tragedies are not dealing with transitory political problems. What comes across when we watch them is that history repeats itself. Political upheavals are simply part of the universal pattern of human folly.

How does The Day the Fish Came Out *fit into your work as a whole?*

It fits because it attacks today's power structures which create and manufacture machines of wholesale death. What appals me even more about this is that it can happen in an underhanded, secretive way and bring disaster on our heads without our knowing or even suspecting. The film was motivated by the incident in Spain around that time when a plane accidentally dropped some of its atomic cargo. It was a big shock when we discovered that there were planes flying over our heads in readiness, loaded with atomic weapons.

Sweet Country *belongs to this category, too, doesn't it?*

Absolutely; those were American atom bombs. The Russians were doing it at the same time. What was just as shocking was that, although people reacted with horror, practically within days they were turning it all into a joke.

Back to your films of Greek tragedy. What about the use of modern languages? Does modern Greek express tragedy as well as classical Greek?

And what about English, the language you used for The Trojan Women?

Great texts survive in any language. My earlier parallel to Shakespeare applies here, too. Some of the best Shakespeare productions, especially on film, were not made in English or by the English. In Greece the plays are performed not in the original but in modern Greek, and translating them is almost as challenging a task as it is to translate them into English. Edith Hamilton's translation of *The Trojan Women*, I think, is masterly. I doubt that the play has been translated into any language as well, including modern Greek. Sartre, who had been commissioned to do the French translation which I staged in Paris, did a freer adaptation, brilliant in parts but not as consistent in power.

When you film in Greece, do you feel that the countryside can add something to the film? Mycenae, obviously, seems to do just that.

Certainly with *Iphigenia* and *Electra,* which is a pastoral tragedy, but it depends on the subject matter. With *The Trojan Women* it was less so, because I saw its setting as a parallel to a concentration camp in a foreign country, in this case Troy. I made the film in Spain, where I found a better location than I could in Greece, a huge expanse of walls surrounding a city in ruins. Making films of that quality is problematic, and not only in Greece, because they do not fit into any accepted commercial patterns. Afterwards everybody says, "How wonderful," but believe me, such films are made with spit and blood. They are not produced with enough money. It's like begging for favors to get any backing for them.

What do you think about the Greek film industry? Is there anything you respect, or do you think it's being sucked into commercialism?

It's not being sucked in because directors heroically go on making films on the tight budgets provided by the state. But they cannot compete commercially with today's huge spectacles, like the science fiction films that the young people in Greece run to see. There's a leveling of culture all around the world. It's all American, in a sense. It's American-bred, so you have the kids here all wearing blue jeans and walking around with their walkmen and reading comics.

What is your working relationship with Giorgos Arvanitis, who was the cinematographer on your Iphigenia *in 1976? Were you influenced by his visual sense or style?*

I don't think he imposes his style. No man other than the director can, or at least should, do that.

So you basically tell your cinematographer what to do?

Well, you do, but you also rely on his talent to deliver what you want. I ask for a certain light, for example, to convey the harshness of the landscape.

In Iphigenia, *that worked very well; both the landscape and the heat came across with great power.*

Theodore Angelopoulos [whose 1975 film, *The Traveling Players,* Arvanitis had photographed] goes for a very different visual style. He is much more aesthetic than I am in his imagery. The degree of stylization in my films is dictated by the emotional impact I am aiming at. I don't just want to dazzle people's eyes. I want to get to their hearts, to move them—shock them and move them. That way I arrive at a kind of cathartic experience.

What do you think about the cinematic treatments of tragedy by other directors?

I don't believe in updating the tragedies, forcing the characters into modern dress, which amounts to diminishing their dramatic power, or in setting them in some mythical limbo. There is a serious misunderstanding in that approach. For instance, Pasolini and Greek tragedy: Pasolini did not make Greek tragedy. He made very striking films about the myths on which tragedy is based. My aim was to make films about the tragic dimension given to the myths by great writers, not to discard it for the bare bones of a plot. What makes the plots work from my point of view is the timeless power given to them by the playwrights. Pasolini's *Oedipus* is set in a very primitive society. And absolutely no inner torment of Oedipus is suggested. But, of course, he was aiming at something totally different. It has nothing to do with Greek tragedy. It has to do with mythology. There is a great confusion about the two.

What are your plans now?

I am finishing a script about the Byzantine Empress Zoë. I'll have to invest a tremendous amount of work in it because there no longer is a Byzantium. Although it is closer to us in time than ancient Greece, there are very few relics left. We have churches but no palaces, no cities, except in ruins. It's all been destroyed or adapted to Turkish architecture. What we have is the music, and a wealth of icons and mosaics, also a lot of literature and detailed chronicles about every aspect of life. It's an extraordinary civilization that has never been explored except in a few novels. Visually, in a film, it can be very exciting.

Are you planning to have Irene Papas in it?

Yes; she is quite an extraordinary woman.

You seem to go back to strong women. Do you connect that with feminism?

Well, feminism is there, isn't it? You don't have to link it with anything. It's on your shirt-sleeve.

Do you plan to go back to the classics?

Maybe. But I don't know which tragedy to make. It should be something different, either *Medea* or *Oedipus*.

What attracted you to Zorba the Greek? *Did you see any connections between the society in that film with ancient Greek society, in particular concerning the village and the widow?*

I suppose organically, but not explicitly. The novel is so huge, the range it covers so wide, that someone else could have made a completely different film from it. What challenged me was its complexity, its uninhibited shifting of mood. I thought, why not make a film which can't be pigeonholed—a tragedy, a comedy, a philosophical treatise. Orchestrating these elements into something as diverse and unpredictable as life itself was a risky undertaking. But the end result of *Zorba* was enormously positive. It gave me the satisfaction of knowing that it helped people, individually and as groups and even as nations, to cope with fundamental difficulties and tragic experiences. For instance, both Jews and

Palestinians adopted Zorba as a kind of symbol for endurance and survival.

Why did you create such a striking death scene for the widow? In ancient tragedy acts of violence occurred offstage.

Yes, but you had to be aware of the violence because you saw its end results. You were supposed to be tremendously shocked. To see Oedipus staggering out, bleeding, is a culmination of the horror which occurs offstage but is transmitted by the messenger in mercilessly realistic detail, building up to a final cathartic scream.

What is your opinion about eliminating masks, which you don't use in your films? Without them you would see blood running down Oedipus' face.

To me, the human face seen in huge close-up on the screen is even a kind of mask. The ancient Greeks used a lot of effects by way of their stage machinery, which was very advanced. They loved spectacle. Of course, I don't know to what extent they used blood streaming down masks and clothing. But I would not imagine that they evoked pity by downplaying the horror.

Tyrone Guthrie used masks in his Oedipus.

Guthrie only filmed his theatrical production. When he staged *Oedipus* with Laurence Olivier in London, mercifully he didn't substitute a mask for his face.

Harrison's Oresteia, *the BBC production, was also filmed with masks.*

Again, they only filmed the play. That's a different thing. A mask on the screen would be an absurdity. Even in the theater, I don't like using masks. Masks were used in ancient times because they were shaped in such a way that they could project the actors' voices and also because the parts of women were played by men. So they had to use masks. When today's directors use masks, they even put them on the women. So it doesn't really make any sense. The mask was a convention, acceptable to audiences at that time. When staging the plays today, you have to take into consideration the sensibilities of today's audience. I don't use masks because that way I would only tell the audience, "You are looking at a museum piece." Why should I put such a barrier between audience and author? I would in effect be saying, "I'm doing a conducted tour for you, an academic reproduction of how the tragedies were done." We don't even know exactly how they were done, because we have no record of that. What is certain is that the authors aimed at the most immediate impact.

When you look back on your work with Greek tragedy as a whole, what overall impression do your films give you?

You know, people forget, or rather, they are allowed to forget by the distributors' neglect. It's already been so many years since I made these films, and sometimes I feel as if the tide had swept over them. Every now and then they are shown on late-night television or in art theaters, but I don't believe that their appeal is restricted to an elitist kind of audience. In France, for instance, *Electra* was a big success, playing for nine months in the center of Paris, yet you can't get the distributor to revive it. That's the disheartening thing about film: it is the most popular art, if you want; at the same time, it is the most expendable. You have to keep reprinting copies at great expense, and the print itself is very easily damaged and useless after a time. One can't help feeling a little frustrated, after all [*laughs*]. I desperately want to preserve my films. On the other hand, I am thinking of what I can still do, not of what I have done. That's what keeps me alive, in a sense, not to sit down and say, "Well, you haven't done too badly," and stop creating. There is comfort to be drawn from the fact that all three playwrights—Aeschylus, Sophocles, and Euripides—were active until a ripe old age. And they created masterpieces. But they, one adds with a sigh, were geniuses. And they didn't have to waste their energy chasing after vulgar moguls for funds.

INTERVIEW WITH IRENE PAPAS

How do you feel about the role of classics in modern cinema? Do you think the classics still speak to us today?

By producing and acting in them, you show what you feel about them. This means that you trust the philosophy that exists in the words and the plot situations, and these can be transferred into modern means of communication because cinema is a modern word for communicating. But when you express the emotions and thoughts of ancient people, they need modern means of expression. The classics have the same things to say, in a different way, in any period. I believe that, because a classic is a classic, it is also the most modern, the most appropriate for any time. Otherwise the classics wouldn't be alive. If these texts didn't tell people the same truths all the time, they wouldn't be meaningful. There have been many writers whose works survived because of their quality and their truthfulness, and, as art, they are the most timeless and most important things in the world.

Do you think their quality lies in the poetry?

Well, these works can't be put into categories. They have everything, they are not one-dimensional. They have poetry, they have ideas, they have truthfulness, they have form, they have emotions. They are very much a whole. That's why they have been imitated so much. My father used to say that one phrase of ancient wisdom was worth volumes of modern words because the modern world likes to dilute things. Ancient thought is a concentration in the most simple and direct way. As the Greeks say, the best and shortest road to a point is the direct one.

Do you think special acting techniques are necessary in dealing with these texts?

No, I don't believe that. I believe that there is the same way of feeling, then and now. On the classical stage you might have used a louder voice, because some people were seated far away, but you always use the same soul. On the other hand, sometimes you need certain powers that otherwise you don't need. The power of the voice to convey the power of emotions is extremely important. An actor needs to be at his best, physically and mentally, to perform well. We have to. If you don't have your body, the instrument of your profession, always at your disposal, you are limited. That's why I want to open an acting school where you work, technically, with yourself, in your present condition, so that you can portray the clarity of the ancient tragedies. I would create an institute of ancient drama in Greece.

You seem to have great physical power and presence in your roles.

If I were to direct a school I would try to train people the way the

Japanese do in their theater. I know that in Japan you must have training, so it's like polishing the roots of your soul.

You don't distinguish between playing a part written by Aeschylus, Sophocles, or Euripides?

I don't, no.

Do you use methods different from your stage technique when you are acting in films?

Not at all. It's the same process; the only difference is that you decide about the appropriate means at the particular moment of filming.

Do you have a different technique for ancient and modern parts, such as Electra or the politician's widow in Z?

Again, no. The method of expressing yourself is the same. It may take different shapes or forms.

You have said that you prefer films to the stage.

That's because I can see what I do, and I like to have a record of it—you can give your best and correct what you don't like. And you can give the public what you think is the best you can do at the time. Once you have done that, it's like a finished work of art: it exists by itself. You don't have to repeat it. And you don't later ruin it by an inferior performance, either. On the stage you do the same thing again and again, and once you have squeezed out of yourself whatever you can do, it becomes forced work. You do your best for your audience, but soon you become a machine repeating the same thing every night.

On both stage and screen, you often impress your audience with the independence and zest which you bring to your work. Is there a driving force inside you, a particular creative principle?

I have no secret. I think it is your attitude to death that makes you behave and act in certain ways. Death is the greatest catalyst in human life—how you approach it, what it means to you. All people have to face it and make a decision about it which affects their lives: whether to go on living or to commit suicide, whether to wait for death or not to wait for it. While you're waiting, what are you doing with your life? Are you doing right, or are you doing wrong?

Do you think ancient literature, especially tragedy, can help answer this question?

I don't know. When I was doing *Iphigenia in Aulis* in New York and the Vietnam War was raging, I felt that Euripides hadn't done a thing to stop wars. Poor Clytemnestra was shouting, "Murder, murder!" while people in Vietnam were being killed. So what good did Euripides do? None. And he was the best of all.

Aristotle speaks about the pleasure of tragedy in his Poetics. *Doesn't a tragedy present its audience with both a learning process and a pleasurable experience?*

It is not that pleasurable. I don't like to act, to tell you the truth.

You don't like to act?

No, it's nerveracking. But then life doesn't usually permit me to be as truthful as I can be doing tragedy.

Why do you think we should care about literature and art? To educate?

I don't know. Nobody has answered that question yet. There is no objective measure in art—nor in acting.

When you are playing a part in a tragedy, do you think you strike a universal chord in human beings?

I don't know if I do. I have no means to know that. I only know when I feel right. Then something happens.

Do you see a political message in the ancient plays?

I believe in everyday life, in everyday decisions. Of course, you act politically, and this is the same thing in the films and in the ancient dramas. But party politics is a completely different matter. It's one thing to be a Republican, Democrat, Communist, or whatever; it is another thing to be a political human being. As Aristotle said, man is a political creature, and every decision you make is

political. I think ancient Greek drama goes beyond mere behavior; it addresses human existence itself. There are political
films or plays which deal only with questions of behavior, so they
last a decade or twenty years, but when the political system
changes, they are forgotten.

Costa-Gavras makes political films, such as Z, *in which you acted.*

Costa-Gavras uses situations that are factually true, so it is very
natural that he will make overtly political films. His talent is to
take situations chronicled in a newspaper and to turn them into
tragedies, not simply politics. He's very talented that way and
makes beautiful films because he extends bare facts beyond their
time, making them eternal and addressing lasting truths. Michael
[Cacoyannis] takes things that are both political and mythic-eter-
nal in form, but Gavras takes a political event and from that he
extends it into a tragedy. Really, however, both deal with something which goes beyond mere reality.

*Michael Cacoyannis has said that the mythology he uses is, in a sense, also
historical.*

That is his talent. He takes myth and makes it true, and Gavras
takes truth and makes it myth.

When you acted the part of the wife of the politician who is assassinated in
Z, *did you feel or experience something different from playing Clytemnestra in Cacoyannis's* Iphigenia?

In *Iphigenia*, I had a challenging part. *Z* was much easier, because
it was a small and very definite part. I think that Clytemnestra is a
victim of the situation.

Does playing a realistic, modern role affect your acting?

If I don't play a realistic Clytemnestra, I am done for. I don't play
her like somebody who doesn't exist. I play her as if she were
existing right now, as a real person.

So you make the women in both kinds of parts our living contemporaries?

That's right.

Did you have the freedom to create your parts?

That depends on how closely you work with the director—how you coincide with the point of view the director has, because he is the one who decides in the end. So you are not the absolute creator, but you are part of a creation that is also somebody else's. But I had the great fortune to work with Michael [Cacoyannis] close to his point of view. So I participate in bringing out what a particular role means, what we are going to make out of it, which choices we are going to take.

So the two of you shape your roles together?

Oh, sure. I bring in ideas and practical suggestions, and we talk at length about how he sees the part and the whole situation. Of course, I cannot say I am the director, but I contribute to the creation of my role, also theoretically. Sometimes you are called on to interpret only practically, and the theoretical framework is decided by the director. But with Michael I have both.

Cacoyannis said that he made certain of his films with you in mind.

Yes, Michael likes my way of acting. The realism. And he prefers me because I'm not an obstacle to his way of seeing things. Sometimes an actress, even if she is very, very good, may have a technique that is incompatible with the director's; it can be an obstacle inhibiting the director's passion. In such a case the creative passion of Michael cannot function.

Cacoyannis implied that you have certain physical qualities besides your acting ability, and when you portray somebody pushed to extremes you can feel it inside yourself.

Well, I cannot see myself from the outside, but I know that I don't hold back. In a way, the responsibility of an actress is to be generous. It's like a confession, an emotional generosity. Why should you be an actor if you are hiding something? That would be impossible.

Is there a difference between Cacoyannis's and Costa-Gavras's directing styles?

Of course, people are different, but I love them both, and in one way or another I was creative with both of them because I liked the subjects they were filming and, in general, the way they make films. Michael has peaks of passion; he is masterly with moments of strong passion. On the other hand, Gavras has what could be described as a cool passion, which creates emotional peaks in the audience. He treats his subject matter with detachment. He presents more of a counterpoint; Michael just throws himself into the fire. But both are very passionate people.

Does Costa-Gavras allow you to shape your roles in the same way Cacoyannis does? Do you have a similar rapport with him?

Well, I didn't play a big role for him. In *Z* I was a figure of silence and deep emotions, but with Michael I played the most beautiful roles I have ever had.

Do you consider yourself to be the center of his films?

That's not what I mean, but that the roles are so immense and multifaceted. I can't compare that with what I have done with Costa. After all, I've made only one film with him.

What about the technical aspects of filmmaking, such as the camera?

I don't interfere with that. I admire people when they are doing their work well, but sometimes I don't care. Sometimes I do have an opinion which I tell Michael but not the technical crew.

Would you tell us something about your roles in his films of Euripides?

The first part I played was Electra, and it was very exciting. It was breathtaking for me, and I was there from the beginning to the end. I saw every shot as it was done, and I would participate. At the end, when we finished shooting, I had a fever for three days! It was too intense for me. In *The Trojan Women*, I had a smaller responsibility for reasons that had to do with the production. I wasn't there all the time. I had a very big part again in *Iphigenia*, and I was closer and participated a lot more.

Did you prefer playing one particular role to any other?

I can't answer that, because it is not possible to answer. To prefer Electra to Clytemnestra, to prefer Clytemnestra to Electra—you just can't do that.

You once mentioned that you wanted to play Andromache in The Trojan
Women, *but that Cacoyannis saw much more of Helen in you. Would you
have preferred playing Andromache?*

I wanted Andromache because she has that terrific scene with the
boy [Astyanax]. For an actress, that is a gift. But the other part,
Helen, was a very big challenge for me. So, finally, Michael was
right because that part needs more acting; more meaning had to
be put into it. Andromache would have been easier. It's difficult
when you play a role that is more ambiguous. It is not advan-
tageous, the role of Helen. Andromache by nature takes your
heart away. As Helen, you really have to sweat.

*As Helen, you have a kind of burning, intense beauty—the audience can
understand why men would die for you.*

Well, but that's not acting. I don't believe that physical attributes
are either your fault or your merit. What you choose to do with
them, and how you approach your part, that is your art.

How does the film industry in Greece compare with that of other countries?

The Greek industry does not have money to compete interna-
tionally, and because of this it appears to have great geniuses
because a few individuals do everything. They do the acting; they
do the directing; they direct the photography. They do everything because there is no money to pay a lot of people. A Greek
film costs as much as an Italian or American film, but the market-
ing here cannot bring the money back, even if a film is the greatest
success. So there is a problem with Greek cinema: there is no
market. It is an expensive project to make a film, and if you don't
have the money to do it, it is very difficult. There are lots of
geniuses who never cross the border.

How do you see the future of films in Greece?

The films might fall into co-productions. Or, if the European
market provides a pool of money and distributes it to people who
then could have bigger budgets, you might have better films.

Why do you think it important to film the ancient plays?

I would like to see all the Greek tragedies done as films, just as
Shakespeare is done on film and television. I think they should be

done this way because it's our new means of communication. If Sophocles were alive today, he would even do computer graphics for his plays, just as he did the *skenographia* [scene-painting] then.

Cacoyannis mentioned making an Oedipus *or a* Medea. *And you're planning to do* Zoë, Empress of Byzantium *with him.*

We are still searching for the money. He has the script ready, and it seems commercially attractive, too, so he might find money from commercial sources.

Is there a feminist strain in his films, in the way he deals with the women who are at the center of the tragedies?

It is Euripides who's for women. He saw the underdogs in them, just as in the slaves. He also antagonized the fascist society of ancient Greece.

What about the Empress Zoë as a central and powerful figure?

During the Byzantine Empire, because of the laws of the country, there were a lot of women who became notorious because they had power. The law gave them the power to develop. It is not only Zoë who is interesting; there are many women who are powerful and very important to the history of Byzantium. My purpose is to try to show the world something about this empire which permitted women to flourish. I would like to play certain women to promote the knowledge of Byzantium. There would be some big, beautiful parts.

You have given concerts with Byzantine songs.

They've really taught me a lot of things. I'm very grateful that I've been able to do them.

What are your feelings about the way women were treated and represented in ancient as opposed to modern Greece? Do you think women have more freedom now? Do you see any connections, continuity, or progress?

Women in ancient times were shut in by four walls. If you read Euripides' *Iphigenia among the Taurians,* you realize that they didn't know how to read or write. Iphigenia was waiting for a sailor to write for her. The only women who had any freedom at that time were the concubines. But what kind of freedom was that?

Through the penis. Now the world is much better. Women have more freedom, more rights, except in the Muslim countries. But this new political leader in Pakistan, Benazir Bhutto—that she's a prime minister is very significant, particularly because she was elected in a Muslim society.

Haven't women gained more rights in Greece since Papandreou, in comparison with the time of the junta?

Under a junta, no one gains anything. Everybody loses: personality, freedom, opinion. I mean, you only become a soldier.

In Greece there still is male chauvinism, the philotimo. . . .

In a manner of speaking, we're a very new country because we do not even have a hundred years of freedom, and certain parts of Greece do not have even a hundred years of freedom from the Turks. So I think the males are still under the influence of Muslims. But I think they are slowly getting over it [*laughs*].

Should women educate the men?

Oh, I don't think we can educate anybody. I think economics educates people, because our society is more bound to freedom through money. Money has become equal to freedom in our society. The more women have money and responsibility, in industry and politics, the more men will feel equal to them. In a family of rich people, if a woman has a bastard, it doesn't mean a thing. But in a village, in a family of five people, she is going to be killed because there is no money to feed her or to send her away. So our society still binds up morality with sex. We're not yet free of that. Sexuality is considered a sin. Modern society is against the body, but the ancient Greeks were not that way.

You played the widow in Zorba the Greek *who was stoned and killed for her behavior. Do you think that something like this could happen in Greece now?*

Oh, sure. If the situations are the same. But I don't think that in general Greek men are more chauvinistic than, for instance, Americans; in fact, I think that being macho is much more prevalent in America.

When women are faced with war, isn't that another form of male domination?

It's again money: who will make wars if money isn't involved?

If women had political and economic power, do you think we would have fewer wars?

Who knows what we would do? We cannot prophesy things. I don't know, but I think women, because they are mothers and preservers of life, would think twice about making war. Aristophanes said in *Lysistrata* that women would not propose wars.

You mentioned earlier that you felt Euripides was sympathetic toward women.

That's because they were a kind of suffering animal.

In Electra, *he portrayed Clytemnestra more sympathetically than Cacoyannis did in his film version.*

Sometimes, when I see *Electra*, I think that Euripides might be angry with us because we gave Electra all the rights. It's a modern interpretation. When I played the Sophoclean Electra, I felt it was not that her mother is not right, but that her mother in being so afraid of revenge behaved very badly to her children—conflicting rights and duties, as so often in tragedy. When you become a dictator you can become subject to what you wanted to rectify. When you kill somebody for doing something evil you yourself become a killer, somebody evil—so what you wanted to avoid you actually become. Revenge is a vicious circle.

If, in a way, Clytemnestra was a victim, doesn't that make Electra's lack of understanding and her hatred all the more terrible?

Maybe the mother was very cruel to her, because the child was shouting at her. And Clytemnestra buries her, as it were, just to get rid of her. She gives her to a peasant so that Electra cannot have children or a share of the inheritance.

Do you think that Euripides' Electra is more concerned about her own position and her inheritance than about revenge for her father?

Well, why should she have to marry a peasant? Clytemnestra just throws her out. In Euripides sometimes nobody's completely right and nobody's completely wrong. Especially in *The Bacchae*. Nothing is simple. And this is one of the challenges for me, if I open my school of acting. I would do all the tragedies, acting whatever part my age would permit. I would do all Byzantium, I would do all mythology, all the dialogues of Plato, in films and series, all of them.

What in particular would you teach other actresses in your academy?

I would try to facilitate their souls to be free. But to teach a soul is very difficult—to teach truth or truthfulness. I believe that art is the truest thing in the world. And that's what an actor should strive for.

Tragic Features in John Ford's
The Searchers

Martin M. Winkler

George Mason University

ONE of the reasons for the lasting appeal of Greek tragedy lies in its mythical nature. With their archetypal qualities and inherent tragic potential, myths are the foundation of tragedy. In modern society, too, myths have preserved much of their appeal, albeit often appearing in a diluted or not readily apparent form. In American culture, the mythology of the West has given twentieth-century literature and art one of its enduring new archetypes: that of the Westerner. In ways comparable to the Greek tragedians' use of received mythology for social, political, and moral reflection on their day and age, the myths of the West have frequently been used for similar purposes. In the words of director Sam Peckinpah: "The Western is a universal frame within which it is possible to comment on today."[1]

The mythology of the Western hero bears obvious parallels to classical hero myths; such major *topoi* as the quest, arms and violence, and even immortality, with which we are already familiar from archaic and other mythologies, recur prominently in the comparatively recent myths surrounding the Westerner.[2] The greatest significance and the highest emotional and intellectual appeal deriving from the figure of the Westerner are to be found in films which merit our attention as works of art. As in the classical cultures, the archetypes underlying mythology manifest themselves to best effect when they have been reworked into the unity of a literary (or literate) work of art. The principal genres in which this process took place in ancient Greece are epic and drama; in *The Poetics*, Aristotle makes no generic distinction between these two.[3] The popular stories of myth transcend their nonliterary origins when they are molded into the masterpieces of Homer and Hesiod, of Aeschylus, Sophocles, Euripides, and others whose works have not survived. A parallel process obtains for the myth of the American West: well-known plots and figures reappear in the cinema, particularly in the films of such acknowl-

edged masters as John Ford and Howard Hawks. The best Western films can exhibit the features of tragedy discussed by Aristotle. In this paper I will briefly outline some of the chief aspects of
tragedy in connection with the Western film and then turn to a
particular film, *The Searchers* (1956), in greater detail.

In his *Poetics*, Aristotle takes as his point of departure the
concept of mimesis. Poetry, drama, and music are all forms of
representation or imitation, and the same may be held today for
the cinema.[4] To Aristotle, tragedy is a representation of action
and life; in a well-known passage he defines it as follows:

> Tragedy, then, is a representation of an action which is serious,
> complete, and of a certain magnitude—in language which is gar-
> nished in various forms in its different parts—in the mode of dra-
> matic enactment, not narrative—and through the arousal of pity
> [*eleos*] and fear [*phobos*] effecting the *katharsis* of such emotions.[5]

Representation is naturally embodied in and carried out by the
actors appearing on the stage, most importantly by the tragic
protagonist who, according to Aristotle, should be neither wholly
good nor wholly evil but rather someone with whom we may
identify despite the extremity of his situation or fate: "Such a man
is one who is not preeminent in virtue and justice, and one who
falls into affliction not because of evil and wickedness, but because
of a certain fallibility *(hamartia)*."[6] The spectator is affected by his
realization that what takes place on stage may happen to himself:
"There, but for the grace of God, go I"; from this derives a
heightened awareness of the frailty of human life, the fickleness
and unpredictability of fortune, and ultimately a greater consciousness of the bond which holds mankind together: "pity is felt
towards one whose affliction is undeserved, fear towards one who
is like ourselves."[7] Such pity and fear is linked to the suffering
and violence which the principal characters, often including the
chorus, must undergo; according to Aristotle, violence and suffering inflicted by and upon family members in particular increase the viewer's emotional involvement.[8] Pity and fear,
previously latent emotions, are thus stirred up and accumulate in
the spectator. This intense strain is broken at the drama's climax;
in Aristotle's words, the viewer is purged of his heightened sensa-
tions of pity and fear by means of catharsis. Originally a term used
in ancient Greek medicine, catharsis—traditionally rendered in

English as "purification" or "purgation"—restores emotional balance and leads to a temporary psychological calm, even numbness. The decrease in emotional excitement, which catharsis effects, leads to a feeling of pleasurable relief.[9] Psychologically and emotionally the spectator, who has become one with the protagonist, is now released from this identification. To employ a phrase from Aeschylus, the protagonist's suffering *(pathos)* arouses pity and fear; this in turn brings about a learning process *(mathos)* in the viewer.[10] Tragic mimesis and catharsis provide for an increase in knowledge and philosophical consciousness.

In order that the viewer's learning process be effective, the tragic protagonist is placed in a situation where he must decide upon a course of action. His ethical dilemma arises from the fact that he becomes guilty whichever decision he makes; especially in the plays of Aeschylus, "there is a conflict of duties such that while a choice is morally imperative, none is morally possible."[11] At the same time, however, the protagonist is innocent on another level. Thus Oedipus, to cite only the most famous example, is objectively guilty of parricide and incest, but is subjectively innocent because of, e.g., the absence of evil intentions. Nevertheless he accepts the responsibility for his deeds. The simultaneous presence of guilt and innocence in the hero is one of the chief characteristics of Greek tragedy, one of its most complex and fascinating features.

This question of innocence and guilt is also important for the Western film which regularly employs mythical archetypes for its story patterns. Standard Westerns present us with a protagonist who is excessively good and strong; being one-dimensional, he remains outside serious consideration as a figure of art. But when the Westerner, like the hero on the tragic stage, becomes morally questionable, the genre transcends the limits of popular entertainment.[12] As Robert Warshow has observed in his now classic essay on the Westerner: "The truth is that the Westerner comes into the field of serious art only when his moral code, without ceasing to be compelling, is seen also to be imperfect. The Westerner at his best exhibits a moral ambiguity which darkens his image and saves him from absurdity; this ambiguity arises from the fact that, whatever his justifications, he is a killer of men."[13]

The Westerner must both act and react: act in order to preserve his status as hero, react—usually to injustice and violence—to preserve his moral integrity. Thus forced into action, the Westerner is often confronted with a situation which compels him to make a choice. In those films which leave behind the stereotypical "good guy vs. bad guy" format in favor of a more complex and psychologically convincing plot, the Westerner may face conflicting alliances and responsibilities; in choosing a course of action, he is confronted with a problem comparable to that of the tragic protagonist. A well-known example is *High Noon* (1952), in which the hero is caught in a triple bind: responsibility to his wife, to and for the citizens of his town, and to himself (he must not abandon his code of honor). Another example is found in *The Virginian* (1929), an "archetypal Western" based on the novel by Owen Wister. Here the eponymous hero's close friend has been lured by the villain Trampas into stealing cattle; the Virginian, leader of the posse pursuing the thieves, must himself bring about the death of his friend when the latter has been caught. Warshow's observations on the "seriousness of the West" as exemplified in this film serve well to illustrate the similarities between the Westerner and the hero of Greek tragedy: "The Virginian is thus in a tragic dilemma where one moral absolute conflicts with another and the choice of either must leave a moral stain. . . . the movie is . . . a tragedy, for though the hero escapes with his life, he has been forced to confront the ultimate limits of his moral ideas." The tragic quality of the serious Western film gives this genre its "mature sense of limitation and unavoidable guilt." As do the heroes of drama both ancient and modern, the hero of the Western film affects us by an appeal to our sense of compassion; in Warshow's words, "what we finally respond to is not his victory but his defeat."[14] Ultimately, the Westerner is a modern reincarnation of the archetypal mythic and tragic hero, hence largely his universal appeal.[15]

The complexity of the Westerner, in which he is again comparable to some of the classical tragic heroes, may be illustrated by the duality of his nature, combining rationality, experience, ingenuity, and love for peace with violence and destruction. On the Greek stage, it is particularly an authority figure such as the king, ruler of his city-state, who is caught between the demands of order, peace, and justice to ensure the stability and survival of the city and the urges, often irrational and violent, to impose his views upon others and to force them into submission. Even with the best intentions his power can lead him into suspicion, hubris, oppression of dissenters, and a violent crushing of sometimes only imagined opposition. Examples are Sophocles' Oedipus and Creon and Euripides' Pentheus. In the Western film we find a corresponding figure in the harsh patriarch who rules with an iron fist over his cattle empire; a good example, to mention only one, is found in *Broken Lance* (1954), a film with overtones of *King Lear*. The dual nature of the Westerner usually shows itself in his being paired with a badman who is in many ways the hero's alter ego. The hero and his opponent often represent two sides of the same coin; their antagonism, sometimes postponed by an uneasy temporary alliance, finally erupts in a violent showdown at the film's climax. Direct echoes of Greek tragedy by way of intrafamilial and Oedipal conflicts can be seen in *Duel in the Sun* (1946) and *Red River* (1948). Many of Anthony Mann's films reveal this director's preoccupation with both Greek and Elizabethan tragedy; his film, *Winchester 73* (1950), shows the hero's revenge on his brother who had killed their father.[16] The revenge theme in the Western film may be said to derive in no small degree from Jacobean drama. Screenwriter Philip Yordan aimed at tragedy in several of the Westerns he wrote: "I have . . . attempted to discover again the purity of the heroes of classical tragedy. I have always wanted to re-create a tragic mythology, giving a large role to destiny, solitude, nobility. At the same time I've tried to join this type of hero to typically American characters."[17] The use of the American West as a setting for tragedy appears to be an integral feature of American culture, going back at least as far as James Fenimore Cooper's *The Prairie* (1827). In this novel, the tragedy centers on Ishmael Bush, a patriarchal authority figure who metes out harsh and bloody justice to his brother-in-law who had killed Bush's son.[18] Contemporaneously with the actual settlement of the West, tragic archetypes were already inspiring the imagination of popular novelists, a tradition continuing in the twentieth century with, for example, the Western novels of Max Brand. As recently as 1966, Frederick Manfred's novel *King of Spades* presents a nearly undisguised retelling of the Oedipus myth set in the West. With the cinema superseding literature as the chief medium of popular American culture, it is not surprising that one of the foremost examples of the tragic hero should be encountered in what may be the most important work by John Ford, America's greatest filmmaker. To this film I would now like to turn. Since the tragic nature of *The Searchers* is most clearly present in Ford's film and, at least to me, largely missing from its source, the 1954 novel by Alan LeMay, I proceed from the assumption that Ford, as director, is to be credited for *The Searchers* being the enduring work of popular art that it is.[19] This is in keeping not only with the *auteur* theory of cinema but also parallels the practice of ancient and later tragedians to use received material which they then turned into their lasting works of art.

In one of his influential articles Jean-Pierre Vernant asks the following questions about the tragic hero:

> What is this being that tragedy describes as a *deinos,* an incomprehensible and baffling monster, both an agent and one acted upon, guilty and innocent, lucid and blind, whose industrious mind can dominate the whole of nature yet who is incapable of governing himself? What is the relationship of this man to the actions upon which we see him deliberate on the stage and for which he takes the initiative and responsibility but whose real meaning is beyond him and escapes him so that it is not so much the agent who explains the action but rather the action that, revealing its true significance after the event, recoils upon the agent and discloses what he is and what he has really, unwittingly, done? Finally, what is this man's place in a world that is at once social, natural, divine, and ambiguous, rent by contradictions. . . ?[20]

These questions may be applied to Ethan Edwards, the central character in *The Searchers,* with regard to the tragic quality of this film.[21]

Three years after the end of the Civil War, in which he had fought for the Confederacy, Ethan returns to his brother's homestead in the Texas wilderness and, as if precipitated by his unexpected return, a series of catastrophes begins. Hostile Comanche Indians under their war chief, Scar, massacre Ethan's brother, sister-in-law, and nephew and abduct Ethan's two young nieces. Ethan, after many years still secretly in love with his brother's wife, embarks upon a desperate search for the girls, accompanied by Martin Pawley, a young man of partly Indian origin whom the Edwardses had reared as their own son. When Ethan discovers the raped and mutilated body of his older niece, Lucy, his determination to save Debbie, the younger girl, who could be his own daughter, grows even stronger. His search, however, remains unsuccessful for several years. His anguish and despair over Debbie then gradually change into a murderous obsession to kill her once he realizes that she has grown up and must have become one of Scar's wives.

Ethan is the psychologically most complex and ambivalent figure created in the history of the Western film. That Ford cast John Wayne, the archetypal icon of the Westerner, in the part of a

man "not conspicuous for virtue and justice," only enhances the
film's dramatic power. In keeping with heroic and tragic tradition,
Ethan is first and foremost a man of action. After the end of the
Civil War he has resorted to marauding; he possesses "fresh-
minted Yankee dollars," and his description appears on several
"Wanted" posters. Although fallen on hard times, he remains a
figure of authority which he does not hesitate to assert: "I'm
giving the orders." The uniform coat he still wears points to his
former rank as officer and to his inability to adjust to a peaceful
life. His own words characterize him well: "I still got my sabre . . .
didn't turn it into no plowshare, neither." Violence is the key to
Ethan's character; it exposes his increasing madness and
viciousness in the course of the film. There is also a pronounced
streak of racial bigotry toward Indians in Ethan; this reveals itself,
for instance, in his gruff, even hostile, treatment of Martin whom
he has no scruples to use as bait for a trap. His ugly and crazed
laugh at Martin's Indian bride underscores his hatred and contempt of the Indians. In all likelihood, Ethan is such a racist
because he is aware, without conscious knowledge, that he is in
many ways like an Indian himself: savage, violent, and without a
permanent home. Not only is Ethan well-versed in Indian languages, customs, and religion, but he also knows much about
Indian strategy and psychology. He understands the diversionary
tactics of Scar's raid and realizes that his only chance in catching
up with Scar lies in perseverance greater than the Indians'. A
visual clue to the Indian aspects of his nature is the scabbard in
which he keeps his rifle; it has long fringes and looks Indian-
made. Ethan is a man who exists on the borderline between
savagery and civilization. That he is by no means the usual clean-
cut (and clean-shaven) Western hero becomes overwhelmingly
clear in the course of the film. Early on, he defiles a dead Indian's
body by shooting the corpse's eyes out, an indication that his
hatred of Indians goes even beyond death. Ethan's reason for this
is his knowledge that, in the Indians' belief, such loss of their eyes
will prevent their souls from entering the spirit land and condemn them "to wander forever between the winds." As startling
and morally questionable as the defilement of a dead enemy's
body is, it is nevertheless within the heroic tradition. In the *Iliad*,
Achilles defiles Hector's corpse and, denying it proper burial,
intends to prevent Hector's shade from entering the underworld;
this is Achilles' ultimate revenge.[22] That Ethan, like Achilles, goes
beyond the limits of heroic behavior becomes evident on several
other occasions. At a skirmish with Scar's warriors by the riverside

he attempts to shoot Indians whose backs are turned in retreat; later on, he sets a trap for the treacherous white trader Futterman and his two henchmen, killing all three by shooting them in the back. A close-up of Ethan's rifle at this point emphasizes that this act is in direct violation of the traditional code of honor usually upheld in the American Western film.

I have remarked earlier upon the duality of the Western hero in terms of his close association with his antagonist, an association which points to the morality-play quality of the Western film: the struggle between good and evil. A significant variation of this theme occurs in *The Searchers* in the figures of Ethan and Scar. Just as Ethan, despite his negative traits, is a superior Westerner, Scar is a skillful leader. On two significant occasions in the film, Ford emphasizes the heroic theme by showing Scar as he is putting on his war bonnet. The fact that both times Ethan then shoots Scar's horse from under him foreshadows the latter's eventual defeat and death. Before the skirmish at the river begins, Ford cuts from a close-up of Ethan directly to one of Scar, emphasizing the tension between the two. A similar series of fast cuts occurs when Ethan, Martin, and Scar finally meet face to face in front of Scar's tent: Ford cuts from Scar to Ethan, back to Scar, and to Martin. In the heroic tradition, a verbal duel between Ethan and Scar ensues in which Ethan insults Scar, while Scar acknowledges Ethan's prowess and tenacity. Ethan and Scar's closeness to each other is reinforced at this moment by the parallelism in their exchange on language.[23] Both of them bear wounds, Scar physically, Ethan in his soul: "Scar, as the name suggests, is Ethan's mark of Cain."[24] That the part of Scar is played by a white actor takes on added meaning in this context.[25]

The motif of the search or quest is one of the basic themes of mythology; Jason and the Argonauts in classical and Parsifal's search for the Grail in medieval literature are prominent examples. Frequently in the mythological tradition of such travels, the hero's ultimate goal is the attainment of self-knowledge and the ideal of achieving moral goodness. For Ethan, however, the five-year quest for his niece is not so much a journey of glorious heroism, but rather one of obsession and defeat which eventually will drive him to the brink of madness. His social decline from officer to renegade is paralleled and intensified by his fall into savagery during his search: in this as in other films by John Ford, "the sense of duty that sustains his individuals also commonly leads them astray into aberrations or death."[26] For this reason Ethan resembles less the mythological hero of epic or the chivalrous knight of romance than the tragic sufferer of the Greek stage. Ethan's increasing obsession with finding his niece and avenging his family's destruction upon Scar, coupled with his racism toward the Indians, represents the film's true tragic theme. What Vernant observes about Eteocles in Aeschylus' *Seven against Thebes* may, *mutatis mutandis*, describe Ethan as well:

> The murderous madness that henceforth characterizes his *ethos* is not simply a human emotion; it is a daemonic power in every way beyond him. It envelops him in the black cloud of *atē*, penetrating him . . . from within, in a form of *mania*, a *lussa*, a delirium that breeds criminal acts of *hubris*.[27]

As H. A. Mason has noted: "The greatest poets have always found the greatest pathos by taking away from the hero's mind what we call the rational faculty and giving him a greater hold over us by making him *mad*."[28] It attests to the subtlety with which Ford structures the development of his narrative that the theme of Ethan's obsession is made explicit only intermittently and unobtrusively so that a casual spectator might overlook it. Nevertheless, its dramatic force increases steadily until it culminates in Ethan's last confrontation with Scar, by then dead. Added momentum derives from the underlying subject of miscegenation and sexual jealousy and frustration. The catalyst for this is Ethan's secret and hopeless love for his brother's wife. Ford introduces this topic as the starting point for the film.

The Searchers begins with the camera following Martha Edwards, Ethan's sister-in-law, as she opens the door of her house and walks out onto the porch, having noticed a horseman approaching. This moment contains the first indication of an intimate bond between herself and Ethan, the man arriving. Cinematic tradition induces a viewer to assume that this woman is expecting the return of her husband. Martha is the first to greet Ethan, who responds by gently kissing her on the forehead. He later lifts up little Debbie as if she were his own daughter. Next morning, when Ethan prepares to leave with a posse of Texas Rangers led by the Reverend Clayton in order to retrieve the settlers' stolen cattle, Martha, gone to fetch Ethan's coat and thinking herself alone, tenderly strokes it. This is observed, however, by Clayton who discreetly turns his gaze away. His eyes speak volumes.[29] At the end of this moving and justly famous scene, Martha and Debbie wave and look after Ethan riding off just as a departing man's wife and daughter would do. This is Martha's last glimpse of Ethan. With utter economy Ford here suggests a deep-seated but hopeless love between them. It is most likely because of this love that Ethan left his home years ago, joined the Confederate army, and stayed away for three years even after the war had ended. Ethan, the would-be husband of Martha, by extension becomes the would-be father of her children. This partly accounts for his unceasing pursuit of Scar, who had raped and killed the woman Ethan had chastely loved from afar. That Scar raped Martha before killing her may be inferred from the scene in which Ethan finds the bodies of Martha, his brother, and his nephew. Later, Ethan will discover Lucy in a canyon where she had been abandoned after being raped and killed and probably mutilated as well; he buries her in the cloak which Martha had brought him before his departure. Hence, his obsession to kill Scar and thus to avenge Martha's dishonor becomes an overpowering force which will relentlessly drive him on. Ethan knows that Scar has defiled and destroyed what has been unattainable and most sacred to himself. This is another bond between Ethan and Scar, perhaps the strongest one. At the outset of the search, Ethan is motivated by two powerful impulses: avenging Martha and rescuing Debbie, who could be his own daughter. A third driving force will eventually overshadow both of these.

Ford develops Ethan's journey into obsession and madness in psychologically convincing and, to the spectator, increasingly involving stages. First doubts about Ethan's mental state arise both in his companion, Martin Pawley, and in the viewer when Ethan, reluctantly agreeing to take Martin and Brad Jorgensen, Lucy's boyfriend, with him on the search, asserts his authority over the two young men. This prompts Martin's question: "Just one reason we're here, ain't it? To find Debbie and Lucy?" Ethan does not reply, and suspicion begins to grow in Martin's mind, as it does in the spectator's, about Ethan's true motivation. Things are spelled out more clearly later when Ethan decides to turn back for the winter and to continue his search in the spring: "She's alive, she's safe for a while. They'll . . . keep her to raise as one of their own until—until she's of an age to. . . ." He breaks off, but it is clear that Ethan is thinking of Martha's violation by Scar and of Debbie's future fate. That Scar will eventually force his captive into sexual relations with him represents, to Ethan's mind, a fate worse than, and worthy of, death; that Scar will have had intercourse with both mother and daughter is a thought unbearable to him.

This brief scene in the film marks the turning point in Ethan's character: from now on he is bent on revenge and destruction and will seek the deaths of Scar, Debbie, and of Indians in general. Ethan's suppressed intensity effectively contrasts with the quiet beauty of nature: a peaceful winter forest, gently falling snow, and complete silence. While nature is pure and calm, a violent rage is stirring in man. The first open revelation of this occurs at the beginning of the film's cavalry sequence, which also takes place in winter. Ethan and Martin have come upon a herd of buffalo, and Ethan begins to shoot as many of them as he can. When Martin tries to prevent such meaningless slaughter, Ethan for the first time explicitly reveals his obsession. Brutally knocking Martin down, he exclaims: "Hunger, empty bellies . . . at least *they* won't feed any Comanch' this winter." Then, at the cavalry fort, the searchers find some mad white girls of Debbie's age who had lived among Indians and have now been "liberated" by the army. It is important to note that their madness is not caused by mistreatment at the hands of "the savages," but rather by the brutality of the cavalry. Nevertheless, Ethan blames the Indians for the girls' fate: "They ain't white—anymore. They're Comanch'." The camera now moves in to a close-up of Ethan's face, and a different kind of madness is clearly written on his features. The very rarity of a camera movement such as this attests to its utmost significance; it reveals Ethan's murderous obsession. The moment is emphasized by the predominant dark colors of this scene, and Ethan's face is partly obscured by shadow. With the inexorable logic of paranoia, Ethan later attempts to shoot Debbie once he has caught up with her. (Ironically, she has come to warn him and Martin against an impending attack by Scar.) Martin shields Debbie with his body as Ethan, gun drawn, is wounded by an Indian's arrow. The impending intrafamilial bloodshed is thus avoided at the last moment. The nefarious nature of Ethan's attempt on his niece's life is visually underscored in that Ethan draws his gun in a sweeping, circular movement; this is the same manner in which he had earlier shot out the dead Indian's eyes. The identity of the gesture indicates an identical inhumanity underlying both acts and points to the fact that, to Ethan, Debbie is no longer white. His rejection of her is made chillingly explicit in two verbal exchanges he has with Martin in later scenes in the film. In his last will and testament he renounces her as not being his "blood kin" because "she's been living with a buck." More explicitly, before the whites' final attack on Scar, Martin pleads not to destroy the entire Indian camp, as the Rangers are planning to do. As Ethan admits to him, he hopes that Debbie will not survive the indiscriminate slaughter; he adds: "Living with Comanches ain't being alive." These words and the Rangers' scorched-earth tactics will no doubt have reminded viewers at the time of the film's initial release of parallels with recent history.

Cinematically, Ethan's madness is revealed to the viewer through extreme close-ups of his face. While Ford usually shows us both the people and the environment in which they act—he is well-known for his long shots indoors and extreme long shots outdoors which dwarf the human figures—there are some highly significant moments when the camera and with it the viewer move in for a closer look. The close-ups of Ethan powerfully depict the turmoil inside him. As Béla Balász has emphasized: "Close-ups are often dramatic revelations of what is really happening under the surface of appearances."[30] Ford prepares the viewer for the impact of these close-ups early in the film when he shows Ethan in a medium shot after he has realized what strategy lies behind the Indians' theft of the white settlers' cattle. Knowing that it is too late to bring help, he allows his horse to rest while the others return in futile haste. To judge from his words and actions during this scene, Ethan is calm and self-controlled, but when we see him more closely, mechanically rubbing down his horse and staring vacantly into the distance, the expression on his face tells us differently: "He is contemplating the unthinkable."[31] Watching Ethan's partly shadowed face, we can see in our minds exactly what he sees with his mind's eye: the rape and slaughter taking place some forty miles away at his brother's home. Ethan's feelings of helplessness, anxiety, grief, and despair are thus forcefully communicated to us. With this brief shot Ford makes the filming of the actual carnage unnecessary. At this moment the spectator begins to be drawn irresistibly into the tragedy about to unfold. A full close-up of Ethan then logically occurs when he actually comes upon the aftermath of the slaughter. When Ethan forcibly restrains Martin from rushing into the shed where the dead bodies of his foster parents have been thrown, and when later, after finding Lucy, he behaves in a manner strange and inexplicable to Martin, the viewers can themselves picture what Ethan has seen and can feel with him. Ethan's discoveries of the bodies of Martha and Lucy are not presented to us in gruesome detail: instead, Ford eschews luridness by only showing us the emotional shock which these grisly moments have on Ethan. Ford's discreet handling of such instances of high emotional strain, obliquely depicting the results of savage violence against helpless victims, is in a direct line of tradition from Greek tragedy where acts of violence take place offstage and are reported by a messenger or eyewitness. On the Greek tragic stage and in artistic cinema, the spectators' task is to fill in the terrifying details themselves; in this way playwright and film director ensure the audience's emotional involvement and call forth their feelings of pity and fear.

These emotions rise in the viewer at several crucial moments in *The Searchers*. At the beginning, we fear for the survival of Ethan's relatives while they are being stalked by an unseen enemy; the greater is our shock when we first see Scar, his shadow falling over the crouching figure of little Debbie and his face decorated with war paint. Next we fear for the fate of the two abducted girls and hope that Ethan will find them; later, after we have become aware of Ethan's obsession, we begin to hope that he will not find Debbie. More extended scenes of pity and fear in *The Searchers* are contained in the cavalry sequence: Ethan and Martin come upon the aftermath of the cavalry's massacre of an entire Indian village, with tepees burning and bloody corpses of humans and animals lying about and left to freeze in the winter cold, a scene of documentary realism. Shortly after, the searchers witness the white man's "civilizing" influence when they interrogate the mad girls. Our sympathy for the victims, particularly women and children, is enhanced by the visual contrast of the cavalry sequence to the rest of the film. With the exception of the brief scene of dialogue in which Ethan decides to break off the search, the cavalry sequence is the only part of the film taking place in winter; it is also the only sequence of location filming outside Monument Valley. The predominant colors of the cavalry sequence are red (blood shed, fires burning), white (the snow covering the land and the dead like a shroud), and blue (the cavalry uniforms), hardly an accidental scheme. The violence in the cavalry sequence, underscored by its cold colors which contrast with the warm brownred of Monument Valley, foreshadows Ethan's cold-blooded attempt on his niece's life.

As the preceding will already have indicated, the tragic quality of *The Searchers* is grounded in its natural setting. The landscape, one of the basic aspects of meaning in the Western genre, in this film is Monument Valley, the Western landscape par excellence, whose iconography is most closely associated with John Ford.[32] The cyclopean rocks form the perfect background to the film's human actions and impart an overwhelming sense of doom to the film; towering cliffs dwarf the protagonists and implacably look down upon the deeds and sufferings of the people living or moving among them. This landscape, in which both whites and Indians are carving out their existence, underscores the duality of both races' ways of life, a rudimentary social organization enveloped by savagery. It is not by accident that Ethan is photographed with a sheer wall of rock rising up behind him at the moment he commits his first inhuman act, blinding the dead Indian. Monument Valley does not function as mere pictorialism, but rather possesses thematic meaning as Ford's "moral universe."[33] As he himself has noted about Monument Valley: "the real star of my Westerns has always been the land." Ford also implies moral regeneration arising from the Western landscape in an almost cathartic experience: "When I come back from making a Western on location, I feel a better man for it."[34] Thus Ethan's journey into madness takes on an almost unbearable poignancy; a sense of both timelessness and doom permeates *The Searchers*. When Ethan and Martin are pursued by Scar and his warriors, we see them fleeing toward a cave, just as later Debbie, fleeing from Ethan, will run toward a cave of almost identical appearance (a scene to be discussed below). In both instances the camera observes the fugitives from inside. The impression is that of nature implacably watching the acts of men. But nature as such is not altogether hostile; the camera placement suggests its readiness to receive, shelter, and protect. Thus Martin finds life-saving water dripping from the barren rock when he and Ethan are secure in the cave. Nature's ambivalence mirrors the ambiguous nature of man.

The effects of classical tragedy are heightened by the complexity of its plot. Aristotle calls those plays complex whose plots contain *anagnorisis* and *peripeteia*. The former term denotes the discovery of someone's identity, while peripety, a reversal of fortune, occurs as a result of actions and sufferings whose implications, unknown before but then revealed through *anagnorisis*, lead to the hero's tragic fall.[35] Both recognition and peripety represent a passage from ignorance to knowledge and self-awareness and thus complement the workings of catharsis. Forms of recognition and peripety often recur in the later dramatic tradition and occasionally in the medium of film.

Recognition and peripety, respectively, occur in two key scenes in *The Searchers*. The former takes place in three separate stages during a council of Ethan, Martin, and Scar in the chief's tent. Scar calls upon one of his wives to show Ethan and Martin some of the scalps he has taken to avenge his sons killed by whites. Ethan recognizes, as he will later tell Martin, one of the scalps to be that of Martin's mother; evidently, Scar has been the white settlers' nemesis for longer than they themselves had realized. This first recognition leads directly to another. Scar now draws attention to the medal he wears on his chest among other decorations; Ethan recognizes it as the one he gave as a present to little Debbie upon his return home after the Civil War. This is the first proof, rather than the circumstantial evidence Ethan has come upon so far, that it is indeed Scar who has kidnapped Debbie. A rapid tracking shot underscores the importance of the moment, the camera moving in to a close-up of the medal from Ethan's point of view. This particular piece of camera work serves a double purpose: it closely links Ethan and Scar and also prepares Ethan and the viewer for their first glimpse of Debbie after her kidnapping. Ethan and Martin now look up simultaneously at Scar's young wife holding the scalps in front of them; both immediately recognize Debbie in her. Their long and arduous search has finally come to an end. Nevertheless, they are at the moment powerless to take her away from Scar.

Peripety is linked to catharsis in what must be the most gripping and emotionally draining sequence in the entire film. Before the Rangers' and Ethan's final attack on Scar's village, Martin has crept into Scar's tepee to save Debbie from the indiscriminate slaughter which is imminent. Surprised by Scar, Martin shoots and kills him. After the Rangers' massacre of the village Ethan, bent on murder and revenge, finds the chief dead in his tent. Thus Ethan is denied one of the hero's basic exploits, the show-down with his enemy. Scar's death is intentionally anticlimactic, a deliberate revision of the traditional code of combat which goes back to the duel of Achilles and Hector in *The Iliad*. Ethan, denied heroic stature, now defiles a corpse for the second time: he scalps Scar. While Ford does not show the actual scalping on the screen, he cuts away only at the last possible moment, thereby emphasizing both its terror and its significance. Although probably introduced by whites, the custom of scalping has traditionally become associated almost exclusively with the Indians as a symbol of their perceived lack of civilization. Thus a white man, unless presented as wholly dehumanized—i.e., like a savage Indian—would not usually commit such an act.[36] Ethan's deed represents the moral nadir down to which his obsession has brought him. This is the moment of his greatest self-abasement as a human being. His savagery is emphasized when we see him riding out of Scar's tent, holding the dripping scalp in his hand. He appears like a gruesome angel of death, and Ford gives us a close-up of his face. Once outside the tepee, Ethan sees Debbie who turns and flees in terror, pursued by her uncle.

The viewer's emotions of pity and fear begin to reach their peak at this moment, enhanced by the fact that Martin, who had saved Debbie's life once before, now is helpless in the face of Ethan's frenzy; when Martin tries to stop him, Ethan simply rides him down. Ethan finally catches up with Debbie at the entrance to a cave; the exhausted girl, fallen to the ground, recoils in horror from her pursuer who has dismounted and is approaching her. But now a surprising reversal of the girl's—and the viewer's— expectations occurs: instead of killing her, Ethan picks her up in his arms, just as he had done on first seeing her after his return home, and takes her back to white society. The explanation for this dramatic peripety must be that all the hatred, violence, and obsession, accumulated in Ethan during the years spent in pursuit of Scar and Debbie, have drained from him at the moment of his meanest act, the scalping of Scar. The brief period of time elapsed between Ethan riding down Martin and catching up with Debbie must have brought him back to his senses; finally acknowledging the ties of blood kinship which he has denied for so long, Ethan is at last saved from what seemed up to now an inevitable fall into savagery and inhumanity. The draining of violence from Ethan parallels the viewer's cathartic experience; the scene just described is the best proof for the film's tragic nature.[37]

That Ford eschews a violent climax—such as Ethan killing Debbie and later paying with his own life for this—might at first speak against the tragic quality of the film. But "happy endings" are part of the ancient tradition of tragedy. All three Athenian dramatists wrote plays in which murder and bloodshed were avoided. In *The Eumenides*, the conclusion of Aeschylus' *Oresteia*, the Furies are placated and Orestes is absolved from blood guilt; in Sophocles' *Philoctetes*, the eponymous hero forbears from killing his arch-enemy Odysseus and agrees to help the Greeks before Troy; in Euripides' *Iphigenia among the Taurians*, Orestes is saved from immolation upon the altar of Artemis at his sister's hands, who is the goddess's priestess; Euripides' lost play, *Antigone*, ended with the wedding of Antigone and Haemon, and his *Ion* and *Helen* end happily as well. In chapter 14 of his *Poetics*, Aristotle even prefers an avoidance of intrafamilial killing.[38] For the protagonist of the Western film, we have Robert Warshow's observation that "his story need not end with his death (and usually does not)."[39] Even so, Ford avoids a superficial denouement. Debbie is restored to civilization when Ethan takes her to the Jorgensens, who will, presumably, keep her as a member of their family; but Ethan himself remains an outcast from society, homeless and alone. In the film's famous last scene, after everybody else has gone inside, Ethan is left behind on the doorstep. His look follows the others; he then turns away and slowly begins to walk back into the desert wilderness while the door closes upon him. Thematically, and cinematically through its camera setup, this parallels the film's opening scene, providing a perfect example of ring composition which emphasizes the Aristotelian unity of time, place, and action. In addition, it summarizes the protagonist's state of mind: Ethan, drained of emotions and beyond violence, resigns himself to the status of an outcast and loner. While Ethan is not punished by death, his survival hardly constitutes a redemption. In a reversal of the case of Oedipus, who is guilty in deed but innocent in intention, Ethan has been guilty in intention—killing his niece— and innocent of the deed, but he is by no means absolved from guilt, as his status of social outcast attests. And just as Oedipus exiled himself from Thebes, Ethan takes upon himself a voluntary exile to the wilderness. Vernant's comments on Sophocles' *Oedipus* emphasize the duality inherent in the tragic protagonist thus exiled: "the tragedy is based on the idea that the same man . . . on whom the prosperity of the earth, of the herds, and of the women depends . . . is at the same time considered to be something dreadfully dangerous, a sort of incarnation of *hubris,* which must be expelled."[40] The task of finding his niece accomplished, Ethan has become superfluous to a society which, from now on, will live in peace, no longer threatened by Indian raids and no longer needing the archaic man of violence for its protection. When Ethan hugs his right arm with his left hand before turning away, this gesture of loneliness indicates that he has outlived his usefulness to society. It attests to Ford's mastery that these last moments in the film are completely wordless (except for the title song returning on the soundtrack). Nobody explains anything; the implications are nevertheless overwhelmingly clear. The subtlety of this closure to the film even surpasses that in the scene where Ford revealed Martha's love for Ethan. Ethan now receives the reward for his sacrilegious obsession; as critics have observed, he, too, will "wander forever between the winds," refused entry into the land of home and family, peace and civilization.[41] Like Ahasver, he is condemned to roam restlessly and aimlessly. In this context the names of the Edwards brothers, Ethan and Aaron, take on added meaning through their biblical connotations: Aaron is the brother of Moses, the wanderer in the desert who may not enter the Promised Land. It is worth noting that both names are changed from those the brothers carried in LeMay's novel. Both Ethan and his alter ego Scar represent necessary steps in the historical evolution of the country from savagery to civilization; they must live violent lives to prepare the way for future peace and justice, but they themselves have no part in this. It is the Westerner's task to aid in the transformation of nature from cruel and barren wilderness to a blossoming garden made fertile and tended by man, but he is not meant to participate in the result.[42] In *The Searchers,* the movement from violence to order is represented primarily in the figure of Ethan; his tragedy lies in the fact that he helps bring about this development but, belonging only to the archaic side, is himself unable to make the transition. When he tells Debbie, "Let's go home," he can only take her home and hand her over to others, but he cannot go home himself. Ethan, like other Fordian heroes, takes up "with resignation his burden as scapegoat and saviour. These transitional figures accept the stigma of all heroes since the beginning of society, and their characters often have mythical or Biblical overtones."[43] Our emotional involvement in the visual poetry of the film's final moments derives from our awareness of this; the ending also bears out Warshow's observation that we primarily respond to the hero's defeat. The theme of violence and disorder giving way to culture, law, and a stable society is perhaps the most fundamental subject in the history of Western literature. Among its most prominent ancient examples is *The Theogony,* Hesiod's epic on the creation of the world and the gods, in which the movement from *chaos* to *kosmos,* the order of the universe as ruled by divine justice, is embodied in the myth of the three generations of gods who successively rule over the world.

One of the most distinctive features of Greek drama is the chorus. Far from being a mere adornment to the action of the play, choral lyrics form an integral part of both tragedy and comedy; indeed, as far as we know, Greek drama may have developed out of originally static choral recitations. The tragic chorus finds its chief function in commenting upon the protagonist's words and deeds; voicing the author's thoughts and opinions, the chorus provides an important link to the audience.

Its integration into the plot can range from detached observation to active participation. While, in the history of theater, the chorus has not preserved its importance beyond the ancient stage, traces of its function are still to be found in later developments of tragedy; Shakespearean drama with its fools and clowns immediately comes to mind. Continuing this tradition, in the cinema comment upon the action is frequently assigned not to a group of observers, but to one or more individual characters who are often closely associated with the hero. In artistically meaningful films, a character's comments upon the protagonist's deeds or attitudes may provide as close a bond to the audience as did the chorus on the classical stage. Not surprisingly, characters of a choric nature are to be found in *The Searchers* also. One of these is old Mose Harper, a divine fool in an almost Shakespearean sense, reminiscent of the fool in *King Lear*.[44] Mose does not play a major part in the film, being on screen for only a comparatively short time; nevertheless, he is present during some of the film's key scenes. Mose is one of Ford's most memorable creations, providing the richness of detail and characterization unique to the characters who people his best films. In this way, even marginal figures may become essential. Thus the figure of Mose is important on different levels. For one, he provides comic relief from the film's stark tragedy.[45] Under a less accomplished director than Ford, these comic touches could easily destroy the film's dramatic equilibrium; as it is, the viewer's apprehension of impending tragedy even increases. More importantly, Mose is also an experienced Westerner. He immediately grasps the reason why Ethan blinds the dead Indian, and on two occasions he gives Ethan decisive information about Debbie after Ethan has lost all traces of her. For this, Mose even suffers great physical exhaustion. The bald and emaciated old man ends as a figure of pity and woe; Ford uses Christian imagery to emphasize his long suffering when, toward the end of the film, Mose is supported by a soldier on either side of him, his arms outstretched in a Christ-like pose. In contrast to the greed of Futterman, the trader who sells Ethan information about Debbie, Mose has no desire for material rewards: "Don't want no money . . . just a roof over old Mose's head, and a rocking chair by the fire." His awareness of old age and encroaching death and his selfless loyalty endow him with quiet dignity; it is fitting that the old man will find a permanent home with the Jorgensens. Mose, as his name implies, has been a homeless wanderer for most of his life; he, too, is in this sense an alter ego of Ethan. This is reinforced by the slight touches of childishness and harmless madness in Mose of which he is himself aware. But since he is a gentle and innocent soul, his end will be different from Ethan's.

More directly than Mose Harper, the figure of Mrs. Jorgensen serves as a choric commentator. Not only is she the archetypal hardy pioneer woman, but she also embodies pragmatism and common sense in the face of the men's more emotional and irrational reactions to the tragic events in their lives. She is an example of what Ford described as "the home women who helped break the land, bear and raise children and make a home for their families. These were hard times for women and they acquitted themselves nobly."[46] After the Edwards family's funeral, Mrs. Jorgensen's is the voice of restraint which counsels against meaningless and ruinous revenge. She implores Ethan to refrain from drawing Martin and her son Brad into a useless crusade against the Indians: "If the girls are dead, don't let the boys waste their lives in vengeance—promise me, Ethan!" She receives no reply. As usual, the voice of reason goes unheeded. Mrs. Jorgensen's urgent plea foreshadows her son's death; when he learns about Lucy's fate, Brad impulsively rushes off to the Indian camp to avenge her, but falls into Scar's trap. When we next see his mother again, more than a year later in narrative time, she has come to terms with her son's fate, with the harshness of the settlers' existence, and with the hostility of the land in which the pioneers are struggling to survive. In one of the film's key scenes—this is after Ethan and Martin's temporary return from their search—Mr. Jorgensen submits to his grief over Brad's death: "Oh, Ethan, this country . . . it's this country killed my boy." His quiet despair contrasts with his wife's stoic acceptance of her son's death. She characterizes the pioneers' life on the edge of civilization as being "way out on a limb, this year and next, maybe for a hundred more, but I don't think it'll be forever. Someday this country is gonna be a fine, good place to be. Maybe it needs our bones in the ground before that time can come." Her awareness of the necessity of sacrifices gives her the strength to endure; savagery and violence will eventually be overcome, and there is hope for peace in the future. Her words perfectly summarize the underlying theme of The Searchers and of most of Ford's other Westerns: the evolution from savagery to civilization, the change in the land from wilderness to garden. Her words point to her own generation's part in this process and to the knowledge that she and the other settlers will not live to see the task completed. In addition, they foreshadow Ethan's eventual fate. Significantly, the setting of this short scene, memorable for its peace and quiet, is the Jorgensens' porch at evening. In a touch typical for his reversals from seriousness to humor or vice versa, Ford circumvents melodramatic emotionalism at this point by having Mr. Jorgensen explain his wife's eloquence to Ethan: "She was a school teacher, you know." The Jorgensens' is the kind of home which Ethan can only visit for a time but not belong to. The affirmation of hope for the future contrasts with the increasing disappointment of this hope which is found in the later films of John Ford. *The Searchers* thus takes on added significance if considered in the context of Ford's complete oeuvre. But even when examined on its own terms, this film most likely represents the director's foremost achievement. In no small degree this is due to the fact that Ford makes such powerful use of mythic and dramatic archetypes and successfully translates them into a modern medium. In the questions quoted at the beginning of my discussion of *The Searchers*, Vernant emphasized the ambiguities inherent in the tragic hero and in his environs. That Ethan is a modern example of a tragic *deinos* I have attempted to show on the preceding pages. When Ford, albeit using the term loosely, described *The Searchers* as "the tragedy of a loner," his remark came closer to the film's true nature than he himself may have realized.[47]

NOTES

1. The quotation is taken from Paul Seydor, *Peckinpah: The Western Films* (Urbana: University of Illinois Press, 1980), 270.

2. I have traced parallels between classical mythological heroes and the Western hero in my "Classical Mythology and the Western Film," *Comparative Literature Studies* 22 (1985): 516–40. On the history and mythology of the Western and its origins see especially Henry Nash Smith, *Virgin Land: The American West as Symbol and Myth* (1950; reprint, Cambridge: Harvard University Press, 1970), 51–120.

3. For Aristotle on the links between epic and tragedy see *Poetics* 4, 5, 23, 24, and 26. On tragedy in Homer see, e.g., James M. Redfield, *Nature and Culture in the "Iliad": The Tragedy of Hector* (Chicago: University of Chicago Press, 1975). Aeschylus, who wrote a trilogy about Achilles which has not come down to us, considered his tragedies to be "slices from the large meals of Homer" (Athenaeus, *The Deipnosophists* 8.347e).

4. *Poetics* 3. On classical mimesis see now Stephen Halliwell, *Aristotle's Poetics* (London: Duckworth, 1986), 109–37. On mimesis and film see Gerald Mast, *Film/Cinema/Movie* (1977; reprint, Chicago: University of Chicago Press, 1983), 38–61.

5. *Poetics* 6; the translation is from Halliwell, *The Poetics of Aristotle: Translation and Commentary* (Chapel Hill: University of North Carolina Press, 1987), 37.

6. *Poetics* 13; quoted from Halliwell, ibid., 44.

7. Ibid. On tragedy's quality of *nostra res agitur* see, e.g., Albin Lesky, *Die griechische Tragödie*, 5th ed. (Stuttgart: Kröner, 1984), 22–23.

8. *Poetics* 14.

9. For a recent examination of the evidence and the controversies surrounding Aristotelian catharsis see Halliwell, *Aristotle's Poetics*, 168–201 and 350–56.

10. Aeschylus, *Agamemnon*, line 177: *pathei mathos* (learning through suffering); see also line 250.

11. Benjamin Apthorp Gould Fuller, "The Conflict of Moral Obligation in the Trilogy of Aeschylus," *Harvard Theological Review* 8 (1915):460. See also the detailed discussion by Richmond Lattimore, *Story Patterns in Greek Tragedy* (Ann Arbor: University of Michigan Press, 1964), 29–49.

12. On formula and genre in American literature and film see in particular John G. Cawelti, *Adventure, Mystery, and Romance: Formula Stories as Art and Popular Culture* (Chicago: University of Chicago Press, 1976), esp. 192–259, and *The Six-Gun Mystique* (Bowling Green, Ohio: Bowling Green University Popular Press, n.d.), esp. 26–34; also Stanley J. Solomon, *Beyond Formula* (Chicago: Harcourt Brace Jovanovich, 1976), 12–29. See in addition Joseph W. Reed, *Three American Originals: John Ford, William Faulkner, and Charles Ives* (Middletown, Conn.: Wesleyan University Press, 1984), 143–49.

13. Robert Warshow, "The Westerner," in *The Immediate Experience* (1962; reprint, New York: Atheneum, 1972), 142. This essay first appeared in *Partisan Review* of March–April, 1954.

14. This quotation and the four preceding it are from Warshow, "The Westerner," 142–43.

15. "The Western hero is necessarily an archaic figure" (ibid., 154); on the universality of the Westerner, exemplified by the eponymous hero of *Shane* (1953), see ibid., 150–51.

16. See Christopher Wicking and Barrie Pattison, "Interviews with Anthony Mann," *Screen* 10, no. 4 (1969):41–42, and Jim Kitses, *Horizons West: Anthony Mann, Budd Boetticher, Sam Peckinpah: Studies of Authorship within the Western* (London: Thames & Hudson, 1969), 72–73 (also 46–59 and 73–77). At the time of his death Mann planned to film *King Lear* as a Western (Kitses, 80). Borden Chase, one of the most distinguished Western novelists and screenwriters, reverses his *Winchester 73* theme in his script for *Backlash* (1956) with the figure of a guilty father instead of a guilty son.

17. Quoted from *The BFI Companion to the Western*, ed. Edward Buscombe (London: Deutsch/British Film Institute, 1988), 397. The most remarkable of the films written or co-written by Yordan are *Johnny Guitar* (1953), *The Man from Laramie* (1955, directed by Mann), *The Bravados* (1958), and *Day of the Outlaw* (1959).

18. On this see D. H. Lawrence, *Studies in Classic American Literature* (1923; reprint, Harmondsworth: Penguin, 1981), 62–63; Smith, *Virgin Land*, 221–22; and Cawelti, *Adventure, Mystery, and Romance*, 201–2. See also Eric Rohmer, "Rediscovering America," in *Cahiers du Cinéma: The 1950s*, ed. Jim Hillier (Cambridge: Harvard University Press, 1985), 90–91.

19. Some of the differences between novel and film are discussed by James Van Dyck Card, "The 'Searchers' by Alan LeMay and by John Ford," *Literature/Film Quarterly* 16 (1988):2–9.

20. Jean-Pierre Vernant, "Tensions and Ambiguities in Greek Tragedy," in Vernant and Pierre Vidal-Naquet, *Myth and Tragedy in Ancient Greece*, trans. Janet Lloyd (1981; reprint, New York: Zone Books, 1988), 32.

21. The following are among the standard sources on John Ford; page references are to *The Searchers:* John Baxter, *The Cinema of John Ford* (New York: Barnes, 1971), 144–52; J. A. Place, *The Western Films of John Ford* (Secaucus, N.J.: Citadel Press, 1974), 160–73; Joseph McBride and Michael Wilmington, *John Ford* (1974; reprint, New York: Da Capo, 1975), 147–63; Andrew Sarris, *The John Ford Movie Mystery* (Bloomington: Indiana University Press, 1975), 170–75; Peter Stowell, *John Ford* (Boston: Twayne, 1986), 122–40; and Tag Gallagher, *John Ford: The Man and His Films* (Berkeley: University of California Press, 1986), 324–38.

22. See Charles Segal, *The Theme of the Mutilation of the Corpse in the "Iliad"* (Leiden: Brill, 1971).

23. Ethan: "Scar, eh? Plain to see how you got your name." Then: "You speak pretty good American—someone teach you?" Moments later, Scar has the last word on Ethan: "You speak good Comanch'—someone teach you?"

24. Stowell, *John Ford*, 135.

25. See McBride and Wilmington, *John Ford*, 152.

26. Gallagher, *John Ford*, 274.

27. Vernant, "Tensions and Ambiguity in Greek Tragedy," 35.

28. H. A. Mason, *The Tragic Plane* (Oxford: Clarendon Press, 1985), 146.

29. On this brief moment see Andrew Sarris, *The American Cinema: Directors and Directions: 1929–1968* (New York: Dutton, 1968), 47, and *The John Ford Movie Mystery*, 172; see also Baxter, *The Cinema of John Ford*, 150, and Ford's own remarks as stated in Peter Bogdanovich, *John Ford*, rev. ed. (Berkeley: University of California Press, 1978), 93–94.

30. Béla Balász, "The Close-Up" (from *Theory of the Film* [1945]), reprinted in *Film Theory and Criticism: Introductory Readings*, ed. Gerald Mast and Marshall Cohen, 3d ed. (New York: Oxford University Press, 1985), 256. Cf. Soviet theorist and director Sergei Eisenstein on the function of the close-up: it is "not so much to *show* or to *present* as to *signify*, to *give meaning, to designate*" (quoted in *Film Theory and Criticism*, 239).

31. McBride and Wilmington, *John Ford*, 160. Stowell, *John Ford*, 139, characterizes Ethan's expression at this moment as "powerfully tragic."

32. On landscape in the Western see Warshow, "The Westerner," 139; Philip French, *Westerns: Aspects of a Movie Genre*, 2d ed. (London: Secker & Warburg, 1977), 100–113; Cawelti, *The Six-Gun Mystique*, 39–44; and Solomon, *Beyond Formula*, 12–17. In general see Smith, *Virgin Land*. For the literary roots of the meaning of the Western's landscape see *The BFI Companion to the Western*, 169.

33. French, *Westerns*, 104; on Ford and Monument Valley see also McBride and Wilmington, *John Ford*, 36–37 ("Monument Valley is a moral battleground").

34. Both quotations are from Bill Libby, "The Old Wrangler Rides Again," *Cosmopolitan* (March 1964), 21 and 14 (interview with Ford).

35. On *anagnorisis* and peripety see *Poetics* 10 and 11.

36. Evan S. Connell, *Son of the Morning Star: Custer and the Little Bighorn* (1984; reprint, New York: Harper & Row, 1985), 162–63, traces the custom of scalping back to antiquity.

37. Sarris, *The John Ford Movie Mystery*, 173: "a man picks up a girl in his arms and is miraculously delivered of all the racist, revenge-seeking furies that have seared his soul." Cf. Lattimore, *Story Patterns in Greek Tragedy*, 8, on *anagnorisis* and peripety: "And this is the moment of truth or revelation or recognition when the hero in drama sees the shape of the action in which he is involved." As Ford himself has stated about the protagonists of his films: "the tragic moment . . . permits them to define themselves, to become conscious of what they are. . . . to exalt man 'in depth,' this is the dramatic device I like." (Trans. by Gallagher, *John Ford*, 302, from an interview with Jean Mitry, first published in French in *Cahiers du Cinéma* 45 [March 1955]:6).

38. On this aspect of Greek tragedy see also Lattimore, *Story Patterns in Greek Tragedy*, 13 and 76–77, n. 39.

39. Warshow, "The Westerner," 143.

40. Jean-Pierre Vernant, "Greek Tragedy: Problems of Interpretation," in *The Languages of Criticism and the Sciences of Man*, ed. Richard Macksey and Eugenio Donato (Baltimore: Johns Hopkins University Press, 1970), 277. Jaan Puhvel, *Comparative Mythology* (Baltimore: Johns Hopkins University Press, 1987), 242, makes a similar point about the Indo-European tradition of heroic myth: "The warrior thus had an ambivalent role as single champion or part of a self-centered corps or coterie, both a society's external defender and its potential internal menace."

41. Thus McBride and Wilmington, *John Ford*, 163.

42. On this pervasive theme in American intellectual history see Smith, *Virgin Land*, 121–260, esp. 123–32 and 250–60, the latter passage on Frederick Jackson Turner's 1893 frontier hypothesis ("The Significance of the Frontier in American History"). In this landmark essay Turner called the frontier "the meeting point between savagery and civilization."

43. Baxter, *The Cinema of John Ford*, 21. In antiquity the hero's acceptance of his burden finds its most moving expression in Vergil's description of Aeneas taking up his shield (*Aeneid* 8.729–31); in his discussion of these lines Jasper Griffin, *Virgil* (New York: Oxford University Press, 1986), 67, speaks of "the pathos of the pioneer who must work for a result which he will never see."

44. Cf. Baxter, *The Cinema of John Ford*, 19.

45. Ford's narrative mastery in this film is evidenced by his seamless integration of two comic subplots into the main tragic plot. This, too, is in keeping with Greek tragedy, which could contain comic elements; see Bernd Seidensticker, *Palintonos Harmonia: Studien zu komischen Elementen in der griechischen Tragödie* (Göttingen: Vandenhoeck & Ruprecht, 1982). While humor is present even in its serious moments, the film in its second half switches back and forth between tragedy and comedy with effortless grace. As Ford said before beginning work on *The Searchers:* "I should like to do a tragedy, the most serious in the world, that turned into the ridiculous." (The quotation is from Michael Goodwin, "John Ford: A Poet Who Shot Great Movies," *Moving Image* 1, no. 3 [December 1981]:62.) See also Andrew Sinclair, *John Ford* (New York: Dial Press/Wade, 1979), 213–14, on Ford's interest in tragedy and on his place in the history of tragedy as a popular art form; cf. Solomon, *Beyond Formula*, 46. The two comic strands in the film involve Martin's inadvertent acquisition of an Indian girl as a bride; this reverts to stark tragedy when Ethan later finds her killed by the cavalry. In the courtship of Laurie Jorgensen by Charlie McCorry, an archetypal redneck, and in his subsequent brawl over Laurie with Martin, the comedy in the film comes close to farce. Cf. McBride and Wilmington, *John Ford*, 32: "In [Ford's] greatest works, the plot line oscillates freely between the tragic and the ridiculous, with the comic elements providing a continuous commentary on the meaning of the drama." As Sarris, *The John Ford Movie Mystery*, 174, has noted on the humor in *The Searchers:* "If Ford had been more solemn, *The Searchers* would have been less sublime." There is even a fair share of ridicule of the military in the film: whereas the army is characterized as indiscriminate butchers of Indians in the cavalry sequence, its second appearance—indeed, interference—at the film's close gives Ford occasion to satirize it for nepotism, bureaucracy, and incompetence.

46. *Cosmopolitan* interview, 17.

47. Quoted from Bogdanovich, *John Ford*, 92.

An American Tragedy: *Chinatown*

Mary-Kay Gamel

University of California, Santa Cruz

> History is what hurts.
> —Fredric Jameson, *The Political Unconscious*

IN the late twentieth century generic distinctions in the arts seem to be rapidly breaking down as old genres merge and new ones arise. In contemporary literary studies, genre criticism is often dismissed.[1] In film, however, genre remains a system of classification widely used by producers, critics, and consumers.[2] The importance of genre in the production, presentation, discussion, and evaluation of ancient literature suggests that valuable insights might result from a wide-ranging, systematic discussion of genre both in that literature and in film, but comparisons so far have been limited.[3] Given the close connections between theater and film, the relationship between ancient drama and film seems an especially promising topic.[4] Greek drama and film share certain formal, thematic, and affective features: like drama, film is the product not of an individual but of the combined talents of author, director, actors, and musicians.[5] Material aspects are crucial to both media, and the success of individual films, like that of drama, is affected by the financial support of the producer. Like ancient dramas, films are presented as examples of specific genres, and in both cases the large audience comprises all classes of society and expresses strong responses to what it sees.[6] Such similarities suggest that a significant comparison between these media could be achieved by utilizing existing analyses of their complex relationship to their respective social contexts.[7] But most discussions of Greek tragedy and cinema discuss only filmic treatments of ancient dramas.[8]

One critical study which does draw formal and thematic comparisons is Thomas Sobchack's "Genre Film: A Classical Experience."[9] Sobchack ascribes to all "genre films" a "classical" status established by three elements. First, they emphasize form, in particular "a profound respect for Aristotelian dramatic values"

209

(105). Second, they imitate past models and conform to generic expectations: "Classical theory insists upon the primacy of the original. It is that which must be imitated, and the basic and fundamental elements must not be changed. . . . A genre film . . . is capable of creating the classical experience because of this insistence on the familiar" (104–5). The third "classical" element is ahistoricity: "The contemporary and the particular are inimical to the prevailing idea in classical thought that knowledge is found in the general conclusions that have stood the test of time" (102). The setting of genre films is "an ideal plane, a utopia, as far removed from our world as was the world of kings and nobles and Olympian gods from the lives of the Athenians who attended the plays" (108). Yet as always formal considerations have social implications: "The genre film, like all classical art, is basically conservative, both aesthetically and politically" (112). The effect of such "classical" films on the audience is not intellectual stimulation; rather, "given the appropriate ending, these emotions [pity and fear] are dissipated, leaving viewers in a state of calm" (109). Films which violate conventional expectations induce in the audience "a kind of irrational radicalism as opposed to a reasonable conformism. . . . This is not what ordinary people—fated to a life in society in which they are relatively powerless to change the course of things—like to comfort themselves with" (112).

The issues Sobchack raises—especially about the relationship between genre, ideology, and cultural products—have been more thoughtfully discussed elsewhere.[10] I have dwelt on his article because his uncritical acceptance of Aristotelian categories and his quietistic social views echo conservative educators' defense of the established literary canon because of its "timeless" or "universal" values. Such assumptions about "the classics" as unconnected to their political and social context, although widely held, are not based on a thoughtful examination of ancient drama. Rather, the idea of the "classic" is constructed as a term in a binary opposition with a polemical aim; its function is to define (hence to praise or condemn) its opposite as "modern," "progressive," or, alternatively, as "corrupt," "decadent."[11]

To test the validity of such definitions of "classicism" I will examine a film which shares conspicuous formal and thematic characteristics with Greek tragedy: *Chinatown* (1974), written by Robert Towne and directed by Roman Polanski.[12] In making this comparison I am not trying to honor an especially worthy film by comparing it to past "masterpieces." Intertextuality works both ways, and an assessment of connections between ancient drama and film benefits the former as much as the latter. Reading *Chinatown* in terms of tragedy raises questions about the "classical" status of tragedy as well.

I

The plot: in 1937 Los Angeles, private detective Jake Gittes (played by Jack Nicholson) is engaged by a woman who calls herself Evelyn Mulwray to ascertain whether her husband Hollis, City Commissioner of Water and Power, is having an affair. Gittes follows Mulwray and takes photos of him with a young girl. After these photos appear in a newspaper article, the real Mrs. Mulwray (played by Faye Dunaway) sues Gittes. Soon after Gittes sets out to discover who arranged the deception, Mulwray is found dead. Gittes gradually discovers that Mulwray's death is part of a huge scheme masterminded by Noah Cross (played by John Huston), who is both Evelyn Mulwray's father and Hollis Mulwray's former business partner. Cross is secretly buying land in the San Fernando Valley and secretly promoting the construction of a new dam which the L. A. citizens think will serve their city. The dam will actually irrigate Cross's land, which he will then be able to sell for huge profits. The young girl is not Mulwray's mistress but Evelyn's daughter and sister Katherine, the product of incest with her own father. She and Hollis have brought Katherine up in Mexico, hidden from Cross. Gittes's efforts to solve Hollis Mulwray's murder, help Evelyn, and thwart Cross result instead in Cross's triumph and Evelyn's death.

Chinatown has the intensity and economy of Greek tragedy. The plot is concentrated, the events all taking place within a few days, and the passage of time is carefully marked. Scenes are shot in various locations, but the overall setting, Los Angeles, is constantly referred to verbally and visually. The film thus conforms to Aristotle's prescription for temporal and spatial unity (*Poetics* 1450b). The number of characters is limited, and every character introduced, even the most minor, plays a crucial role. The action is punctuated by physical violence and culminates in a shocking death, but the violence, used sparingly and closely connected to the film's semiotic pattern, has the same function as in Greek tragedy: to underline the importance of the issues at stake. The dialogue, while apparently naturalistic, is tightly knit; every line, every exchange either advances the plot or touches on its themes. Every shot is carefully planned and contains meaningful ele-

ments. The names of many characters are as significant as those of
Oedipus, Aias, Hippolytus, Orestes, and Electra. Gittes's name
(which Noah Cross purposefully mispronounces "gits") is pointedly different from the phallic names of other hard-boiled detectives like Sam Spade or Mike Hammer, suggesting that he tries to
"git his" and then "git out." Lou Escobar, the police lieutenant
who worked with Gittes in the past, may be a new broom trying to
sweep clean, but Claude Mulvehill, Noah Cross's hired thug, is a
clod and Escobar's fellow cop Loach (whose shot kills Evelyn) is
louche, a low roach. Evelyn's name suggests that she may be evil, an
Eve tempting man to sin. Most significant of all is Noah Cross, an
Old Testament patriarch who controls the waters.

The film's protagonist and structure resemble those of Sophocles' *Oedipus the King* in striking ways.[13] Like Oedipus, Gittes at
first seems intelligent, powerful, in control. He dresses nattily
(meeting him again, Escobar notes: "looks like you've done all
right for yourself"), has a nice office, employs "operatives" and a
cute secretary. (Her name is Sophie; like the flute girl in Plato's
Symposium she is sent out of the room when male wisdom needs to
be heard.) Like Oedipus he sets out on an investigation confident
of results. He gets information even from unwilling sources. He
lectures his employees Walsh and Duffy on "finesse" and delivers
snappy comeuppances to those he considers his inferiors. He
pursues his investigation with purpose, using professional tricks
(leaving watches under parked car wheels to time a suspect's
movements, breaking the taillight on Evelyn's car so as to follow
her at night without being spotted). He thinks and acts quickly.
Gittes experiences not only lies and threats but also violence;
his nose is slit, he is beaten up and shot at. Like Oedipus, he
seems heroic when he courageously continues his investigation
nonetheless.

Gittes also fits Aristotle's prescription for a protagonist who is
morally "between the extremes" (*Poetics* 1453a). Divorce work,
shunned by other hard-boiled detectives, is Gittes's "meetiyay."[14]
He is generous to working-class Curly, but decides to overcharge
Mrs. Mulwray as soon as he finds out that her husband is Chief
Engineer at Water and Power. He reacts indignantly when ac-
cused of trading on scandal ("I make an honest living! People only
come to me when they're in a desperate situation—I help 'em
out"). But while nobly shielding Evelyn Mulwray from reporters'
questions and flashbulbs he tries to get publicity for himself
("Gittes—two t's and an e!"). His primary motive for continuing
the investigation may not be desire for the truth, but worry about

losing his reputation as a businessman: "I'm not supposed to be the one caught with my pants down." He negotiates contracts for large sums with both Evelyn and Noah Cross, despite obvious signs that they are at odds with one another.

His understanding, too, is deeply flawed. As Noah Cross says to him, "You may think you know what you're dealing with here, but believe me, you don't." Gittes ignores important clues and fails to draw obvious conclusions—for example, that Hollis is spending his nights on his own investigation, not with his "mistress," or that by following a useful tip he himself will endanger the informant who gave it to him. Like Oedipus, Gittes impulsively jumps to wrong conclusions, accusing Yelburton, Hollis Mulwray's successor, and then Evelyn of Mulwray's murder. His misplaced self-confidence even leads him to stage a showdown with Noah Cross, whereupon Cross, who has brought along a gunman, forces Gittes to take him to Katherine.[15] As a result the objects of Gittes's scorn like Mulvehill and Loach triumph over him. Thus his wounded nose does not disappear as do most film injuries but stays in prominent view for the entire film. Covered with a comic bandage or revealing its stitches, the wound becomes a sign not of courage but, like Oedipus' pierced ankles, a symbol of the hero's vulnerability.

The final result of Gittes's investigation, like that of Oedipus, is that he turns out to be part of the problem rather than the solution, "the murderer of the king whose murderer you seek," as Teiresias says (line 362). In the past Gittes "was trying to keep somebody from getting hurt and ended up making sure that she was hurt," and he does exactly the same this time. The film's denouement can be described in terms of elements identified by Aristotle: *peripeteia* and *anagnorisis* (reversal and recognition, *Poetics* 1452a). Evelyn's revelation of the incest with her father is the film's *peripeteia*, which causes Jake to try to help her instead of blocking her, and her death causes him to experience *anagnorisis*, recognition not only of Noah Cross's schemes but also of his own failure, lack of understanding, and complicity in the outcome.[16] This recognition comes, however—as to Hippolytus, Theseus, Heracles, Creon, and Oedipus—only when it is too late to avert disaster. As Escobar says, "You never learn, do you, Jake?" The film is bracketed by suggestions that knowledge only serves to increase pain. "You're better off not knowing," says Gittes to the fake Mrs. Mulwray at the beginning, and the film's last line is "Forget it, Jake, it's Chinatown."

Chinatown displays a complex of visual imagery which resembles the verbal imagery of many Greek tragedies.[17] Gittes seems to be an expert manipulator of specular technology (binoculars, camera, magnifying glass), but imperfect knowledge, his and others', is consistently represented by visual images of flawed sight—pairs of glasses with one broken lens, the broken taillight on Evelyn's car. When the dead Mulwray is dragged from the reservoir, his glasses are gone and he is pop-eyed as if in amazement at what he has seen. The punishment of Curly's wife for "seeing" another man is a large black eye. Evelyn has a flaw in the iris of her left eye which she describes as "a sort of birthmark" and that eye, blasted by Loach's bullet, is the audience's last view of her. As Katherine screams at the sight of her dead mother, Noah Cross covers her eyes, suggesting that he will be able to control her as he did Evelyn. By contrast, Noah Cross wears bifocals, here a sign not of feeble age but of duplicity of vision: the ability to see Evelyn both as daughter and lover, to see private profit in the public domain.[18]

Many times mechanical means which should aid vision instead obstruct it. When Gittes perches on a roof to get photographs of Hollis with his "girlfriend," the shot moves away from the couple below to focus on his face obscured by his camera. The reversed image of Mulwray and Katherine in his camera lens, like the images in Gittes's car mirror as he follows Hollis, indicates that he is getting things backward. As Gittes drives up to the reservoir, the camera, positioned behind his right shoulder, shows a closed gate framed in the windshield of his car, suggesting that the windshield too is a barrier rather than a visual conduit. The photographs Gittes takes of Hollis with Katherine are interpreted incorrectly—by the newspapers as proof of a "love nest," by Escobar as proof that Gittes is guilty of extortion.[19] Similarly, the constant presence of Venetian blinds is not just visual homage to thirties films but another barrier to sight.

The theme of flawed sight is further reinforced by ironic use of cinematic techniques.[20] The editing of the film is primarily mise-en-scène, featuring long takes and establishing relationships between characters and surroundings. The use of this editing style rather than that of montage, which calls attention to the director's manipulation of the image, suggests that the viewer is getting the whole, undistorted picture.[21] So does the use of undiffused light, which creates hard edges, and the consistent use of deep focus, which renders visible all objects in the frame. But because here, as in *Oedipus,* seeing does not lead to understanding, these techniques underline the inadequacy and deceptiveness of sight, reminding viewers that their sight, the primary means of understanding motion "pictures," is flawed too. The close-up, normally used to mark an object as specially important, is used deceptively when a manicure kit in Mulwray's office drawer and documents in the wallet of Ida Sessions, who had impersonated Mrs. Mulwray, are "clues" that lead nowhere.

As in *Oedipus,* the protagonist's point of view—his "private eye"—dominates the film. Not only does Gittes appear in every scene, but the camera is frequently placed near his shoulder so that the audience sees from his point of view, and the film's only dissolve occurs when Gittes is knocked unconscious by angry farmers. When he watches a Mexican boy on a white horse talking to Mulwray, they are shown in a double iris shot so that the audience looks through the binoculars with Gittes and sees exactly what he sees. Gittes is frequently shown making his observations from a high position—a bluff over the sea, the bank of the Los Angeles River, a roof overlooking Katherine's apartment. Such a position might suggest that his vision is godlike, Olympian. But not so: at the apartment he dislodges a roof tile and has to jump back to keep from being seen. The result of this identification with Gittes is to implicate the viewer in his fallibility.

Visual evidence, moreover, is incomplete without words.[22] His binoculars let Gittes see Hollis talking to the Mexican boy, but he cannot hear their words; Walsh takes pictures of Cross and Mulwray arguing but hears only the words "apple core." When spying on Katherine Gittes does not hear that she is speaking Spanish with Hollis at the "love nest" and with Evelyn at the safe house, where Gittes sees them through a closed window. Gittes disregards verbal clues such as Cross's evading his question about the argument Cross had with Mulwray, Evelyn's stammering whenever her father is mentioned, and the Japanese gardener's "Velly bad for glass," a double clue, to both the salt water in the Mulwrays' pond and the glasses lost there. Flawed sight as a metaphor for the difficulty of knowledge, and the need for other kinds of knowledge than intellectual understanding, are Sophoclean themes: as Teiresias says to Oedipus, "you are blind in mind and ears as well as in your eyes" (371).[23] Euripidean drama often emphasizes the need to integrate verbal with visual evidence, the two modes of understanding fundamental to theatrical experience, as in the contrast, for example, in *Electra* between the criminal Clytemnestra described by Electra and the contrite, compassionate mother who later comes on stage. When featured in drama and film, such epistemological themes raise important metatheatrical and metacinematic issues about the validity of the understanding these media seem to provide. By problematizing their own status as media, theater and film demonstrate that simple mimesis is impossible, that all experience is mediated.

Chinatown does not simply indict Gittes as an individual. Its central theme is the complexity and obscurity of human experience, which makes understanding difficult. Chinatown, where "you can't always tell what's going on," is a metaphor for the reality experienced by the film's characters and audience. As Oedipus thinks he has escaped from Corinth, Gittes thinks he's "outta Chinatown," but he, Escobar, Evelyn, Cross, and Katherine are all inevitably drawn back to the crossroads to play out the catastrophe. The world of *Chinatown* is not only more complex and enigmatic but more evil than Gittes could ever have imagined. What his investigation discovers is corruption so pervasive, a corporate conspiracy so immense, that no individual can get to the bottom of it or do anything about it, and almost anybody may be complicit in it. Whether Yelburton or Loach are part of the scheme is never established (even the film's conclusion withholds from the audience the illusion of complete knowledge), but there are constant suggestions that public officials have been bought. "Who's paying you?" Hollis is asked. Visitors to Noah Cross's ranch "paid $5000 each towards the sheriff's re-election," and the hood Mulvehill is identified as a corrupt former sheriff. When Gittes says he'll sue "the big boys who are making the payoffs," his employee Duffy scoffs: "People like that are liable to be having dinner with the judges trying the suit." Escobar seems to be a good cop, but when asked if he's honest, Gittes responds: "As far as it goes—of course, he has to swim in the same water we all do." When Gittes pleads with Evelyn to let the police handle her father, she screams "He owns the police!" The end of the film reverses the conclusion of *Oedipus:* Noah Cross, the father who has had his "son" Hollis killed and caused his daughter's death, is not driven away by the revelation of his guilt, but remains firmly in power.

In this complex, corrupt world causality is intricate, involving institutions as well as individuals. As in many Greek tragedies, the catastrophe is rooted in the family.[24] The film depicts the founding of a city with the ambivalence about urban values evident in *The Eumenides, Medea,* and *The Bacchae.* As murderer, incestuous paterfamilias, and scheming city "father," the figure of Noah Cross combines individual and institutional transgression. His scheme will make him millions on real estate, yet his motive is not money but power: he expresses admiration for Hollis Mulwray who "built this city." When Gittes asks: "How much better can you eat, what can you buy that you can't already afford?" Cross answers, "The future, Mr. Gits! The future!" Cross is presented not as a monster but as an example of human nature at its most basic: when Gittes confronts him with his incest he replies "I don't blame myself. Most people never have to face the fact that at the right time and the right place they're capable of anything." Cross's and Mulwray's partnership ("Hollis Mulwray and I were a lot closer than Evelyn realized"), Cross's and Evelyn's sexual involvement, even the similarity in the names Mulwray and Mulvehill, indicate that no one is innocent.[25] Hence history is presented as cyclical, progress as impossible, and people as fated to repeat past actions, however evil or disastrous. Mulwray describes having been convinced by Cross to build a dam which later collapsed and killed several hundred people; he now opposes plans for the new dam, swearing, "I won't make the same mistake twice." But his disgrace and death clear the way for that dam to be built. Like Mulvehill, Gittes has been a police officer. While serving in Chinatown, he had been told to "do as little as possible," and these are his last words in the film, whispered to himself as he stares at Evelyn's body. Jake again makes the mistake of hurting someone he was trying to help, and Noah Cross will be able to commit incest again, this time with a daughter who is also his granddaughter.

The setting for the film's events is literally elemental. Cross is able to control not only individuals and institutions but also land and water. The action takes place during a drought exacerbated by a heat wave: LOS ANGELES IS DYING OF THIRST proclaims a handbill, and the mayor warns that the city is caught "between the desert and the Pacific Ocean." The subtle brown-beige tone with which the film was washed (to increase its period look) also increases the sense of heat and drought. Set against this are constant images of water (lake, reservoirs, channels, surf, Mulwray's tidepool, the spouting radiator of Gittes's crashed car, even glasses of iced tea), as well as verbal references to it: "Water again!" exclaims Gittes, Curly is a fisherman, Hollis has "water on the brain," and the retirement home is called Mar Vista (a bilingual clue: besides combining the themes of water and sight, it suggests that Cross's scheme will disfigure the landscape). There are even liquid sound effects—water drips ominously into a sink as Gittes discovers the body of Ida Sessions, who gave him the Mar Vista clue; water thunders down run-off channels or splashes gently as Evelyn offers Gittes a drink. These are aural clues that water is the key to the whole mystery, but they also indicate that water is a contradictory symbol that can represent either danger (when it drowns Mulwray or almost sweeps Gittes away) or refreshment and safety. Immediately before the drink scene Evelyn has rescued Jake from danger; now she tenderly nurses him, and they end up making love.

This elemental imagery evokes mythical themes and imbues the film with allegorical meanings.[26] Los Angeles is a Waste Land, a sterile kingdom with a drowned man and a wounded king, waiting for the water of redemption. But no redeemer comes; the wound is not healed. Cross is an Old Testament patriarch who will not give up his power to the new generation.[27] Hollis thinks that "the public should own the water," but Cross keeps private what should be public, the water, the land, and his daughter(s). His sexual and his political behavior are both incestuous, and the final result is sterility. Evelyn hates him and dies trying to keep Katherine from him; his agents dump water, poison wells, and blow up water tanks ("pretty funny irrigation," observes the owner of an orange grove) in order to transform ripe agricultural land into an arid city.

In this context the use of Christian references is ironic. Cross is a double-crosser, an Antichrist who crucifies others, a fisher of men who picks bad rather than good. "You have a nasty reputation," he says to Gittes; "I like that." A fish seen in silhouette (resembling the ICHTHYS symbol) appears on the flag of the Albacore Club, which Cross owns, but here it symbolizes not Christian benevolence but elemental rapacity. He dispenses alms to the residents of Mar Vista not as an act of Christian charity but to increase his own power. As Cross and Gittes eat lunch, the camera focuses on a fish's eye staring up from the plate and Cross comments "I believe fish should be served with the head." In the argument between Mulwray and Cross Walsh hears "apple core" for "Albacore," suggesting that Los Angeles is another Eden destroyed by greed, but for this original sin there is no redemption. As in the films of Sam Peckinpah, Mexico (represented by the boy on the white horse and as the refuge of Katherine) seems to symbolize a place and time of innocence and beauty, an early, unspoiled California. But Noah Cross dresses like a Spanish grandee and lives in a Spanish-style ranch house, so that symbol too is tainted.

Chinatown resembles Greek tragedy, then, in raising significant issues in individual, familial, political, even cosmic terms in an extremely intense and condensed format; in suggesting that individual characters stand for human experience in general; in heightening contrasts and posing choices between extreme alternatives. Perhaps the most important resemblance is its emphasis on stasis and hierarchy in both plot and character, suggesting that the past inevitably recurs, that progress is impossible, that individuals' power to act is constrained by stronger human beings or even extra-human forces. All of this might seem to support Sobchack's thesis that creating "classical" art depends on imitating past models. Hence even Polanski's casting himself in the role of a hood, making himself the hireling of John Huston, director of such film "classics" as *The Maltese Falcon* (1941) and *The Treasure of Sierra Madre* (1948), may be read as his admission that a contemporary director can only follow the old masters.[28]

II

My point in connecting *Chinatown* and Greek tragedy is not to demonstrate conscious imitation or influence. Screenwriter Towne drew upon the novels of Dashiell Hammett, Raymond Chandler, and John Fante, and director Polanski upon American black-and-white films of the thirties and forties such as *The Maltese Falcon*, Orson Welles's *Citizen Kane* (1941), and Howard Hawks's *The Big Sleep*. Nor am I suggesting that *Chinatown*'s "classical" features support a theory of recurring archetypes (such as Joseph Campbell's, based on Jung), or conscious use of an Aristotelian or neo-Aristotelian model (such as Northrop Frye's) of organic development of genres. It is possible that Towne, who was educated at Pomona College, was consciously following Aristotelian ideas. Even if not, the influence, often second or thirdhand, of Aristotle on "well-made" plays and films is pervasive, though often unacknowledged or even unrecognized. For all its emphasis on repetition, inevitability, and closure, *Chinatown* is not a closed text which imitates the ideal form of past models and avoids contemporary reference and relevance. In fact—and this is my central point in this paper—it is *Chinatown*'s "classic" elements which most clearly establish its connections to the historical, political, and aesthetic circumstances of its own production. The comparison I have been presenting up to this point, based on formal similarities between *Chinatown* and tragedy, maintains the approach for which I criticize Sobchack. As Hans Robert Jauss says: "Even the most highly developed practice of comparison tells us neither what should enter into the comparison (and what not), nor to what end. The relevance and thereby the selection of the comparison cannot be drawn directly from the compared elements themselves; even when in the end significance apparently 'springs out' on its own, it nonetheless presupposes hermeneutically a preconception, however often unadmitted."[29] Formal or "timeless" comparison appears to be "a high-level dialogue between illustrious spirits, with the philologist only needing to eavesdrop in order to understand" (112). But this apparently objective procedure ignores the historical processes of "preservation, suppression, and omission" which are part of all "formations of tradition" and the process of "approval as well as disapproval in which the judgment of the particular present either takes over or gives up past experience, either renews it or rejects it" (112). To avoid the reductiveness of the timeless comparison, Jauss argues, an interpreter must locate the individual works in their own historical contexts and also discover "the contemporary horizon of interest of the interpreter who is comparatively questioning them" (113). A classicist's "horizon of interest" will probably be the continued value of ancient themes or forms, whereas the preconception which motivates Sobchack's comparison of genre film and Greek tragedy is that the established order (social and aesthetic) must not be questioned; hence he approves of "progenitors" and disapproves of "antigenre" films.

But there are many other possible horizons. For example, the generic tradition in which *Chinatown* most obviously belongs is *film noir*. This term refers to a group of American films made in the forties and fifties; Billy Wilder's *Double Indemnity* (1944) is often considered the first, Orson Welles's *Touch of Evil* (1958) the last. Since these films cut across many of the traditional genres, critics are divided about whether to define *film noir* by its semantic loci (such as crime) or by visual style (such as high-contrast lighting, complex composition, symbolic use of camera angles), or by mood (pessimism, alienation, dread).[30] *Chinatown* includes many of the semantic features associated with different films from the *noir* period. In his fallibility and moral ambiguity Gittes resembles Walter Neff in *Double Indemnity* (1944). His dark past from which he cannot escape recalls Jeff Bailey in Jacques Tourneur's *Out of the Past* (1947). Despite his tough appearance he is vulnerable, like the characters played by Burt Lancaster in Robert Siodmak's *The Killers* (1946) and *Criss Cross* (1949; in this film a cast on his broken arm functions like the bandage on Jake's nose). Evelyn Mulwray resembles many mysterious *noir* women, from Phyllis Dietrichson in *Double Indemnity* to Vivian Sternwood in *The Big Sleep* to Elsa

Bannister in Welles's *The Lady from Shanghai* (1948). The escalation from an individual crime to a political network recalls Sam Fuller's *Pickup on South Street* (1953). The alienation of *Chinatown*'s characters, its strained, increasingly threatening mood, its sense of inevitability and its pessimistic conclusion, as well as some of its stylistic features such as framing devices (windows, mirrors, windshields, hats, veils), nonrationalized lighting, complex mise-en-scène, even its thirties-style opening credits and musical score, allude to earlier films. Other films made after the fifties also use *noir* themes and techniques, but none so consistently as *Chinatown*.[31]

Many of the formal and thematic similarities to Greek tragedy I have noted in *Chinatown*, then, can also be discerned in the original *films noirs*. And there are others. For example, many *noir* films feature extreme close-ups in which an actor's face fills the screen, producing an effect of alienation rather than intimacy. As Foster Hirsch says: "The performers most closely identified with the genre have masklike faces, their features frozen not in mid- but in pre-expression. The *noir* actor is an icon . . . embodying a type."[32] The use of low-key lighting (in which the ratio of key light to fill light is great, creating sharp contrasts between black and white) also renders characters and situations more abstract and indicates that strong, fundamental issues are at stake, that characters must choose between extreme alternatives, neither of which is bearable.

Introducing *film noir* into a comparison between *Chinatown* and tragedy triangulates and opens up the closed binary opposition. As Polanski himself said, *Chinatown*'s combination of period setting and echoes of *film noir* with seventies film techniques keeps it from being a simple imitation.[33] The use of Panavision, for example, instead of the 1.33 aspect ratio used in the forties, breaks the claustrophobia typical of *noir* films. The setting ranges beyond city streets to include natural landscapes.[34] And the film is shot in color instead of high-contrast black and white. The wide screen suggests that escape is possible, the landscapes that nature cannot be contained by Cross's schemes. Part of the film's tragic irony is created by the use of the wide screen and the views of nature to raise expectations which are then disappointed. The color scheme, muted from the beginning, gradually simplifies as the film approaches the final scene which frames white car in black night, speckled only by neon and blood. Yet the tensions between setting and technology remain.

Chinatown also swerves emphatically away from *noir* semantic conventions. Evelyn Mulwray, for example, seems a perfect *noir* "black widow," the mysterious femme fatale who uses her sexuality to entrap men and is finally revealed as a killer.[35] As if he had seen these *noir* portrayals, Gittes shows his "finesse" by doubting and suspecting Evelyn from the start, accusing her of lying and murder, but she is complex, not just deceptive. She turns out to be a victim, yet she is smart enough and strong enough to rescue Gittes twice and to defy her father, and her plan for escape would have worked except for Gittes's intervention. She is portrayed as both sensual and nurturing. Although sexually unfaithful to her husband, she speaks of him with deep emotion and hires Gittes to find his murderer. It is not only her deceptiveness but also Gittes's preconceptions about her and about women in general (for example, that the only relationship possible between women is sexual rivalry over a man) which make him unable to understand her. The representation of Chinese motifs and characters has been similarly transformed. In *The Big Sleep*, Chinese furniture and art in Arthur Geiger's house is used to signal drugs, criminality, and sexual perversity. In *The Lady from Shanghai*, the eponymous heroine has lived in China, speaks Chinese, and has a Chinese servant—all indications that she is deceptive and deadly. In *Chinatown* the female and the Oriental as Other are connected by Faye Dunaway's appearance: makeup and lighting make her look as Oriental as possible. But here the Chinese servants and the references to Chinatown, even the long joke about Chinese-style sex, say nothing about Orientals; they signal Gittes's prejudices and inability to see with any eyes but his own inadequate ones.

Similarly, in earlier films, the protagonist's individualism is prized; he can depend only on himself, and his isolation keeps him free from corruption.[36] But *Chinatown* depicts Gittes's inability to join with others as a failing. Again and again he misses opportunities to make common cause with people like Escobar, Evelyn, or the orange growers, who could give him information and help. He remains a private I: asked at one point whether he is alone, he quips "Isn't everyone?" He lumps others into categories and derides them: he makes a joke out of discrimination against Jews, calls a hood a "midget" and in return has his nose slit, calls an orange grower a "dumb Okie" and is knocked out. The point of the "Chinaman" joke—which involves a man practicing coitus interruptus "like the Chinese" with his own wife only to have her exclaim "What's the matter with you? You're screwing like a Chinaman!"—is not only that Orientals are bizarre but that women are untrustworthy. Jake likes this joke because he has already "learned" this lesson from his profession, as the opening sequence about Curly's unfaithful wife shows. The joke also indicates, quite early in the film, that expected climaxes may be deferred or avoided altogether.

On a few occasions love is proffered as a response to the bleakness of this world. "Do you love your husband?" Gittes asks the fake Mrs. Mulwray. "Of course."—"Then go home and forget the whole thing." The two scenes at Evelyn's house contain the only moments of tenderness and relaxation in the entire film, but Gittes and Evelyn are too scarred and too scared to love. In bed she asks him about himself, but he brushes her off. When she must leave abruptly, she begs him to stay: "I need you here. Trust me this much." Instead he follows her and breaks the security of Katherine's hiding place. In a long scene in her car, she tells him, with great difficulty, that Katherine is her sister. This crucial scene, the hinge of the entire film, epitomizes Gittes's inability to go beyond appearances ("That's not what it looks like"), his acceptance of easy answers (for example, her too-quick agreement to his suggestion that she is maintaining secrecy because of her sister's affair with her husband), and his distrust of genuine, complex emotions. When she speaks of her husband and weeps, Gittes pulls away and gets out of the car; she asks him to come home with her. With the car window separating them, his lower face in shadow, he refuses: "I'm tired, *Mrs. Mulwray*," implying that she's only interested in sex. Evelyn's death is explicitly foreshadowed in this scene: "I don't want to hurt you," says Gittes, and in pain she drops her head forward onto the steering wheel, sounding the horn. In the final scene, the car in which she is taking Katherine away speeds directly away from the camera down the dark Chinatown street. After Loach fires, the moan of the horn is the signal that his bullet has found its mark. The interconnections between these two scenes indicate that Gittes's inability to make connections with others destroys Evelyn, hurts himself, and keeps Noah Cross in power.

The film's critique of traditional masculine behavior and individualism reflects the social values celebrated during the decade previous to the film's production. The explicit political focus of *Chinatown* also marks it as a film of the seventies, distinguishing it from the concentration on individual and domestic problems usually found in *film noir*. The conspiracy is depicted in much more specific terms than in those in Fritz Lang's *The Big Heat* (1953) or in *Pickup on South Street*. Noah Cross's greed and lust for power may be primeval, but capitalism is shown as the justification for and institutionalization of individual rapacity. And the plot's foundation in specific historical events, however transformed, counterbalances the film's mythical and allegorical tendencies. Depicting 1937 through the lens of seventies film technology and socio-political attitudes does not take *Chinatown* out of history into some timeless place. Instead, it puts 1937 and 1974 in a dialectical relationship which evokes both continuities (capitalism, corruption) and discontinuities (gender roles, attitudes toward race). Thus the film problematizes the relation between present and past just as it does the relation between sight and knowledge. Considered as an historical document, moreover, *Chinatown* suggests that "history" is not some abstract truth but rather an attempt to confer meaning and permanence on immediate events by presenting them in an appropriate aesthetic form.

To counteract the "timeless comparison" dismissed by Jauss, Fredric Jameson suggests that immanent formal analysis of an individual text be coordinated with "the twin diachronic perspective of the history of forms and the evolution of social life. . . . The third variable in such analysis is necessarily history itself, as an absent cause."[37] Trying to find *Chinatown's* "absent cause," I might note that it was the first film Polanski made in America after his wife's brutal murder and the sensational treatment of that event in the press. In his autobiography he writes of his anger, guilt, and pessimism, and calls Los Angeles, the site of the murder, the most beautiful city in the world, "provided it's seen by night and from a distance."[38] In terms of American history, 1974 was the year in which revelations about involvement in criminal activity, misuse of funds, and a massive cover-up conspiracy forced, for the first time in history, the resignation of a president of the United States. And in 1974 the United States was enmeshed in a politically and morally questionable war which was costing money and lives and dividing the country. It was a war which the mysterious Oriental enemy did not wage according to Western ideas of confrontation; a *bellum interruptum* with no definitive climax, it was apparently never going to end. Gittes's mixture of altruism and selfishness, his misplaced heroics, and his inability to get beyond his own limited perspective make him a figure for American involvement in Vietnam.[39] American leaders' inability to comprehend a culture completely different from their own and to learn from the past led to a repetition of many of the mistakes made by the French colonial powers there.[40] The genre of American history has traditionally been romance; *Chinatown* rewrites it as tragedy, but deprives us of the "catharsis."

Like film, ancient drama gains meaning when located in its historical context. The use of myth in Greek tragedy, for example, is often seen as a technique for avoiding particular political and ideological meanings. But dramatists shaped myths to suit their particular ends. Like *Chinatown*'s period setting, the use of myth establishes a complex, ironic relationship between present and past, between Athens and (for example) Thebes, between the Peloponnesian War and the Trojan War, between audience and characters. Bernard Knox observes: "The audience which watched Oedipus in the theater of Dionysus was watching itself," and Jean-Pierre Vernant has said of tragedy's dialectic that "tragedy is born when myth starts to be considered from the point of view of a citizen. But it is not only the world of myth which loses its consistency and dissolves in this focus. By the same token the world of the city is called into question and its fundamental values are challenged by the ensuing debate."[41]

Other considerations are raised by juxtaposing contemporary films with ancient dramas. First, the very abundance of films means that any individual film must be considered in the context of others—in a generic tradition—rather than in isolation. And the abundance may remind us that the surviving works of tragedy are only a small fraction of the total corpus, that our judgments of surviving plays need to be tempered by whatever information we can obtain about lost works. Second, having resources which are not available for ancient drama, such as accounts of those involved in making a film, audience and critical responses, and detailed historical information from various sources, may make us aware of the multiplicity of factors which influence a work's meaning and question positivistic and univocal readings. Third, film reminds us of the importance of thinking about drama as performance. For Aristotle, as for many modern academics, performance is unimportant; drama means only the literary text.[42] The equivalent in film criticism would be to ignore the finished film while discussing only the screenplay. Particular aspects of ancient drama, such as the use of masks, often described as lifting the particular action to a transcendent, universal plane, also need to be reconsidered. Considering critics' insistence on tensions between various aspects of film, we might postulate a similar tension in the performance of tragedy—for example, between the intense emotion expressed by the voice and the still façade of the mask, between the mythical character and his embodiment by a living actor.[43]

Finally, many of the features which I have evoked, often considered as items in a flat Aristotelian checklist, are precisely those which prohibit closure. Characters' moral ambiguity and a complex web of causality preclude resolution into binary oppositions, such as guilt/innocence, free will/predestination, and avoid the danger endemic to tragedy of degenerating into melodrama.[44] Epistemological questions and reminders that the audience's vision is as flawed as that of the characters raise questions about the status of the film as a way of knowing, and indicate that the audience uses the work to produce its own meaning. The film's conclusion, too, like those of many tragedies, sustains rather than resolves the questions it has raised about responsibility and justice. Polanski did not want to induce "calm" in his audiences; Towne's original script called for Evelyn to kill her father and escape to Mexico with her daughter, but Polanski insisted, "if *Chinatown* was to be special, not just another thriller where the good guys triumph in the final reel, Evelyn had to die. Its dramatic impact would be lost unless audiences left their seats with a sense of outrage at the injustice of it all."[45] Despite the director's expressed desire for straightforward reaction, however, the very last shot of the film is not didactic. As the camera rises for the only crane shot in the film, Gittes, now very small, walks away from disaster down the dark Chinatown street. The audience is thus offered the "Olympian" position of distance and superiority to Gittes which he took earlier in the film, but here again such distance literally keeps us from seeing clearly as he disappears into the darkness of both Chinatown and *Chinatown*. This film suggests that real knowledge, personal and political, is gained not by abstraction but in immediate interactions. This apparently abstract idea clearly marks *Chinatown* as a film of the seventies.

Identifying "tragedy" as a transhistorical entity misses the point that genre, like an individual work, is located within history. "The existence of certain genres in a society and their absence in another reveal a central ideology, and enable us to establish it with considerable certainty. It is not chance that the epic is possible during one era, the novel during another . . ." observes Tzvetan Todorov, and Jameson concurs that the presence or absence of a particular genre at a particular historical moment "alerts us to the historical ground . . . in which the original structure was meaningful."[46] What historical ground can be identified in fifth-century Athens in which tragedy was meaningful? This ground will, of course, include a variety of factors whose interactions with individual texts should be worked out in detail, as I have here tried to do for *Chinatown*.[47] But there is an interesting parallel between 1974 America and the Athens of the late fifth century, the era from which most of the surviving tragedies come. Each of these states had been the glorious leader in a war which led to the defeat of a power conceived as formidable and evil. Each had then become embroiled in a war in which the enemy was no longer the alien Other, a war which deeply divided the populace and raised questions about the ethics of leaders and the moral foundation of the state itself. Are these not historical grounds in which human vision is likely to be seen as flawed, in which cruelty and self-interest will be seen as stronger than love or compassion? Are these not circumstances in which considering individual human agency completely responsible for the course of events would be morally unbearable? If instead events are seen as directed or influenced by superhuman forces, inscrutable and malevolent, according to fixed and irresistible patterns, will this not provide some psychological and political absolution?[48]

Notes

1. For an overview of genre criticism, including references to the work of contemporary critics, see Heather Dubrow, *Genre* (London: Methuen, 1982). Even Fredric Jameson, who dismisses genre criticism as "thoroughly discredited by modern literary theory and practice," takes up the issue in "Magical Narratives," in *The Political Unconscious* (Ithaca: Cornell University Press, 1981), 103–50.

2. For discussions of genre in film see Barry Keith Grant, ed., *Film Genre Reader* (Austin: University of Texas Press, 1986); Gerald Mast and Marshall Cohen, eds., *Film Theory and Criticism: Introductory Readings*, 3d ed. (New York: Oxford University Press, 1985); Bill Nichols, ed., *Movies and Methods* (Berkeley: University of California Press, 1976); Stuart Kaminsky, *American Film Genres* (Dayton, Ohio: Pflaum, 1974).

3. Most discussions have concentrated on exploring connections between epic and the American Western; see, for example, Vincent Marston's brief "Epics and Westerns," *The Classical Outlook* 54 (1976–77): 76–79. Derek Elley, *The Epic Film* (London: Routledge, 1984), focuses not on form but content (films dealing with periods up to the end of the Dark Ages); his last chapter includes some interesting remarks on epic elements in other kinds of films.

4. See Susan Sontag's "Film and Theatre" and Andre Bazin's "Theater and Cinema" in Mast and Cohen, *Film Theory*, 340–55 and 356–69.

5. Since the nineteenth century classical scholars, heavily influenced by romanticism, have focused on the literary text as the product of individual genius. The influence of New Criticism also isolated the individual work from its historical context. *Auteur* theory in film similarly focuses on the individual talent.

6. Both Plato and Aristotle speak with disdain of tragedy's appeal to a mass audience: *Gorgias* 501–2, *Laws* 658d, *Poetics* 1462a. For audience reactions see Arthur Pickard-Cambridge, *The Dramatic Festivals of Athens*, rev. ed. (Oxford: Clarendon Press, 1988), 272–78; W. B. Stanford, *Greek Tragedy and the Emotions* (London: Routledge, 1983). For a general discussion of theories of mass culture including tragedy see Patrick Brantlinger, *Bread & Circuses* (Ithaca: Cornell University Press, 1983).

7. Recent studies which locate tragedy in its sociopolitical context are J. Peter Euben, ed., *Greek Tragedy and Political Theory* (Berkeley: University of California Press, 1986) and John J. Winkler and Froma Zeitlin, eds., *Nothing to Do with Dionysos?* (Princeton: Princeton University Press, 1990). Older studies include Victor Ehrenberg, *Sophocles and Pericles* (Oxford: Blackwell, 1954); G. Zuntz, *The Political Plays of Euripides* (Manchester: Manchester University Press, 1955); George Thomson, *Aeschylus and Athens*, 3d ed. (London: Lawrence & Wishart, 1966); Anthony J. Podlecki, *The Political Background of Aeschylean Tragedy* (Ann Arbor: University of Michigan Press, 1966); Karen Hermassi, *Polity and Theatre in Historical Perspective* (Berkeley: University of California Press, 1977). On American films in historical/political context see John Baxter, *Hollywood in the Thirties* (New York: Penguin, 1978); Charles Higham and Joel Greenberg, *Hollywood in the Forties* (New York: Barnes, 1968); Andrew Dowdy, *The Films of the Fifties* (New York: Morrow, 1973); Peter Biskind, *Seeing Is Believing* (New York: Pantheon, 1983).

8. For discussions of filmed versions of tragedy see Kenneth MacKinnon, *Greek Tragedy into Film* (Rutherford, N.J.: Fairleigh Dickinson University Press, 1986), and Jon Solomon, *The Ancient World in the Cinema* (Cranbury, N.J.: Barnes, 1978). Martin M. Winkler, "Classical Mythology and the Western Film," *Comparative Literature Studies* 22 (1985): 516–40, discusses tragic patterns in film.

9. Originally published in *Literature/Film Quarterly* 3 (1975): 196–204; reprinted in Grant, *Film Genre*, 102–13. Page references in my text refer to the latter.

10. For discussions specifically of film see Stephen Neale, *Genre* (London: British Film Institute, 1980) and Barbara Klinger, " 'Cinema/Ideology/Criticism' Revisited: The Progressive Genre," in Grant, *Film Genre*, 74–90.

11. In "Literary Genres and Textual Genericity," for example, Jean-Marie Schaeffer uses "the classical era" to refer to all literature before romanticism (in Ralph Cohen, ed., *The Future of Literary Theory* [New York: Routledge, 1989], 167–87). In "Genre Films and the Status Quo" (Grant, *Film Genre*, 41–49), Judith Hess Wright takes Sobchack's position in order to condemn genre films for helping maintain an unjust political structure.

12. Polanski demonstrated strong interest in genre in an interview shortly before the film's opening: "I want to do every genre of film—horror, Western, detective, and this is my latter!" Quoted from Tom Burke, "The Restoration of Roman Polanski," *Rolling Stone*, 18 July 1974, 42. In "The Gangster as Tragic Hero," Robert Warshow argues that the gangster film is a tragic form (in *The Immediate Experience* [New York: Doubleday, 1954], 127–33). This article raises some promising issues, but brevity and overgeneralizations limit its value. Sobchack's essay is basically an amplification of Warshow's remarks.

13. Wayne D. McGinnis, "*Chinatown:* Roman Polanski's Contemporary Oedipus Story," *Literature/Film Quarterly* 3 (1975): 249–51, makes the comparison very sketchily. Deborah Linderman, "Oedipus in Chinatown," *enclitic* (special issue, 1982), 190–203, employs Freudian theory rather than the ancient text.

14. As John G. Cawelti points out, "one of the most deeply symbolic clichés of the traditional hard-boiled formula is the hero's refusal to do divorce business. . . . By this choice the traditional private eye of the myth established both his personal sense of honor and his transcendent vocation." ("*Chinatown* and Generic Transformation in Recent American Films," in Mast and Cohen, *Film Theory*, 565). Gittes thus more closely resembles the unscrupulous "bedroom dick" Mike Hammer of Robert Aldrich's *Kiss Me Deadly* (1955) than Sam Spade or Philip Marlowe.

15. Gittes's botched confrontation inverts the typical scene in the hard-boiled plot wherein the hero confronts, hears the confession of, and sometimes executes the criminal; see Cawelti, "Generic Transformation," 562–63. In other films characters from whom information is demanded protect others by refusing to divulge it, even at the price of

beating (Candy in Sam Fuller's *Pickup on South Street* [1953]) or death (Harry Jones in Howard Hawks's *The Big Sleep* [1946]).

16. I am using the term *anagnorisis* not in the strict Aristotelian sense (recognition of the identity of persons previously unknown), but in the more general sense of intellectual and moral understanding.

17. On the complex verbal imagery in the *Oresteia*, for example, see Anne Lebeck, *The Oresteia: A Study in Language and Structure* (Cambridge: Harvard University Press, 1971), and Pierre Vidal-Naquet, "Hunting and Sacrifice in Aeschylus' *Oresteia*," in Jean-Pierre Vernant and Pierre Vidal-Naquet, *Tragedy and Myth in Ancient Greece*, trans. Janet Lloyd (Atlantic Highlands, N.J.: Humanities Press, 1981), 150–74. On Aeschylean visual imagery in performance, see Oliver Taplin, *The Stagecraft of Aeschylus* (Oxford: Oxford University Press, 1977), 12–49 and passim.

18. The walking stick seen in Cross's hand in the photographs taken by Walsh has a similar double meaning: instead of an old man's cane, it suggests both a patriarch's staff and Cross's phallic power.

19. The motif of photography as inadequate mimesis which must be interpreted and supplemented owes much to Michelangelo Antonioni's *Blow-Up* (1966), but that film is far less dark than *Chinatown*.

20. William J. Palmer's excellent discussion of *Chinatown* in *The Films of the Seventies: A Social History* (Metuchen, N.J.: Scarecrow Press, 1987), 117–78, includes an extended analysis of the relationship between the film's themes and its cinematic techniques. See also Virginia Wright Wexman, "*Chinatown:* The Generic Synthesis," in *Roman Polanski* (Boston: Twayne, 1985), 91–106.

21. For the distinction between mise-en-scène and montage editing see Thomas Sobchack and Vivian C. Sobchack, *An Introduction to Film* (Boston: Little, Brown 1980), 104–24.

22. Francis Ford Coppola's *The Conversation* (1977) is thematically the converse of *Chinatown*. In this film an eavesdropping expert learns words must be complemented by visual information.

23. As one of many analyses of Sophocles' use of verbal imagery involving sight see David Seale, *Vision and Stagecraft in Sophocles* (Chicago: University of Chicago Press, 1982).

24. Aristotle says that violence between family members most effectively arouses pity and fear (*Poetics* 1453b); in keeping with his focus on natural forms, the family is not considered a political institution.

25. The name of the engineer in charge of the Owens Valley water project, the historical event on which the plot of *Chinatown* is based, was William Mulholland. Unlike Mulwray, Mulholland was the prime mover of the project; he is memorialized as a founding father of modern California. Towne used Carey McWilliams, *Southern California Country: An Island on the Land* (New York: Duell, Sloan & Pearce, 1946), as his source; for a full discussion of the project see William L. Kahrl, *Water and Power* (Berkeley: University of California Press, 1982).

26. See Cawelti, "Generic Transformation," 567, and Garrett Stewart, "*The Long Goodbye* from *Chinatown*," *Film Quarterly* 28 (1974): 25–32.

27. Casting John Huston as Noah Cross has significant intertextual overtones: Huston had portrayed a folksy, comic Noah in his own film *The Bible* (1966).

28. This is Stewart's view in "*Long Goodbye*," 30–32.

29. Hans Robert Jauss, *Toward an Aesthetic of Reception*, trans. Timothy Bahti (Minneapolis: University of Minnesota Press, 1982), 110; further page references will be cited in the text.

30. As examples of each of these types of definition, see Foster Hirsch, *The Dark Side of*

the Screen: Film Noir (New York: Barnes, 1981). 167–97; J. A. Place and L. S. Peterson, "Some Visual Motifs of *Film Noir*," in Nichols, *Movies and Methods*, 325–38; Robert G. Porforio, "No Way Out: Existential Motifs in the Film Noir," *Sight and Sound* 45 (1976): 212–17.

31. *Farewell, My Lovely* was remade in 1975, *The Big Sleep* in 1978, *D.O.A.* in 1988. *Against All Odds* (1984; based on *Out of the Past*) and Robert Altman's *The Long Goodbye* (1973) so radically changed their sources that they have little connection with *film noir*. *Body Heat* (1982), *Blood Simple* (1983), and *Black Widow* (1987) also show strong *noir* influences. Of these only *Farewell, My Lovely* is set in period.

32. Hirsch, *Dark Side of the Screen*, 146.

33. "I saw *Chinatown* not as a 'retro' piece or conscious imitation of classic movies shot in black and white, but as a film about the thirties seen through the camera eye of the seventies. . . . I wanted the style of the period conveyed by a scrupulously accurate reconstruction of decor, costume, and idiom—not by a deliberate imitation, in 1973, of thirties film techniques." Quoted from *Roman by Polanski* (New York: Morrow, 1984), 349.

34. Rural settings are rare in *film noir*. When they do appear they usually suggest an ideal which the doomed protagonist cannot attain, as in Tourneur's *Out of the Past*, and the finale of Huston's *The Asphalt Jungle* (1950).

35. See E. Ann Kaplan, ed., *Women in Film Noir* (London: British Film Institute, 1978).

36. See Cawelti, "Generic Transformation," 561–64.

37. Jameson, "Magical Narratives," 105 and 146.

38. *Roman by Polanski*, 348.

39. Vietnam was certainly an "absent cause" in the cinema while the war continued; before 1975 only four American films explicitly dealt with the topic. Now films about the war appear regularly.

40. On intellectual and cultural differences and their effect on policy see Frances FitzGerald, *Fire in the Lake* (Boston: Little, Brown, 1972). In *The Two VietᵣNams: A Political and Military Analysis* (New York: Praeger, 1967) Bernard B. Fall observes that the 2,000-year history of Vietnam "seems destined to a course like that of a Greek drama" (390).

41. Bernard M. W. Knox, *Oedipus at Thebes* (New York: Norton, 1971), 77; Vernant, "Tensions and Ambiguities in Greek Tragedy," in *Tragedy and Myth*, 9. See also Raymond Williams, *Modern Tragedy* (Stanford: Stanford University Press, 1966), 17–18.

42. "Tragedy fulfills its function even without a public performance and actors" (*Poetics* 1450b); "when it is merely read the tragic force is clearly manifested" (1462a). Challenging this position, contemporary performance criticism examines how performance interacts with the verbal text; for a good introduction see Oliver Taplin, *Greek Tragedy in Action* (Berkeley: University of California Press, 1978).

43. See Hirsch, *Dark Side of the Screen*, 150.

44. When Evelyn reveals the incest Jake asks: "He raped you?" She shakes her head—not an unambiguous "no," perhaps, but certainly not a clear "yes." Yet a number of critics (for example, Stanley J. Solomon, in *Beyond Formula: American Film Genres* [New York: Harcourt Brace Jovanovich, 1976], 239) insists that Cross did rape his daughter, thereby reducing the complexity of both Evelyn's character and the moral situation to melodrama.

45. *Roman by Polanski*, 348. Towne himself never accepted Polanski's "relentlessly cynical" ending. Gerald Mast, in *Film/Cinema/Movie* (New York: Harper & Row, 1977), 43, calls *Chinatown* "a perfect universe of essential ugliness and injustice." Two reviewers in *Jump Cut* 3 (1974) disagreed on what they took to be the film's political message: to James Kavanaugh, it offered "a deeper and more shattering vision of bourgeois society than much professedly radical political propaganda" (1), but to Murray Sperber "Polanski's point is that we should accept Cross' mastery as total and inevitable and thus we should accept the pessimism of the film's conclusion as equally inevitable" (8). Such reactions

indicate that Polanski's violation of generic conventions succeeded in provoking his audiences. For a list of reviews, see Gretchen Bisplinghoff and Virginia Wright Wexman, *Roman Polanski: A Guide to References and Resources* (Boston: Hall, 1979).

46. Tzvetan Todorov, "The Origin of Genres," *New Literary History* 8 (1976): 164; Jameson, "Magical Narratives," 146.

47. The relationship between democracy and tragedy has been a frequent focus of discussion; see, e.g., Friedrich Nietzsche, *The Birth of Tragedy;* Thomson, *Aeschylus and Athens;* M. I. Finley, *The Ancient Greeks* (New York: Viking, 1964); Gerald F. Else, *The Origin and Early Form of Greek Tragedy* (Cambridge: Harvard University Press, 1965). Just as *film noir* is often connected to American postwar guilt and readjustment anxieties, especially about gender roles, other films I would define as tragic are illuminated by being located in their historical context: Coppola's *Godfather* films (1972, 1976) use the family as a metaphor for the disintegration of American society during the Vietnam era, and John MacKenzie's *The Long Good Friday* (1980) reflects the impasse created in Great Britain by Thatcherite policies, especially the stance toward Northern Ireland.

48. I am grateful to David Kirk and Kenneth McKenzie of the McHenry Library at the University of California, Santa Cruz; to Janet Lorenz of the Margaret Herrick Library at the Academy of Motion Picture Arts and Sciences; to H. Marshall Leicester for access to his fine collection of *film noir;* to Daniel L. Selden, Peter Richardson, and most of all to Thomas A. Vogler for their valuable suggestions.

9 to 5 as Aristophanic Comedy

James R. Baron

College of William and Mary

T HERE has been considerable progress in the critical study of
film genres in the last two decades, including the analysis and
classification of the subgenres within the wide and diverse category of film comedy.[1] However, the actual products of creative
minds, ancient or modern, seldom fit perfectly into the schemata
which scholars devise; this is certainly the case with the film *9 to 5*
(1980).[2] Although the shenanigans of the film's three heroines are
as zany as those of the heroines of the classic "screwball" comedies
of Howard Hawks, romance plays no part in the plot, whereas it is
essential to its resolution in the "screwball" genre. *9 to 5* steals
several stock scenes from the "clown" tradition; clowning and
slapstick are, nevertheless, by no means the essence of the film,
but hold the same place as they do in the plays of Aristophanes, as
I shall point out in this paper. *9 to 5* is not predominantly "ironic"
comedy either. One does not experience the thrill of the irony of
the superior knowledge of the "divinely omniscient spectator" of
the plays of Plautus and his imitators, nor does one perceive the
ironic form of complex social-political commentary discussed by
Gerald Mast when he classifies such diverse films as Ingmar
Bergman's *Smiles of a Summer Night* (1955) and Stanley Kubrick's
Dr. Strangelove (1963) as ironic. Finally, it would certainly be
difficult to fit *9 to 5* into the branches of the "dialogue" or "literary" traditions of film comedy derived from the "high" comic
stage. *9 to 5* is a film which has some elements of most of the
above, but blended in just about the same ways as the ancient
Greek "Old" comedies of Aristophanes from the late fifth and
early fourth centuries B.C., which also share with *9 to 5* certain
other features of form and content which will be discussed in this
paper.[3]

Scholarship on Aristophanes' works has been very fruitful in
recent decades. The evidence is too limited to allow for any
universal agreement on the details of lines of influence and contact and the relative weight of its various cultural components, but
we are now aware that Attic Old Comedy was the result of a very

complex fusion of diverse ritual and festival elements which were not unique to Attica in the fifth century B.C., nor to ancient Greece or the Mediterranean basin, but are present in some form or another in almost all human societies. It is not my purpose in this paper, however, to advocate any particular position about the origins and development of Attic Comedy, but rather to demonstrate how closely *9 to 5* corresponds to an eclectic view of the form and style of Aristophanes' plays, the sort of general picture which might be absorbed by reading the most readily available translations and popular commentaries. The first part of my paper will focus on formal and stylistic aspects of the film. I hope to demonstrate that *9 to 5* matches not one particular ancient play but rather the typical features of Old Comedy which scholars have inferred from the surviving plays of Aristophanes at least as well as many of the plays of Aristophanes themselves, which are quite varied in nature.[4] The second part of the paper attempts to show that the three main female characters of *9 to 5* are not just typical Aristophanic heroes, but correspond specifically to three of the main female roles of *Lysistrata*.

I

One of the most distinctive features of Aristophanes' comedies is the outrageous, fantastic "happy idea" or "grand scheme" which provides whatever there is of a plot.[5] The happy idea may be presented to the audience in several different ways: in some plays, such as *Lysistrata* and *Frogs*, the comic heroine or hero has already conceived the scheme before the play begins and merely spells it out in the prologue and first episode; in others, such as *Wasps*, *Birds*, and *Clouds*, the hero begins the play with a plan which, however, is dropped in favor of a new option or undergoes as many metamorphoses as do the characters themselves in response to opposition and opportunities. Like *Acharnians*, *9 to 5* is in a third category: the prologue only serves to present the main character or characters, who initially have no clue about a solution to their distress, but then invent a fantastic scheme before our very eyes in the early episodes as an extemporaneous response to the forces oppressing them. In *9 to 5*, what might pass for the equivalents of an Aristophanic prologue and *parodos* (the processional ode sung by the chorus as they enter) are interwoven as the main characters are awakened at the beginning of a workday, each by a style of alarm clock appropriate to her personality, and then join the

throng of clerical workers, whose clocklike, synchronized, marching legs are emphasized by several sidewalk-level shots inter-
spersed among other morning rush-hour scenes during the
opening credits. There is also a bit of foreshadowing of the critical
role that coffee, especially spilled coffee, will play in the plot, but
there is not the slightest hint of any grand scheme in 9 *to* 5 until
the film has run through nearly half of its 110-minute length.
Contrary to Aristophanes' concentration on a single hero or heroine, the writers of the screenplay have taken great care to draw all
three of the major female characters in depth and in the context
of three different problems of modern working women: Doralee
Rhodes is a target of sexual harassment, Violet Newstead is a
victim of discrimination in opportunities for promotion and the
assignment of office tasks, and has the credit for her managerial
accomplishments stolen by her immediate supervisor (a male),
and Judy Bernly has been the victim of an immature, totally
egocentric husband whose divorce has now deposited her into the
working world without any preparation. Furthermore, as
McLeish has pointed out,[6] performance of the *parodos,* the *agōn*
(mock debate), and the *parabasis* (choral address to the audience)
could easily fill the first half of the performance time of some of
Aristophanes' plays before the action becomes frenetic. Only
when the trio is enjoying its first *kōmos* (revel), which begins with
alcohol at "Charlie's Bar" and progresses to "Maui Wowie" (a high
grade of marijuana, according to the film) at Doralee Rhodes's
apartment, does each of them muster the courage to describe to
the others her individual fantasy about overthrowing the old
order of the office in a truly Aristophanic combination of binding,
castration, and death symbols.[7] The *kōmos* of a play of
Aristophanes frequently comes near the end. It is a scene in which
the hero or heroine abandons inhibitions and often sobriety to
celebrate the restoration of the pleasures of peacetime, wine,
food, and sometimes sex, as a result of the victory of the happy
idea. *Acharnians,* however, is an exception which provides a close
parallel to 9 *to* 5. Dicaeopolis starts a celebration of the Rural
Dionysia early in the play (*Acharnians,* 237–79), but he is inter-
rupted by the reality of the threats of violence from the Achar-
nian chorus and does not complete his celebration until the end
(*Acharnians,* 1085–1234).[8] In 9 *to* 5 the joyous intoxication, good
food, and fantasizing of the first revel give way quickly to the
reality of another day's drudgery at the office; like Dicaeopolis,
these women do not drink the toast of ultimate victory until a
second revel at the end of the film.

Although their fantasies are revealed in the first revel scene, no unified plan of action begins to emerge until after the end of the next work day, when, along with forceful reminders of the injustices and irritations which they have been enduring, the accidental (at least on the conscious level) substitution of rat poison for the sweetener in the boss's coffee forces the three to extemporize responses which resemble the fantasies expressed in the revel. This is true to the Aristophanic model; as McLeish points out, the Aristophanic hero moves through a gradual progression from alienation to action in the implementation of his or her idea.[9] The three then begin a series of maneuvers which overthrow the authoritarian, patriarchal establishment and create a new order in the office, using the tools which they each understand best, as well as whatever else falls to hand, as Aristophanic heroes and heroines generally do. The scheme develops in three stages. First, they drive Mr. Hart, bound and gagged, to his own house to try to persuade him that the poisoned coffee was an accident. When that fails, they hold him prisoner (still in his own house) while trying to get the necessary evidence to prove that he is guilty of embezzlement so that they can blackmail him into accepting their story about the poison. Finally, having usurped his place at the office to conceal his absence, they begin to enact the reforms which lead to their final triumph. Once set on their course of revolt, they exult in *poneria* (the behavior of scoundrels) and in the breaking of taboos and legal and social barriers. The prime examples of such conduct in Aristophanes' plays are Dicaeopolis in *Acharnians,* who proceeds, once his own victory is secure, to take unfair advantage of others who are suffering the same distress from which he has just escaped, and Pistheteiros of *Birds,* who uses his new-found strategic advantages to establish himself as a virtual tyrant of the universe.[10] The success of the *poneria* of the three heroines of *9 to 5* also leads, in the end, to the final revel and the proclamation of the beginning of a new regime, grown directly out of their fantastic schemes in perfectly Aristophanic fashion. The nature of *poneria* and its compatibility with Aristophanic heroism will be further discussed below in the section on characterization.

Some scholars think that the *parabasis* is *the* distinguishing feature of Aristophanes' style. In addition to the function of a chorus common to all of Greek drama—to sing songs from the point of view of an ideal spectator and thus to deepen the real audience's understanding of what has been enacted and prepare the mood for what is to follow—the choruses of most of Aristophanes' plays at some point break the flow of the action of the plot to address the audience directly both as a group and through the mouth of the chorus leader. Their words are usually something of an editorial, either praising the merits of the comic poet or offering advice of a popular sort on practical social and political problems.[11] One may think it difficult to find a *parabasis* in a film in which the chorus, if one dare use that term for the roomful of clerical workers, does little but process paperwork and type, and the choral leader, Margaret Foster, is an alcoholic typist, but we should not underestimate her importance in carrying on the ancient chorus's dramatic function as both a representative and shaper of audience opinion. Although her "sure, let's all revolt," is a sarcastic sigh of resignation and a clever bit of foreshadowing rather than a call to arms, she interjects "atta girl," with increasing enthusiasm, each time one of the three main characters storms out of the office toward Charlie's Bar after a series of individual confrontations with Mr. Hart, just before the beginning of the first revel which starts the process of metamorphosis of the three from resentful workers to revolutionary reformers. It is true, nevertheless, that a proper formal *parabasis* is simply impossible in any dramatic tradition which is concerned about dramatic illusion, something which bothered the Greeks very little.[12] If, however, we change our focus from form to content, we find at least one genuine Aristophanic precedent for exactly what happens in *9 to 5* in one of Aristophanes' own frequent deviations from the hypothetical structural schemata which scholars attempt to impose on his surviving works. In *Lysistrata,* the formal *parabasis,* lines 614–705, seems, to judge from the text, to have been a reversion to the kind of stripping, flashing, and "grossing out" by insults which may have been typical of the *parabases* of Aristophanes' predecessors or even competitors, or of an earlier ritual/revel procession which evolved into or at least contributed its spirit to Old Comedy. The presentation of sound advice to the citizens, however, the more usual *content* of Aristophanes' own *parabases,* is given by Lysistrata herself in the striking "wool carding" speech (ll. 567–86), a part of her debate *(agōn)* with the Athenian *proboulos* (commissioner or magistrate).[13] Similarly, in *9 to 5,* Violet Newstead leads the Chairman of the Board, as awesome a figure as a real Athenian *proboulos,* on a tour of the office as successfully rejuvenated by the women's reforms as the city of Athens is in Aristophanes' most optimistic finales. Her description of these reforms takes on a certain note of political oratory like the sudden change of tone to patriotic realism typical of

Aristophanes' *parabases* and of Lysistrata's speech to the commissioner. In formal terms, one must admit, because of its position in the film and triumphant tone it might be better to compare the tour of the office to the victory procession leading up to the final revel of an Aristophanic comedy.[14]

This same appeal to consider content more critical than form might also help us find the *agōn* of *9 to 5*. Whether or not the *agōn* originates in some sort of ritual combat, in Aristophanes' plays it has been transformed into a formalized verbal contest or battle of wits between two characters or between the hero and all or part of the chorus.[15] The veneer of realism of all the parts of the film preceding the first revel, mentioned above, rules out the kind of parodies of courtroom rhetoric which distinguish an Aristophanic *agōn*. In a more general sense of the Greek word, however, the entire first half of the film is a "contest" or struggle of wills between Mr. Hart and the three individual women, each with a separate cause for complaint; there are, indeed, brief moments of verbal confrontation between Ms. Newstead and Mr. Hart and Mrs. Rhodes and Mr. Hart, and these intensify into two separate major confrontations of an agonistic character after the discovery that Ms. Newstead's promotion has been denied. Ms. Bernly, meanwhile, is drawn into the struggle by her sympathy for Ms. Delgrado, a typist fired for revealing her salary, a violation of her rights of free speech. Although previously isolated by false impressions of one another in the first part of the film, the three women discover a common bond in their shared feeling of oppression at the beginning of the first revel, the centerpiece and turning point of the film, which follows immediately after these confrontations. During the afternoon after the day on which the collapse of his office chair saves Mr. Hart from drinking coffee accidentally "sweetened" with rat poison, each of the three women attempts to use persuasion to defend their collective innocence, but Hart refuses to listen long enough for a true *agōn* to develop, even though the heroines' very survival or freedom seems to be at stake, as is the case in a typical Aristophanic *agōn*. Thus, not only the modern expectation that the dramatic illusion be preserved, but also the tripling of the heroines has altered and expanded the manner in which the typical material of an *agōn*, the essential conflict of the drama, is presented throughout the first half of the film.

The Aristophanic hero or heroine has to deal with several specific kinds of antagonists. The three most important types are The Old King, The Imposter, and The Informer.[16] The Old

King is the leading representative of the oppressive old order, who must be driven out, defeated, emasculated, or slain to make room for the new season of happiness. The Imposters impede the progress of the happy idea in various ways: some resist its advance in the name of the old order, but others try to turn the success of the hero to their own selfish advantage. Informers do what the term implies: they spy on the hero for the sake of the antagonists of the scheme. *9 to 5*'s Old King is Mr. Hart, who also fulfills the Imposter role by stealing credit for the "color coding of accounts" idea developed by Ms. Newstead. Rosalind Keith, Mr. Hart's administrative assistant, is a genuine Informer who nearly nips the plot in the bud and is suppressed by being sent to Aspen for French lessons, just as the Athenian informer is crated and shipped like a precious vase to Boeotia by Dicaeopolis in *Acharnians,* 910–58. The slapstick scenes between the hero and his or her adversaries which are typical of the second half of Aristophanes' comedies are exactly where they should be in *9 to 5*: the hilarious theft and return of the anonymous corpse mistaken for Mr. Hart's, his subsequent abduction and escape attempts, not to mention the later snags such as the constant delays in acquiring the Ajax Warehouse inventory, the return of Mrs. Hart and Judy Bernly's ex-husband, and Mr. Hart's refilling of the warehouse, which are all typical Aristophanic threats to the happy idea and are met with an increasingly confident application of *poneria* by the trio.

In spite of the problems presented by Mr. Hart's attempt to restore himself to power, the three women win their victory and celebrate the festive achievement of "fantasy triumphant" (McLeish's term) in a second revel worthy of Aristophanes' final scenes, enjoying a bottle of champagne expropriated from their ex-boss in his former office, soon to be officially occupied by Ms. Newstead upon her promotion. The credits begin to roll by with a series of text-shots which present, in the time-honored style of *Dragnet,* an account of the aftermath, a set of transformations as mythic and Aristophanic as the play-long metamorphoses of the main characters of Aristophanes' *Birds*. Mr. Hart is transferred to Brazil, where he is kidnapped by a tribe of Amazons. (Aristophanes would have loved such mythical-geographical confusion). Doralee Rhodes achieves fame to the point of heroic immortality as a country-western singer; since the part is played by Dolly Parton, this amounts to a humorous violation of dramatic illusion, not unlike some of Aristophanes' references to the real people of Athens in the original audience or cast. Finally, in accordance with the great efforts which F. M. Cornford exerted to find some slim evidence of a *hieros gamos* (a sacred marriage of the new king and queen) at the end of every Aristophanic comedy, it should be pointed out that the text-shots reveal that Judy Bernly joins in a *hieros gamos* of sorts with the Xerox representative.[17]

One cannot, of course, make any comparison to the plays of Aristophanes without dealing with Greek Old Comedy's abundance of sexual and scatological humor and slang.[18] *9 to 5* has no shortage of the sort of material that many people take as the first meaning of the adjective "Aristophanic." Near the beginning of the film, Ms. Newstead expresses her opinion of her boss by holding a manila folder over the nameplate on Franklin Hart's door so that only the letters *F* and *ART* are visible and responds to Rosalind Keith's orders to post an oppressive, authoritarian memo with "I know just where to stick it." She also suddenly and unexpectedly tells the innocent, friendly candy striper at the hospital: "Piss off!" Mr. Hart's favorite expression of surprise is "holy shit!" (He encounters numerous surprises in the course of the film). Upon her return from six weeks of intensive French lessons, Rosalind Keith discovers the three heroines celebrating the overthrow of her boss and says, "holy *merde!*" The most prominent sexual theme is castration.[19] Mr. Hart welcomes Ms. Bernly to the company with a speech about the teamwork needed to "cut the balls off the competition," which is exactly what the team of three women do to him, metaphorically and symbolically speaking. Doralee Rhodes responds to her discovery that Mr. Hart has been making false claims of his success in having an affair with her with a threat to get her pistol from her purse and metamorphosize him "from a rooster to a hen with one shot." Her rapid, slashing gestures while saying this also graphically emphasize the nature of the threat. When she has usurped his identity by forging his signature to enact the reforms in the office, she conceals his absence from Rosalind Keith by leaving a burning cigar, a traditional symbol of male potency, on his desk, and then stubs it out when the ruse succeeds. Furthermore, anyone familiar with scholarly debates about the wearing of oversized leather phalluses during the original performances of Aristophanes' plays should not be startled by the position and angle in front of his fly at which Mr. Hart holds the bottle of champagne presented to him by the Chairman of the Board, a prize which he soon surrenders to Mrs. Rhodes as his emasculating defeat is completed.[20] Mrs. Rhodes, upon learning that her co-workers think that she is having an affair with Mr. Hart, exclaims, "They think I'm screwin' the boss!"—an echo of Ms. Newstead's earlier "she is bangin' the boss" with its truly Aristophanic alliteration. The paperback novel derived from the filmscript contains many more examples of castration, phallic, and ejaculation humor and explicit sexist remarks by both male and female characters, but I have not been able to examine a working script to determine whether these items are the scriptwriters' ideas, perhaps cut to maintain a PG rating, or whether they are additions by the novelist.[21]

Other elements of Aristophanes' complex techniques for eliciting laughter are also present in the film. Not surprisingly, the three fantasies of the *kōmos* each parody a major film genre: jungle adventure films, Westerns, and animated cartoons, but there are also several points of parody of stage tragedy, which is one of Aristophanes' favorite targets.[22] During the argument between Ms. Newstead and her son regarding marijuana, he says, "She [Grandmother] doesn't understand moderation" and "Harm springs from excess," Apollonian maxims from the ideological web of Greek tragedy which the three women exult in breaking during their first revel in the same manner as Dicaeopolis of *Acharnians* and Pistheteiros of *Birds* violate social restraints in exhilaration at the success of their schemes. Another genuinely Aristophanic moment is the mock-tragic crescendo of fears for the future spoken at the hospital by the panicky Ms. Newstead, which culminates in the bathos of "I'm no fool—I've killed the boss—you think they're not going to fire me for a thing like that?" The effect closely matches the sudden change of tone at the end of the mock-tragic dialogue in *Lysistrata*, 706–15: after lamenting in the most tragic of terms and poetic styles the dangerous loss of resolve to continue the sex strike among her corps of Athenian women, Lysistrata suddenly sums up the problem with the shocking word, *"binētiōmen!"*[23] There is also burlesque of myth in *9 to 5*: besides the reference to Amazons in the epilogue, Ms. Bernly's fantasy of revenge is clearly derived from the tale of Artemis (known as Diana to the Romans) and Actaeon: Hart (note the deer name), a sport hunter whose office wall is decorated with a mounted deer head, becomes the hunted as she pursues him around the office with a double-barreled shotgun after he takes refuge there to escape pursuit by the other office workers and their bloodhounds.[24] He runs helplessly back and forth, changing directions after each blast like a shooting gallery's mechanical bear.

To sum up the first half of this article, one can point out reasonable equivalents for all the important typical features of an

Aristophanic play in the film *9 to 5*. There is a fantastic plot based upon a wild scheme and dependent upon plenty of *poneria,* a *kōmos* or two, a series of *agōnes,* something resembling one of Aristophanes' own alternatives to the *parabasis,* and a thoroughly Aristophanic festive close. In addition to these structural features, one finds bawdy humor, bathos, parody of ancient myth and modern film genres, and the right kinds of antagonists. Indeed, *9 to 5* fits the formal paradigm better than many of Aristophanes' plays themselves.

II

The character types of Aristophanes' plays have been studied by scholars from ancient times down to the present.[25] Underlying the substantial variations, there remains one common thread: that the Aristophanic hero is, in varying degrees, a "tolerable scoundrel." Tolerable, partly because he or she fulfills the escapist fantasies widely attested around the world in fairy tales and especially in the comic forms of the trickster myth, and partly because the hero usually begins the play as the innocent victim of an oppressive social situation and progresses from credible idealism to fantastic *poneria* in response to highly unfair treatment or the opposition of genuinely outrageous scoundrels or imposters.[26]

This is true of all three women of *9 to 5*. Almost realistic in the first half of the film, they become as much caricatures as their opponents in the second half. Rather than compare them to Aristophanic heroes in general, I would like to argue that Mss. Newstead, Bernly, and Rhodes match quite accurately the specific characters Lysistrata, Myrrhine, and Lampito of Aristophanes' *Lysistrata.*[27] Each of the three is a different personality type, closely comparable to the personalities of the Aristophanic heroines; in both the ancient play and the film the women's individual situations bring them together in a common feeling of frustration and abuse.

Violet Newstead is Lysistrata. The heroine of Aristophanes' play *Lysistrata* is a woman of strong will balanced by careful restraint of her aggressive urges, as befits the leader of an antiwar conspiracy. She has excellent insight into the social, political, and economic realities of wartime Athens, and yet states her proposals for a solution in terms of wool-working and weaving, the basic ancient symbol of civilized femininity (*Lysistrata,* 567–86). Although her husband is not mentioned in the play, every aspect of her characterization indicates that she is a married woman approaching early middle age. In the typology of Aristophanic heroes, she is a *spoudaia* (competent, visionary yet energetic, and earnest).[28] Ms. Newstead is a widow with four children who has repeatedly lost promotions to less qualified men in spite of her "anything men can do, I can do better" spirit, demonstrated by her competence at everything from installing garage door openers to reforming office procedures and working conditions. She does not dominate the action as Lysistrata does, since the film spreads out its social concern over several different problems plaguing the women of the office, but she is clearly the leader of the group, even when they are carrying out Doralee Rhodes's or Judy Bernly's ideas. It is true that her panic, when she thinks that she has accidently poisoned the boss, goes far beyond the doubt of self and gender group which Lysistrata expresses in the mock-tragic speech mentioned above (*Lysistrata,* 706–15), but it exemplifies the same moment of human weakness exhibited by many of Aristophanes' heroes when their survival or that of the grand scheme seems to be in danger. The film's concluding shots emphasize the irony of her brief panic by running a flashback of her flight through the hospital with the corpse on the gurney while juxtaposing a text which states that she was promoted to Hart's job "because of her ability to remain calm under pressure." Her usual character is better demonstrated by the poise and confidence with which she escorts the Chairman of the Board in a "victory procession" around the reformed office while the defeated Hart trembles in fear even as he is receiving credit for the rejuvenation and revitalization of the office, which have actually been the result of the women's efforts. Athena, a goddess who is patroness of many traditionally masculine crafts and skills and exhibits a personality much like Lysistrata's, would be proud to call Ms. Newstead "sister."

Ms. Newstead's fantasy is presented third at the first revel. It is a Disneyesque fairy tale, "gruesome but cute," as she herself describes it, which grows straight out of the most demeaning aspects of her job. Hart treats her, the senior supervisor of his staff, like an errand girl by making her fetch coffee for him and blames her, rather than the maintenance men, for a constant problem with his office chair, and yet she must do her motherly best to protect the rest of the office staff from other injustices. She therefore imagines herself adding some unspecified crystalline substance from a secret compartment in her ring to Hart's coffee, enough to dissolve the spoon instantly. As the coffee begins to take effect on him, she uses the chair as an ejector seat to hurl him out the twelfth-floor window to the cheers of Bambi, Thumper et al.[29] (All three fantasies involve inflicting upon Hart a violent death involving emasculation, binding, or ritual expulsion like a scapegoat, which is reminiscent of the overthrow of the Old King of the gods in myth.)[30] The rest of the workers, seen in a medieval dungeon, find their chains dropping off as their fairy godmother announces their liberation, just the effect that the "real" reforms later produce.

The next day, distracted by her rage at yet another instance of degrading treatment by Hart, Ms. Newstead carelessly picks up a box of rat poison when she is intending to add "Sweet and Skinny" to Hart's coffee, but, ironically, Hart's defective chair saves him as he tips over backward and spills his coffee without drinking any. When she discovers her mistake, her uncharacteristic panic sets in motion the events which force the women to conspire for their common defense, which in turn leads to the birth of the grand scheme.

Judy Bernly resembles Myrrhine, who is the centerpiece of the most outrageously hilarious scene of Aristophanes' play (ll. 845–1013).[31] Under the direction of Lysistrata, this young woman alternates between flirting with and stalling her amorous husband Kinesias, running off on errand after errand to fetch a bed, a mattress, a pillow, a blanket and perfumes. Her strength of will, however, prevails, and once she has Kinesias' oath to work for peace, she runs off again, keeping her oath to abstain from sex until peace is accomplished and leaving her thoroughly aroused husband unrelieved. Ms. Bernly is attractive, but otherwise an "ordinary housewife," perhaps even a bit atmospherocephalic at first. Very seriously disoriented by the change in lifestyle which her husband's misconduct and the resulting divorce have forced upon her, Ms. Bernly, like Myrrhine, nevertheless finds hidden resources of strength when the chips are really down: when the others are panicking over the discovery that they have the wrong body in the trunk, she shouts them back into order; when her husband attempts to seduce her into a reconciliation, she at first wavers and invites him to lunch the next day, but then sees through his egocentric emptiness and casts him out, the effect on the male being at least psychologically like that of Myrrhine's stalling and ultimate rejection upon the painfully ithyphallic Kinesias. When Hart nearly escapes from his imprisonment, she beats him back into submission—with a pillow, one of the several bedroom items used by Myrrhine in the discomfiting of Kinesias. Her fantasy, which begins with the parody on the myth of Artemis (Diana) and Actaeon mentioned above, shows a side of her personality very different from anything depicted earlier but is in accord with an Artemis-like combination of innocence, reserve, and unrelenting viciousness when angered, and her drill-team twirling of the shotgun recalls the hunter-goddess's archetypal skill with the bow.[32] At the end of the fantasy, Hart is found crouching on a toilet seat like the bewildered men on chamber pots early in Aristophanes' *Ecclesiazusae,* and she accomplishes his final "dethroning" with a single point-blank shot; the squatting, hunched over posture which Hart assumes to try to protect himself, and the next scene, showing his undamaged head mounted in place of the deer's on his office wall, indicate that her aim was not "right between the *eyes.*" Back in reality, late in the afternoon on the day after Hart's emergency trip to the hospital, when chaos breaks out in the office, she does indeed stop his escape (after she, in her naive sympathy, had loosened the telephone cord by which Mrs. Rhodes had bound him) by emptying Doralee Rhodes's revolver at him, although only the office windows and furnishings suffer ill effects.

Doralee Rhodes is the perfect Lampito, the Spartan representative to Lysistrata's conspiratorial council. Her Doric dialect, robust physique, and rural aphorisms were well calculated to draw laughter from the ethnic prejudices of the Athenians; in some ways she might be considered the ancient equivalent of a Polish joke. Doralee Rhodes is the least credible of the three main female characters at the beginning of the film: the scriptwriters have allowed a bit too much of the "Daisy Mae" caricature of the sexy but pure country girl into their efforts. Dolly Parton's Earth Motherish figure has obvious relevance to lines 79–83 of *Lysistrata.*[33] As a Texan, she is exposed to the same kinds of bigotry which the Athenians held against the women of Sparta and other Doric Greek regions, most notably a stereotype of excessively bold, "unladylike" behavior and outlandish speech patterns. Prejudices of ignorance and rusticity about speakers of the southern dialects of American English are so prevalent in other parts of our society that it is only appropriate that Douglass Parker's translation of *Lysistrata* has Lampito speak in a stereotypically hill-billy style; the Jack Lindsay version has her speak Scots dialect, reflecting parallel biases on the British Isles.[34] As far as behavior is concerned, *Dor*alee Rhodes also shows *Dor*ic traits parallel to those hinted at in *Lysistrata*: in line with the "hick" stereotype which the Athenians had of the Spartans, she drives a pick-up truck and drinks beer while the others have more urbane Margueritas or Daiquiris; she is an accomplished rodeo athlete, matching the reputation of Spartan women for athletic competition in public; and she dresses a good bit more boldly than the other office workers, corresponding to the somewhat more revealing character of the Doric *peplos* in contrast to the Attic *chitōn*. Finally, she and her husband seem to have a quite open and equal, albeit unpolished and uninhibited, relationship of a sort found frequently in rural societies, including ancient Sparta.

Mrs. Rhodes's fantasy is an all-out role reversal in the form of a rodeo followed by a barbecue during the course of which Hart is first sexually harassed to the point of emasculation, then calf-roped and hog-tied, and finally roasted, bound to the shaft of a Texas barbecue spit. As in the other women's fantasies, there is enough castration, binding, and "ritual slaughter of the old god" material in these few shots to fulfill every aspect of the hypotheses of not only F. M. Cornford and the other members of the Cambridge School but also the Freudians and neo-Freudians regarding ritual and psychological origins of drama. When the actual overthrow of Hart begins (after her previous threat of castration by pistol shot, mentioned above), he is indeed bound up twice by Mrs. Rhodes: first, he is briefly tied like a rodeo calf in his own office, and then he spends six weeks in a straitjacket which combines features of harness-making from Mrs. Rhodes's expertise with horses with Ms. Newstead's mastery of garage door openers into a perfect parody of the deus ex machina of the theater of Dionysus in Athens, whose perilous operation is commented upon by Trygaeus during his flight on the dung beetle in Aristophanes' *Peace* (ll. 82–176).[35] Similar bindings of males by women occur in *Lysistrata*, 530–38: the commissioner, an ineffectual authority figure parallel in many respects to Hart, is bound with veils and crowned with symbols of death; and in *Thesmophoriazusae*, 929–1015 Euripides' relative Mnesilochus is tied to a plank, the ancient Attic equivalent of handcuffing. Mrs. Rhodes, meanwhile, follows the archetype of the Earth Mother even further by usurping the fallen male's power—perhaps even his identity—by buying the equipment for his binding with his own "Master" card and forging his signature on the memos which announce the first reforms in the office. It is, in fact, this first small step to improve conditions which moves the trio from purely defensive plotting into active usurption of Hart's place in the office and makes possible the positive side of the scheme, the total rejuvenation of their working environment.

The men of the film are caricatures from the beginning and remain such, which is typical of Aristophanic villains such as Lamachos *(Acharnians),* Cleon (as the Paphlagonian in *Knights*), Socrates *(Clouds),* and Cleisthenes *(Thesmophoriazusae).* The women undergo a metamorphosis from credible, albeit stock, characters to caricatures as they pass from helpless suffering through panic and despair to defensive plotting and finally to positively reveling in the success of their scoundrelry. Meanwhile, they release the repressed urges and talents first expressed in their fantasies and become more and more enthusiastic in their Dionysiac smashing of barriers. (Lysistrata does not undergo so radical a transformation, since she begins the play with her plot already developing and retains a certain nobility and dignity even in triumph.) They progress from individual, distinct grievances to the application of the kind of teamwork which Hart had claimed that only real men—those who had played football—could learn. This statement comes back to haunt him through the Chairman of the Board's nonrefusable offer of a place on his company's Brazilian management team. A specific Aristophanic parallel which should be noted is the theme of the importance of pan-hellenic teamwork to rescue the Goddess Peace from the pit in which War has buried her which runs throughout Aristophanes' *Peace;* this theme receives special emphasis in the scene in which the farmers from various parts of Greece have to learn to pull together to hoist her out of the pit (ll. 416–542). But how is it that the team of heroines of *9 to 5* retain our sympathy and even excite our enthusiasm as they resort more and more to skulduggery? After all, not too many people outside the Teamsters' Union would argue that the achievement of fair working conditions justifies assault with a deadly weapon, kidnapping, illegal imprisonment, forgery, and blackmail. (Jimmy Hoffa's missing body is cited as a precedent by Ms. Newstead as she steals what she thinks to be Hart's corpse.) What is found in *9 to 5* is, as suggested at the beginning of this section, the essence of the thrill of watching Aristophanic comedy. The Aristophanic hero abandons all principles and breaks down almost all barriers or inhibitions, whether from social taboos or law, even though the revolt usually arises from and for a good cause. As in *9 to 5*, the opposition is usually left totally vanquished and often in unrelieved distress or pain at the end of Aristophanes' plays, although there are exceptions, such as *Lysistrata,* which revels in reconciliation and reunion at its finale. Cornford saw this kind of scoundrel-like behavior as the comic equivalent of tragic *hybris*: an arrogant self-assertion which leads not to a tragic fall but to the comic reversal of fortunes, in which the oppressed victim becomes triumphant.[36] Whitman argues that the Aristophanic heroes are individualists, out for their own gain regardless of the social benefits for Athens which may sometimes be a side effect of their victories, and points out how this fits the contemporary attitudes of the sophists and of Euripides, whom Aristophanes often seems to be attacking.[37] He also expounds upon the parallels between Aristophanic characterization and surrealistic art in which distortion serves to emphasize the true reality behind outward appearances.[38] But these approaches may be a little oversophisticated. It is quite likely that the appeal of Aristophanes' protagonists and of the three women of *9 to 5* is hidden in every human being's less than noble fantasies of the sort represented by such contemporary colloquial aphorisms as: "Don't get mad, get even!" and "Nothing's illegal if you don't get caught," precisely the kind of fantasies discussed by Sutton and Reckford. Reckford also revives the hypothesis of a "comic catharsis" which makes the release of these fantasies into a cleansing and purifying experience for the soul.[39]

Let me now begin my concluding comment with a reminder that I have made no claim to have proven a direct influence with these preceding comparisons, since I have no direct quotes or other unquestionable borrowings as conclusive evidence. Nevertheless, it would not surprise me to learn that the scriptwriters had some knowledge of or contact with Aristophanes' plays and contemporary scholarship about them. The point that matters is that the Aristophanic spirit is alive and well on the late-night television reruns and in video rental centers throughout the land. In this context, I want to mention one final bit of empirical evidence to support my analysis of *9 to 5* as Aristophanic comedy: when I have taught ancient comedy, nothing other than an actual performance of *Acharnians, Birds,* or *Lysistrata* has been so successful at putting the students closely in touch with the essence of Aristophanes' works as a carefully prepared screening and controlled discussion of this film. Matters such as the structural elements of the ancient plays, the character types, and the possible revelry, festival, and ritual aspects of Old Comedy cease to be abstractions learned from secondary sources and come alive when the students confront them in modern costume. The most important insights gained from viewing *9 to 5,* however, have to do with

those questions of artistic unity and audience response surrounding the metamorphosis of the Aristophanic hero from frustrated
victim to triumphant, uninhibited fulfiller of fantasies, which are
often surprisingly difficult to communicate in a discussion based
upon a printed translation of Aristophanes' plays. After viewing *9
to 5*, students better comprehend the nature of the universal
appeal of the lovable scoundrel, not just to ancient peoples or
simpler societies, but even to space age sophisticates.

NOTES

1. To those with no previous reading in this area, I suggest *Film Genre: Theory and
Criticism*, ed. Barry Grant (Metuchen, N.J.: Scarecrow Press, 1977). On a more specialized
level, there is Gerald Mast, *The Comic Mind* (Indianapolis: Bobbs-Merrill, 1974).

2. Directed by Colin Higgins, screenplay by Higgins and Patricia Resnick, story by
Resnick. In some catalogues the title is given alphabetically as *Nine to Five*.

3. For a discussion of the ways in which farce, comedy, and other forms blend in
Aristophanes see Kenneth McLeish, *The Theatre of Aristophanes* (New York: Taplinger,
1980), 15–22 and 64–66. Much of what McLeish says of Aristophanes' plays also applies to
9 to 5, but the film is not unique in this regard: K. J. Dover, *Aristophanic Comedy* (Berkeley:
University of California Press, 1972), 237–40, discusses Aristophanic aspects of Peter
Ustinov's play, *The Love of Four Colonels* (London: English Theatre Guild, 1951) and
Jacques Feyder's film, *La Kermesse héroïque* (1935). Louis E. Lord, *Aristophanes: His Plays and
His Influence* (New York: Longmans, Green, 1927), 75–175, and Alexis Solomos, *The Living
Aristophanes*, trans. Alexis Solomos and Marvin Felheim (Ann Arbor: University of Michi-
gan Press, 1974), 244–76, provide useful surveys of the high points of Aristophanes'
influence since the Renaissance. "Old" comedy refers to the style of comic drama staged in
Athens from 476 B.C. until the early fourth century B.C., in contrast to "New" comedy,
which begins in the late fourth century B.C. and has much more in common with later
situation comedy and comedy of manners. The sparse fragments surviving from the
"Middle" era indicate only a period of transition, with no distinctive or distinguishing traits
other than a possible tendency to prefer plots which burlesque myth and the disappearance of choral odes written especially for each play.

4. For two very different approaches to the analysis of Aristophanes' basic structural
design see Dover, *Aristophanic Comedy*, 66–77, and F. M. Cornford, *The Origin of Attic
Comedy* (1934; reprint, Gloucester, Mass.: Smith, 1968), 27–77. Although the theories of
the Cambridge School, including Cornford's, have been out of fashion with classicists for
some time because of their narrow focus on fertility ritual as a source of Attic drama, the
great influence of these theories upon creative writers and artists earlier in this century
continues to produce echoes in literature and film. Aristophanes' *Acharnians* and *Birds* are
the plays which best fulfill scholars' paradigms.

5. For a discussion of the progression from reality to fantasy in Aristophanes' structural design and why the happy idea is acceptable in the audience see McLeish, *Theatre of
Aristophanes*, 64–78.

6. Ibid., 50–53.

7. On the festival aspects of Old Comedy, see Kenneth J. Reckford, *Aristophanes' Old-
and-New Comedy* (Chapel Hill: University of North Carolina Press, 1987), 1:3–52 and 443–
98. For the importance of the overthrow of the old order and the binding, emasculation,

or death of the old king in the ritual theory of the origins of Greek drama, see Cornford, *Origin*, 3–55, but see also the more modern and moderate views of Reckford, 39–42, 447–48, 496–97.

8. References to *Acharnians* in this paper are based upon the edition of F. W. Hall and W. M. Geldart, *Aristophanis Comoediae*, vol. 1 (Oxford: Clarendon Press, 1906).

9. McLeish, *Theatre of Aristophanes*, 64–71.

10. See *Acharnians*, 729–958, and *Birds*, 851–1765. The edition of *Birds* used in the preparation of this article is that of Hall and Geldart, *Aristophanis Comoediae*, vol. 1.

11. See Reckford, *Aristophanes' Old-and-New Comedy*, 1:187–91 and 483–91, and G. M. Sifakis, *Parabasis and Animal Choruses* (London: Athlone Press, 1971), 7–70; also Cornford, *Origin*, 91–100, and Dover, *Aristophanic Comedy*, 49–53.

12. See Sifakis, *Parabasis*, 7–22, and William E. Gruber, *Comic Theaters* (Athens: University of Georgia Press, 1986), 11–41.

13. References to *Lysistrata* in this paper are based on the Greek edition of Jeffrey Henderson, *Aristophanes Lysistrata* (Oxford: Clarendon Press, 1987); an English version of this speech, translated by Douglass Parker, may be found in Aristophanes, *Four Comedies*, ed. William Arrowsmith (Ann Arbor: University of Michigan Press, 1969), 44–45.

14. I owe this insight to my colleague, Professor Lewis W. Leadbeater.

15. On the typical Aristophanic *agōn*, see Dover, *Aristophanic Comedy*, 66–68, and Cornford, *Origin*, 27–46.

16. See Cornford, *Origin*, 13–15 and 115–33.

17. On the sacred marriage in the ritual theory, see Cornford, *Origin*, 56–66.

18. For an exhaustive study of the sexual and scatological vocabulary of Aristophanes and its function in the plays, see Jeffrey Henderson, *The Maculate Muse* (New Haven: Yale University Press, 1975); for different views on the nature of the breaking of taboos and the religious and social reasons for this see Dover, *Aristophanic Comedy*, 38–41; McLeish, *Theatre of Aristophanes*, 93–108; Reckford, *Aristophanes' Old-and-New Comedy*, 1:14–15; also Cedric H. Whitman, *Aristophanes and the Comic Hero* (Cambridge: Harvard University Press, 1964), 209–10.

19. On the subtleties of castration and impotence vs. erection humor in *Lysistrata* see Dover, *Aristophanic Comedy*, 150–61.

20. Popping corks and champagne bottles foaming over have been symbols for sexual climax almost from the beginnings of filmmaking. As an obvious *alazōn* (braggart, charlatan) type of Imposter, Franklin Hart invites comparison to Pyrgopolynices of Plautus' *Miles gloriosus (The Braggart Soldier)* and all his later derivatives. Pyrgopolynices is threatened with castration at the end of the play, a traditional Roman punishment for adultery with a citizen's wife. For Aristophanes' Lamachus of *Acharnians* as a comparable braggart soldier, see Solomos, *The Living Aristophanes*, 78–85.

21. Thom Racina, *Nine to Five* (New York: Bantam, 1980).

22. On Aristophanic parodies of tragedy see Dover, *Aristophanic Comedy*, 72–77, 162–64, and 183–89.

23. With apologies to those whose sensibilities may be offended, the fact is that, given the grammatical voice, the desiderative form, and the crudity of the verb *binein*, as demonstrated by Henderson, *Maculate Muse*, 151–52, the only linguistically accurate and contextually appropriate translation of this word is: "We wanna fuck!"

24. Compare Ovid, *Metamorphoses* 3.138–255.

25. For a compact treatment and a convenient chart of the stock types as they appear in Aristophanes' plays see McLeish, *Theatre of Aristophanes*, 53–56 and 127–43. The comic hero, the protagonist, has been the special focus of several monographs; see Whitman, *Aristophanes and the Comic Hero* and Dana Ferrin Sutton, *Self and Society in Aristophanes* (Washington: University Press of America, 1980).

26. See Sutton, *Self and Society*, 17–33, 47–54, and 83–92, Reckford, *Aristophanes' Old-and-New Comedy*, 1:76–112, and, on the trickster myth in general, Joseph Campbell, *The Masks of God: Primitive Mythology* (New York: Viking, 1970), 267–81. The phrase "tolerable scoundrel" is Sutton's.

27. Margaret Foster, the alcoholic typist, might also be compared to Calonice, the bibulous old woman of *Lysistrata*, a stock type of ancient comedy; see *Lysistrata*, 194–208 (distribution of these lines among the various characters is subject to debate). For other examples of women and wine, see Aristophanes, *Thesmophoriazusae*, 630–761; Terence, *Andria*, 228–33.

28. See McLeish, *Theatre of Aristophanes*, 53–56. For another useful summary of Lysistrata's personality see Whitman, *Aristophanes and the Comic Hero*, 201–2.

29. See Sifakis, *Parabasis and Animal Choruses*, 73–103, on the choruses in animal costume in Aristophanes' extant plays *Wasps*, *Birds*, and *Frogs*. In the film, one should also note the brief animalization of the Xerox machine, which belches at Ms. Bernly during her first morning on the job.

30. See above, pp. 237–38 and n. 16.

31. Because of textual problems, some editors and commentators, including Henderson, attribute to Myrrhine or even Lysistrata some or all of the lines suggesting addiction to wine which I feel certain belong to Calonice (*Lysistrata*, 194–208). See above, n. 27, and also Parker's comment in the end notes to his translation, p. 89. On the meaning of the name "Myrrhine," roughly equivalent to American "Pussy," see McLeish, *Theatre of Aristophanes*, 99.

32. For evidence of these characteristics of Artemis see Ovid, *Metamorphoses* 2.401–507 (the transformation of Callisto), 3.138–255 (the death of Actaeon), and 6.148–315 (the slaughter of Niobe's children).

33. The passage in question is a somewhat sarcastic description of the very un-Athenian but stereotypically Spartan athletic physique of Lampito, the result of an active, outdoor lifestyle which her home-bound Athenian counterparts consider unladylike. The key phrase is *to khrēma tōn titthōn* (the abundance of the breasts, l. 83). We should, of course, bear in mind that in ancient Athens Lampito's part was played by a male actor in padded costume, as were all female roles; it is tempting to treat the physical description in this passage and a number of others of similar nature in Aristophanes' plays as "drag" jokes.

34. For Parker's translation, see above, n. 13; the Lindsay translation can be found in *The Complete Plays of Aristophanes*, ed. Moses Hadas (New York: Bantam, 1962), 287–328. Some years ago, within one month, CBS aired two made-for-TV specials in which fictional people who were rural, poor, and uneducated were depicted as such by a random mixture of Georgia, Carolina, and Tennessee phonetics, even though the one film was set near Sacramento, California and the other in Oregon!

35. In the novel version Ms. Newstead refers to Hart as "Peter Pan" (106), an obvious reference to the resemblance of her contrivance to the elaborate deus ex machina used to make Mary Martin fly in the stage and film versions of *Peter Pan*.

36. Cornford, *Origin*, 180–91.

37. Whitman, *Aristophanes and the Comic Hero*, 21–58.

38. Ibid., 259–80.

39. Reckford, *Aristophanes' Old-and-New Comedy*, 1:12–13, 213–14, 231–32, and 272–75. See also the criticism of the catharsis theory on the basis of the literary theories of Frye and the psychological theories of Adler in Sutton, *Self and Society*, 69–90.

The Social Ambience of Petronius'
Satyricon and *Fellini Satyricon*

J. P. Sullivan

University of California, Santa Barbara

*F*ELLINI *Satyricon* has proved something of a puzzle to some critics whose reaction to the film can hardly be construed as favorable. Classicists have been particularly troubled by its syncopation of events, its drastic redistribution of incidents among the characters, and above all, its non-Petronian sources.[1] Perhaps a reevaluation of these sources will throw more light on it. I shall argue that Fellini, faced with the battered torso of this ancient novel, with only a tenth or twentieth of it still extant, felt justified as a director and creative *translator* to supplement the fragmentary narrative with incidents and details from more or less contemporary literary and historical works.[2]

This is not to say that Fellini wished, even creatively, to "adapt" the *Satyricon* as though it were a defective film script based on a historical novel. As he himself insisted: "I've tried first of all to eliminate what is generally called history. . . . Thus the atmosphere is not historical but that of a dream world."[3] But even dreams have a certain logic and usually a consistent tone, often of fear, passivity, pleasure, or some other emotional state. And so the supplementary material is naturally drawn from congenial sources. The atmosphere may be sometimes exotic, but it is never, in any pictorial way, modern. The *Satyricon,* in any case, was an "open" work to begin with, that is to say a work consisting of scarcely related episodes, and it has been further opened by the massive textual losses in the manuscript tradition. This provided an even further stimulus to Fellini's inventive ingenuity which turned for inspiration to the scanty remains of Roman painting and sculpture, as was noticed by Alberto Moravia. It is highly appropriate that the last glimpse the audience has of the film's anti-heroes, Encolpius and Giton, is in a freeze-framed faded fresco of Pompeian colors.

What were these external, non-Petronian materials that Fellini used to flesh out the fragmentary narrative?[4] The basic plot of

Petronius consists of the picaresque adventures of the anti-hero
Encolpius and his young and fickle boyfriend Giton. An early
offence against the sexual divinity Priapus, reinforced by subsequent unwitting offences, causes the god to hound him in various
ways, just as Poseidon hounded Odysseus in the *Odyssey* and Juno
persecuted Aeneas in the *Aeneid*. The *Satyricon* is in this sense a
parody of the *Odyssey* and the *Aeneid*, but it is also a parody of
contemporary Greek love-romances. Encolpius' misadventures—
temple violation, condemnation to the amphitheater, burglary
and murder, and the flight from various avengers—are com-
pounded by his troubles with temporary companions, who try to
take Giton away from him. These are Tryphaena the courtesan,
Ascyltos, his burly and untrustworthy companion for a while, and
the devious and deviant poet Eumolpus. In Croton, living out a
dangerous confidence trick, he adds to his troubles by taking up,
as a pretended slave, with the arrogant Circe, a Roman Lady
Chatterley, who expects the inferior men she prefers to perform
well.[5] She is highly indignant when Priapus' anger induces in
Encolpius a chronic impotence with her. Onto the fantastic narrative thread, already replete with suicide attempts, elaborate
banquets, cannibalism, violence, and trickery Petronius Arbiter
could hang literary digressions relating to contemporary writers,
which Fellini had naturally to forgo, substituting instead the ex-
traneous literary and historical material which he in turn felt was
ben trovato. So he draws upon Juvenal's third satire for the de-
crepit state of his Roman tenements. He borrows medieval material about Vergil the magician for the obscene and fiery fate of the
witch Oenothea, possibly adding here an indecent motif from
Martial (3.93).[6] Encolpius in the novel had at some time been a
gladiator; this is elaborated by Fellini into the gladiatorial mime in
which Encolpius playing the part of Theseus has to fight a gladiator made up as the Minotaur in a labyrinth and then, after
winning Princess Ariadne, has to take her in full sight of a large
audience. His predictable failure and her impatient anger hark
back to Encolpius' failure with Circe in the *Satyricon,* but the scene
as a whole depends on similar episodes in the second extant
Roman novel, written about a century later than the *Satyricon,*
Apuleius' *Golden Ass* (2.31–3.11). Here the anti-hero, Lucius, has
a number of tricks played on him during a festival in honor of the
god of Mirth. For instance, he is tricked into puncturing three
wineskins filled with blood under the impression that he killed
some robbers. He is hauled off to a mock court (in a theater) to

stand trial for his life and is threatened with ghastly tortures before the farce is finally exposed to the great amusement of the assembled townsfolk. This and Lucius' forced copulation later (10.34), while he is still in ass's shape, with a condemned female criminal in the arena, presumably inspired the grotesque "public performances" that Fellini took delight in presenting in the film, most notably in the sexual encounters of Encolpio with Ariadne and then with Oenothea. This aspect of ancient entertainment Fellini could easily have found documented in J. Carcopino's *Daily Life in Ancient Rome,* one of the works he read in preparation for making the film.[7] Martial reports the executions and mutilation on stage in mythological and historical playlets, and nude spectacles by prostitutes were part of the spring rituals of the Floralia in Rome. This would have appealed to Fellini's almost obsessive preoccupation with circuses *(La Strada),* stage performances of an unorthodox kind *(Ginger and Fred),* indeed with exhibitionism in general *(8 ½),* and is not incompatible with his delight in masks. All of this surfaces in the tragic-comic mime scenes and the appearances of Vernacchio, the buffoonish actor who turns up early in *Fellini Satyricon.*

The haunting sequences of the suicides of the handsome upper-class couple in their ornate villa are based on the various stories in Seneca, Martial, and Tacitus of the deaths of Thrasea Paetus, the Stoic opponent of Nero, and his wife Paeta. Their significance in the film is not only to provide a link with the imperial world of the novel, but again to provide a play within a play—this time a tragedy, which will be quickly converted to comedy when the trio of anti-heroes arrives. At first impressed and awed by the mournful spectacle, they are soon engaged in a sexual romp with the young Oriental slave girl they find there. The mood is finally broken by the burning of the body of the master of the villa. Short though the whole sequence is, it provides a good example of how swiftly Fellini, with his eye for detail and coloring, generates a convincing atmosphere or, more generally, ambience in quite brief scenes.

One episode, which has particularly puzzled critics, is the kidnapping by the trio of a frail albino bisexual, who is worshiped as the living god Hermaphroditus, but who dies of thirst and exhaustion in the desert during his abduction. I suggest that this is based on a pseudo-Petronian poem sometimes printed along with the *Satyricon.*[8] This late piece describes the strange debate in heaven over the birth and death of Hermaphroditus: should he die by drowning, stabbing, or crucifixion? In the poem he climbs a tree by a river, transfixes himself with his own sword, and his head falls into the river with his body hanging from the tree.

There is also a possible allusion in the scene depicting the marriage of Lichas and Encolpius to the transvestite emperor Elagabalus, who reigned from A.D. 218 to 222. Born Varius Avitus, the young ruler took his name from the sun god of Emesa, Elah-Gabal, whose hereditary priest he was and whose religion he spent his short life promoting. Reaching Rome in 219, he built two enormous temples for the Oriental deity and celebrated his midsummer festival with outlandish and obscene ceremonies.[9] He and his powerful mother, Julia Soaemias, were eventually murdered by the Praetorians.

For some of the scenes involving Lichas and his "marriage" to the humiliated Encolpius, Fellini has apparently drawn not just on the *Satyricon* but also on certain anecdotes about Nero's mock marriages to his freedmen Doryphorus or Pythagoras, pruriently detailed by the imperial biographer Suetonius and also by Tacitus.[10] Again, these additions are appropriate to the Neronian setting in which the *Satyricon* itself was written.[11]

One could say more about the possible sources, but the fundamental question to be asked is, Why does Fellini allow himself these liberties? Fellini, I suggest, is using the creative translator's method of "equivalences." What cannot come across to the modern audience—for example, the literary and very topical digressions on Neronian literature with their parodies of Seneca and Lucan[12]—Fellini jettisons and substitutes often silent episodes, such as an emperor surrounded and assassinated by soldiers, a monstrous effigy of an emperor's head dragged through the streets (based on the death of Vitellius in A.D. 69), or a new Caesar, dignified and soldierly, marching on Rome. For the literary dimension, impossible to convey on the screen, Fellini has substituted a political dimension. This may be interpreted as the representation of the martial, highly masculine, Rome which the director is undercutting or marginalizing through the sexual mysticism of other, more amplified and indeed grosser, scenes in the film. Fellini has always believed that pagan Rome has certain analogies with our modern world, not least that represented by his own films: *La Dolce Vita* and *Roma*. But for him Rome as an ideal, admittedly pagan ideal, was distorted by Mussolini's fascism, which emphasized its military and organizational virtues. It was also distorted by the moralistic views of Christianity, which rejected as vice what the pagans regarded as happiness and contentment. Fellini's view of ancient and modern Rome is simultaneously pagan and pessimistic, but he is not above parodying the more optimistic alternatives. So the hermaphroditic divinity, who works miracles and is worshiped by peasants, may even be considered a parody of the infant Jesus in his manger, and the cannibalistic scene around the dead Eumolpus toward the end of the *Satyricon* has been heightened by Fellini by "elevating" the solemn reading of Eumolpus' will and the instructions for this cannibalism into a grotesque Last Supper. The Fellini aficionado may be reminded of the enormous flying statue of Christ that opens *La Dolce Vita*.

Where Fellini is astonishingly true to his model is, however, in the *atmosphere* he engenders in his film. Although more graphic and, of course, visual, than his original, he succeeds in expressing its spirit in a number of ways. A few things may be said about Petronius and his audience of which Fellini must have been aware. Here is part of Tacitus' description of Petronius' way of living:

> Gaius Petronius spent his days sleeping and his nights working and enjoying himself. Industry is the usual foundation of success, but with him it was idleness. Unlike most people who throw away their money in dissipation, he was not regarded as an extravagant sensualist, but as one who made luxury a fine art. Yet as proconsul in Bithynia, and later as consul, he showed himself a vigorous and capable administrator. His subsequent return to his old habits, whether this was real or apparent, led to his admission to the small circle of Nero's intimates as his Arbiter of Elegance. In the end Nero's jaded appetite regarded nothing as enjoyable or refined unless Petronius had given his sanction to it. [*Annals* 16.18]

Seneca, Petronius' philosophical opposite and his political rival at court, was familiar with this type of personality and in the *Epistles* severely attacked such an unnatural life-style. Such people were "night-owls"; he says of them, "they pervert the activities of day and night and they don't open their eyes, heavy from yesterday's hangover, before night begins to fall. How can they know how to live who don't know when to live? Do they fear death when they've buried themselves alive?" (122.3). Seneca argues that this depravity of avoiding the day and living at night is part of the viciousness that delights in being completely at odds with nature. It is the aim of luxuriousness to delight in perversity and in departing as far as possible from the correct way of behaving, in fact to do its opposite. Seneca points to the perverse taste for roses and lilies in winter, to transvestite affectations, and to the cultivation of gardens on rooftops (122.8).

He might also have mentioned other perversities of some of his contemporaries, not least Nero's habit of slumming, wandering from his palace in disguise late at night through disreputable parts of Rome, breaking into shops, and playing malicious jokes on whoever he encountered. This is recorded with appropriate distaste by Suetonius; other emperors and at least one Ptolemy shared this taste, and it is presumably a symptom of *nostalgie de la boue,* that longing for degradation, not uncommon in ages when material luxury and artistic sophistication seem to breed a certain decadence and a keen desire for thrills to tickle jaded palates. One thinks of the 1890s in England and France, the period of Joris-Karl Huysmans' *A Rebours* (1884)—*Against Nature* is the title of the English translation—and Oscar Wilde's *The Picture of Dorian Gray* (1891), but one could equally well think of the society portrayed by Fellini himself in *La Dolce Vita.*

The *Satyricon* has to be put in the same class as such works— indeed Huysmans specifically mentions Petronius as one of the works his hero dotes on. Here is the Duc Des Esseintes in his library:

> The author he really loved . . . was Petronius. Petronius was a shrewd observer, a delicate analyst, a marvellous painter; dispassionately, with an entire lack of prejudice or animosity, he described the everyday life of Rome, recording the manners and morals of his time in the lively little chapters of the *Satyricon.*
>
> Noting what he saw as he saw it, he set forth the day-to-day existence of the common people, with all its minor events, its bestial incidents, its obscene antics.
>
> Here we have the Inspector of Lodgings coming to ask for the names of any travellers who have recently arrived; there, a brothel where men circle round naked women standing beside placards giving their price, while through half-open doors couples can be seen disporting themselves in the bedrooms.
>
> Elsewhere, in villas full of insolent luxury where wealth and ostentation run riot, as also in the mean inns described throughout the book, with their unmade trestle beds swarming with fleas, the society of the day has its fling—depraved ruffians, like Ascyltus and Eumolpus, out for what they can get; unnatural old men with their gowns tucked up and their cheeks plastered with white lead and acacia rouge; catamites of sixteen, plump and curly-headed; women having hysterics; legacy-hunters offering their boys and girls to gratify the lusts of rich testators, all these and more scurry across the pages of the *Satyricon,* squabbling in the streets, fingering one another in the baths, beating one another up like characters in a pantomime.
>
> There are lightning sketches of all these people, sprawled round a

table, exchanging the vapid pleasantries of drunken revellers, trotting out mawkish maxims and stupid saws, their heads turned towards Trimalchio, who sits picking his teeth, offers the company chamber-pots, discourses on the state of his bowels, farts to prove his point, and begs his guests to make themselves at home.

This realistic novel, this slice cut from Roman life in the raw, with no thought, whatever people may say, of reforming or satirizing society—this story fascinated Des Esseintes; and in its subtle style, acute observation, and solid construction he could see a curious similarity, a strange analogy with the few modern French novels he could stomach.[13]

This quotation, with only few changes, could very well stand as a description of Fellini's film! *Nostalgie de la boue*, the fascination that rags hold for riches, the urge to wallow in the gutter or stoop to conquer, whether in the male desire for prostitutes or ladies' predilections for slaves, is patently mirrored in both versions of the *Satyricon*.

In Petronius, many of the scenes take place at night. The rites of Priapus are nocturnal (17); Encolpius' crime must be expiated by an all-night vigil in Priapus' honor (21); banquets go on through the night (22); Trimalchio's friend, Habinnas, in particular wants to turn night into day (73), and so the all-night feasting is prolonged by a second bath; only cock-crow breaks up the party, sending the trio wandering through the last shades of night without a torch. The ghost stories of Trimalchio and his guests, about witches and werewolves, all take place in the night (61–63). It is in darkest night on board ship that Encolpius, Giton, and Eumolpus plan their escape from their pursuers and so shave their heads by the light of the moon (103). This atmosphere of darkness, torches, and obscure, dingy dwellings and bathhouses Fellini successfully evokes in the opening scenes of the film.

This psychological complex accounts for much more than the physical atmosphere of both novel and film. It extends also to the social planes on which they operate. Again we are presented only with characters and scenes drawn from the seamier side of Roman society. One particularly interesting character is Circe, the rich and beautiful lady who falls in love at the sight of the pretended slave, Encolpius. She above all expresses *nostalgie de la boue* in her desire for sexual degradation. Here is her maid's description of her to Encolpius:

"You say you're just a poor slave, but you're only exciting her desire to boiling point. Some women get heated up over the absolute dregs and can't feel any passion unless they see slaves or bare-legged messengers. The arena sets some of them on heat, or a mule-driver covered with dust, or actors displayed on the stage. My mistress is one of this type. She jumps across the first fourteen seats from the orchestra and looks for something to love among the lowest of the low."

I said in a voice full of sweetness: "Tell me, are you the one who is in love with me?"

The maid laughed heartily at such an unlikely notion.

"I wouldn't make you so pleased with yourself. I have never yet gone to bed with a slave, and heaven forbid I should ever see a lover of mine crucified. That's for ladies who kiss the whip-marks. Even though I'm a servant, I've never sat anywhere except in the lap of knights."

I couldn't help some surprise at such contrasting sexual desires. I thought it very strange that the maid should cultivate the superior outlook of a lady and the lady the low taste of a maid. [*Sat.* 126][14]

But the theme of sexual degradation has been struck earlier in the tale of the virtuous Widow of Ephesus, who had vowed to remain faithful to her deceased husband till her own death, but falls for a common soldier and saves him by putting her husband's body up on the cross.

The incidental references in the Feast of Trimalchio to mistresses who have affairs with their slaves are not to be omitted from this general picture. This perversion of the natural order of things among the upper-class ladies is paralleled by the pathetic attempts to rise in the social scale on the part of Trimalchio and many of his friends, who hope that through the ostentatious use of their newly acquired money they can ape their betters in taste, luxury, and extravagance. The inspection of the vulgarity of the circle, on Petronius' part, is of course *de haut en bas*, and Fellini's fascination with his Trimalchio is quite unlike the amused and objective coolness which the Roman author brings to his satire, just as Fellini's fondness for the grotesque and the crippled goes beyond the cooler observation of Petronius. Examples of Fellini's eye for the bizarre and the eccentric are especially frequent in his *Satyricon*, but viewers will remember also how pervasive that element is in *La Dolce Vita*, most notably in the monstrous goggle-eyed fish dragged up from the depths near the end of the film, and the troupe of midgets in *Ginger and Fred*.[15] Nevertheless there *are* wizened and oversexed old ladies, gross male prostitutes, and a lecherous old bisexual poet in Petronius' *Satyricon* as well, and the hero himself, after all, is for much of the narrative a hopeless sexual cripple, a facet of the story that Fellini finally confronts directly in the brief scene depicting Encolpius' fiasco with the Princess Ariadne.

The social ambience, then, of Petronius' *Satyricon* is not too unlike that presented, at least in the first half of the film, in *Fellini Satyricon,* if we allow for the greater vividness and shocking detail that the modern visual medium allows and encourages. We go on an intellectual slumming tour in Petronius' company as well as in Fellini's. To observe the lower classes and the criminal elements of Roman society and to have portrayed even upper-class ladies who sink to that level excited a frisson in the highly class-conscious Roman society or, among the respectable members of the senatorial caste, a strong repugnance. Fellini's audience is wider; the differing reactions to his film are worth recalling.[16]

Granted the resemblances and differences between the Roman novel and its cinematic version by Fellini: is there a critical view expressed in Fellini's recreation of that world?

There is a school of thought represented in different nuances that tries to discern in Petronius, a man at home if not enthroned in Nero's court, an elevated and subtle satirist.[17] This critical theory is partly based on T. S. Eliot's use, as an epigraph for *The Waste Land,* of the pathetic story of the Sibyl in the Bottle as told by Trimalchio (*Sat.* 48). When asked by little boys what she wanted, she cried out in Greek: "I want to die."

Helen Bacon elaborated this into a theory about the *Satyricon* as a proto-type of *The Waste Land.*[18] She stressed Trimalchio's obsession with death, the use of food for everything except its proper purpose, money and materialism as the only shared values of the Roman society Petronius depicts, the lack of love, and the world of famine in which luxury tries to tease the satiated senses into the appearance of life. For her the Sibyl symbolizes Petronius' own Waste Land, except that to Petronius the Sibyl does not seem to suggest the possibility of rebirth when longed-for death is achieved. Against this William Arrowsmith has argued:

> Miss Bacon . . . sees that the "Satyricon" is not a symptom of a corrupt society, but a penetrating description of it, remarkably like Fellini's "La Dolce Vita". . . . But when she forces the whole book to yield that Christian, almost Manichaean, desolation of Eliot's "Waste Land," she goes . . . deeply wrong. And when, in order to support this view, she denies that the "Satyricon" is basically comedy, and that the characters are not alive, I think she is violating her text, its plain comic ambitions, and its extraordinary liveliness. . . . Miss Bacon tends to assume either that comedy and moral seriousness are incompatible or that deep gaiety and the description of cultural decay are incompatible. . . . Petronius sets his charming rascals and rogues in sharp contrast to society's greater immorality, hypocrisy, and vulgarity.

Arrowsmith points instead to a hope of which Petronius, even in the midst of so much degradation and death, never loses sight:

> If society has organized itself around the satiety that brings death, man's hope is to recover the old pagan landscape, the radiance here and now, in which everything had *numen,* and nobody needed eternal life because life itself was good and had god in it. . . . Petronius is . . . the last great witness to the pagan sense of life, and the last classical author in whom we can feel the firmness of moral control that underlies the Greek tragedians. . . . Petronius is squarely in the Latin moralist and satirical tradition—and the greatest moralist of them all.[19]

Arrowsmith's interpretation still presents Petronius as ultimately a great moralist, although now he is a *pagan* moralist, satirizing the excesses he sees in Roman society with its emphasis on luxury as a way of escaping death.

How would such an analysis apply to Fellini, particularly when we take into account not only *Fellini Satyricon* but also *La Dolce Vita* and *Roma,* all of which have much in common? Certainly Fellini has a satirical eye and an eye for the grotesque, particularly in his casting for minor roles, and a willingness to exaggerate by emphasis as well. This, incidentally, he can do very effectively with his selection of vivid, sometimes scaring, images: for instance, the handless arm spouting blood that is shown early in *Fellini Satyricon.* But what are his positives?

I suggest that he has, in common with Petronius, an amused tolerance and acceptance of life as it is lived, a willingness to face his perceived reality and an impatience with false solutions, such as Mussolini's fascism. So, like Petronius, he has more of an artist's than a moralist's eye, although *some* social comment is often implicit in his choice of themes.

We have here, then, two contrasting views of Petronius—and the analogies for Fellini are obvious. There is Petronius the complex moralist as described by Arrowsmith and others, and there is Petronius as seen by, e.g., the Duc Des Esseintes in Huysmans' novel. In the latter the comedy of life is seen as irresistible: after a while there is nothing you can do but laugh. To illustrate this point, there are several scenes which Fellini found worth adapting to illustrate this ancient theater of the absurd. References in Petronius to mimic laughter, to the world as a stage, to role-playing and disguises are frequent enough. Fellini plays up this farcical element by introducing his "underground" theater in the film's opening scene and by inventing a new character, the absurd actor Vernacchio, who farts musically, quaffs a beaker of urine, and then cuts off the arm of the pretended Muzio Scevola with a great axe.[20]

Is there a solution to this critical conflict in which Huysmans, Arrowsmith, and Fellini all seem involved? T. S. Eliot in "Tradition and the Individual Talent" (1919) alluded to the phenomenon whereby each new classic rearranged the order of all its predecessors in the great *museé imaginaire* that is Western literature. This in a way was an early and striking statement of the principle nowadays called intertextuality; every literary work has roots and connections that cannot be ignored, however hard we try to treat it as a self-subsistent work of art. Its *history* is part of its *essence*—for us, part of its *lisibilité*. And, to go even further, the reinterpretations become part of the reading we give it, either through reaction to, or sympathy with, earlier readings. This is particularly the case with the Latin and Greek classics; our heads are already full of interpretation, conscious or not, because of what we have had to do just to read them. So no text is sacred.

Interpretations then become preliminary, not unnecessary, of course, to what we nowadays call deconstruction of the work and of the author. Fellini, in a manner of speaking, "deconstructs" Petronius' *Satyricon* and, particularly in the very last shot of his film, lays out the characters in a frozen immobility which transcends the age in which it was written and renders null and void the motives that other critics have attributed to the author. This ending is a clue to one plausible interpretation of *Fellini Satyricon*. The restless cinematographic images of the sometimes inferior actors that have led us such a bewildering dance through the film—and the dance, not the dancers are at issue here—are pinned to a fragmentary mural and so are taken out of time. The random confusion of life, reflected in one way in the fragmentary state of Petronius' own text, is now given a timeless quality. The characters' story becomes history, as it were, not in a conventional sense—which Fellini has rejected anyway—but as a slice of the past held up for aesthetic rather than inquiring contemplation.

To end with a truism: the Greek and Latin classes above all have to be reinvented in every age and for every new audience. Fellini's version of the fragmentary *Satyricon* is a worthy part of that continuing endeavor, and critics' complaints about the lack of fidelity to the often uncertain text are beside the point. The text itself has many meanings; to suggest that only *one* view is the right one is itself to distort that text. Fellini's interpretation, or rather presentation, of Petronius now becomes part of the *Satyricon*'s "literary history" and its meaning for the modern reader.

NOTES

1. Among the reviews of Fellini's film the following three by classical scholars are particularly noteworthy: Gilbert Highet, "Whose *Satyricon*—Petronius's or Fellini's?" *Horizon* 12 (1970), reprinted in *The Classical Papers of Gilbert Highet*, ed. Robert J. Ball (New York: Columbia University Press, 1983), 339–48; Barry Baldwin and Gerald Sandy in *Petronian Society Newsletter* 1, no. 2 (1970): 2–3; and William R. Nethercut in *Classical Bulletin* 47 (1971): 53–59. In addition, see Alberto Moravia, "Dreaming Up Petronius," trans. Raymond Rosenthal, *The New York Review of Books* (26 March 1970), 40–42, reprinted in *Federico Fellini: Essays in Criticism*, ed. Peter Bondanella (New York: Oxford University Press, 1978), 161–68; Charles Samuels, "Puppets: From 'Z' to Zabriskie Point," *The American Scholar* 39 (1970): 678–91; and John Simon, "*Fellini Satyricon,*" in *Movies into Film* (New York: Dial, 1971), 211–19. Those interested in the making of the film may consult Eileen Lanouette Hughes, *On the Set of "Fellini Satyricon": A Behind-the-Scenes Diary* (New York: Morrow, 1971). For the published text of the film see *Fellini's Satyricon*, ed. Dario Zanelli, trans. Eugene Walter and John Matthews (New York: Ballantine, 1970).

2. It should be remembered that Fellini had a number of philological advisers for the film: Luca Canali of the University of Pisa, a Marxist, and the scriptwriter Bernardino Zapponi, who together called on the expertise of Professor Ettore Paratore, the author of a long and inconclusive commentary on Petronius. Not that these would prove any block for Fellini's imagination in his film, *Roma*, when he exercised it on the subject of Nero's Rome, which he seems to see as the substrate underlying the "eternal city" in the twentieth century.

3. Quoted from Edward Murray, *Fellini the Artist*, 2d ed. (New York: Ungar, 1985), 179. Murray's evaluation of the film as a whole is negative (182–83); he describes it as "both artistically and humanistically . . . Fellini's single out-and-out failure" (189).

4. Most of these, but not all, were spotted by Highet, "Whose *Satyricon*?" 342–45.

5. For an analysis of the character type in Latin literature see my "Lady Chatterley in Rome," *Pacific Coast Philology* 15 (1980): 53–62.

6. Thus Domenico Comparetti, *Virgil in the Middle Ages*, trans. E. F. M. Benecke, 2d ed. (New York: Columbia University Press, 1908), followed by Highet, "Whose *Satyricon*?" 343.

7. According to Murray, *Fellini the Artist*, 176.

8. E.g., in the edition of Maurice Rat (Paris: Classiques Garnier, 1938); numbered as Fragment LVII in my Penguin Classics translation: *Petronius: The Satyricon / Seneca: The Apocolocyntosis*, rev. ed. (Harmondsworth: Penguin Books, 1986).

9. Herodian, *History of the Empire* 5.8; Dio Cassius, *Roman History* 79.33 and 80.3–17.

10. Suetonius, *Nero* 29; Tacitus, *Annals* 15.37.

11. On the background of Peronius' *Satyricon* and the audience for which it was written see my *Literature and Politics in the Age of Nero* (Ithaca: Cornell University Press, 1985), 19–73 and 153–79.

12. See the chapter on criticism and parody in my *The Satyricon of Petronius: A Literary Study* (London: Faber, 1968), 158–213.

13. Joris-Karl Huysmans, *Against Nature*, trans. Robert Baldick (Harmondsworth: Penguin Books, 1959), 42–43. Huysmans had borrowed the description of Petronius' work from some edition of Adolf Ebert, *Allgemeine Geschichte der Literatur des Mittelalters im Abendland.*

14. Quoted from my Penguin Classics translation, 142.

15. For further instances see Murray, *Fellini the Artist*, 130 and passim; he also documents the many grotesque minor characters whom Fellini parades in most of his work.

16. E.g., that by Simon, *Movies into Film.*

17. Thus Gilbert Highet, "Petronius the Moralist," *Transactions of the American Philological Association* 72 (1941), reprinted in *Classical Papers,* 191–209; William A. Arrowsmith, "Luxury and Death in the *Satyricon,*" *Arion* 5 (1966): 304–31; Froma I. Zeitlin, "Romanus Petronius: A Study of the *Troiae Halosis* and the *Bellum Civile,*" *Latomus* 30 (1971): 56–82. Contrast these views with that argued in my "Petronius: Artist or Moralist?" *Arion* 8 (1967): 71–88.

18. Helen H. Bacon, "The Sibyl in the Bottle," *Virginia Quarterly Review* 34 (1958): 262–76.

19. Arrowsmith, "Luxury," 325–26 and 329–30.

20. The motif of Mucius Scaevola, the Roman hero who defied the besieging Etruscan king Porsena by burning his right hand in a blazing fire, is actually taken from Martial 1.21; cf. Livy 2.12. If this seems somewhat *recherché,* consider that in Fellini's *Ginger and Fred* the hero claims that his rhyming aphorisms were compared to Martial's epigrams by his highschool Latin teacher.

The Sounds of Cinematic Antiquity

Jon Solomon

University of Arizona

OF the traditional arts, music stands apart from painting, sculpture, and architecture in that its end product is ephemeral. Such well-known, frequently photographed master-pieces as Euphronius' Sarpedon calyx-crater and the Zeus/Poseidon statue from Artemisium still reveal their original artistry. Surface chips and fissures, missing limbs, and added support struts might impair our total aesthetic perception of an ancient objet d'art, but at least such an object exists for our sense of sight to absorb, appreci-ate, and judge. This is actually less so for ancient Greek literature. Most people who read, for example, Sophocles' *Oedipus* do so in translation since they lack the required knowledge of ancient Greek. Nonetheless, with the literary equivalent of chips, fissures, missing limbs, and support struts,[1] and in a language foreign to that in which it was originally written, the play exists in a condition quite satisfactory for both the lay public and the scholar. Modern interpretations of the drama certainly differ from one another as well as from ancient analyses,[2] but Sophocles' tragedy can for the most part be read, visualized, and even staged in a way compara-ble to its original production.

The music which accompanied the poetry of Sophocles and the other Greek tragedians, however, as well as that which accom-panied the poetic libretti of Sappho, Pindar, Terpander, and then also the tubal music which brought the Roman proconsuls home in triumph is lost, apparently and unfortunately, forever. Even if we by this time have recovered over forty fragments of Greco-Roman music, numerous fragments of *auloi* (an instrument sounding somewhat like an oboe or krummhorn), a few thousand depictions of musical instruments on vases, and a dozen ancient musicological treatises, in the end we do not know in fact what ancient Greek music sounded like.[3]

The extent of this loss should not be underestimated either in its scope or in its importance. We cannot hear how Hesiod, Ho-mer, and the other archaic epic poets sang their hexameters,[4] nor do we have the music which originally accompanied the great

264

archaic poets from whom we have considerable literary fragments. Of the approximately three hundred tragedies written by
Aeschylus, Sophocles, and Euripides we have but a very fragmentary dozen or so lines of musical "score."[5] Of Pindar and Bac-
chylides we have nothing. We have nothing either of the
"revolutionary music" of Timotheus and the late-fifth-century
avant-garde contemporaries of Euripides. We do not know what
music Plato heard as a youth, nor do we know exactly what scales
Damon must have been discussing in his ethical categorization of
music.[6] All the music to the songs of Old, Middle, and New
Comedy is completely lost.[7] Besides these lost collections of music,
many great performances were heard only once. The Delphic
performance of Sakadas of Argos, who musically described or
imitated Apollo's slaying of Python, and that of the youthful
Sophocles singing the part of Nausicaa can never again be heard.[8]

During the first few centuries of the Roman Empire, what we
might properly call archaic, classical, and fourth-century Greek
music were already passé. Only antiquarians studied the "music of
the ancients."[9] One of them, Dionysius of Halicarnassus, even
examined in a scholarly fashion a "score" of Euripides' *Orestes*.[10]
At the advent of the Byzantine era the scholarly tradition of
ancient Greek music still dominated both Western—via Boethius
(and, to a lesser extent, Ambrose and Augustine)—and Eastern
empires, but the music itself for several centuries stagnated within
the traditions and rituals associated with the Christian church. By
the time of the Renaissance, ancient Greco-Roman music was
virtually unknown as such.

For centuries this never disturbed any practitioner or scholar of
music. Even in the Renaissance, when most artists developed a
passion for things ancient, music remained confined to the style
and content of its day. The relative lack of understanding and
dissemination of the ancient Greek musical notation, which would
not be fully comprehended for several centuries yet, necessitated
this neglect.[11] While writers and painters from Petrarch to Titian
rediscovered, imitated, and expanded upon ancient texts and
artifacts, musicians for the most part would only continue and
expand upon the medieval tradition. There was for them very
little ancient music to "rediscover" or imitate.

There were exceptions, of course. Ludwig Senfl and Petrus
Tritonius attempted to engineer a genuine renascence in the
sixteenth century. Their goal was to reproduce musically the
quantitative value of ancient poetry, and they achieved respectable results even if harmonically their recreations belong not to

antiquity but to sixteenth-century chordal style.[12] The other notable exception, the Florentine Camerata's nobly intended revival
of Greek lyric monody, resulted in opera—no mean achievement
but still not ancient music.[13]

For the next three centuries, hundreds of competent and scores
of significant musical compositions celebrated mythological and
historical personages from the ancient world. In these three centuries alone there were in England, France, Italy, and Germany
over seventy different operas entitled *Dido and Aeneas*.[14] Caesar,
Dardanus, Jupiter, and Cleopatra came to life again and again.
But all the baroque, classical, and romantic composers who recreated ancient plots, characters, or subject matter contented themselves with contemporary music. That is, they made no attempt to
have their ancient characters, plots, or subject matter identified by
or associated with sounds evocative of ancient music. To hear
Lully's *Theseus* is to hear Lully, not antiquity. The same can be said
of Gluck's *Orfeo ed Eurydice*, Mozart's *Idomeneo*, Beethoven's *Die
Geschöpfe des Prometheus*, and even Strauss's *Elektra*.[15]

With the development of ethnology and ethnomusicology in
the last quarter of the nineteenth century, it became popular to
introduce and blend certain ethnomusicological stereotypes into
the classical orchestral palette of Western romanticism. Berlioz
scored a sistrum for *Les Troyens;* Debussy glorified the syrinx in
L'après-midi d'un faune; an appropriate Egyptian "sound" produced by harp and soprano singing minor-third and half-tone
intervals emerged at the beginning of the second scene of Verdi's
Aïda.[16] Stravinsky then took only a small step in scoring not only a
harp motif for Orpheus in his 1948 ballet of that name but also a
brief melody actually written in an authentically Hellenic Dorian
mode.[17]

This modal technique became the most frequently employed
method to evoke the musical "sounds" of classical antiquity. Most
composers had in their conservatory training at least been exposed to the Ptolemaic-Boethian modes *(tonoi)*. For the most part
its practitioners were European. A second and important example
after Stravinsky was Nino Rota's Dorian melody for harp and
flute, which he used as Gitone's theme in the controversial film,
Fellini Satyricon (1968).[18]

There was another mid-twentieth-century method for attempting to establish historical accuracy in music describing an "ancient" setting. By this time scholars had discovered and
transcribed several dozen fragments of ancient Greek music, so
composers could incorporate one of these authentic ancient

Greek melodies into their own works and thereby imbue them with an archaizing style. André Jolivet, companion and compatriot of Messiaen, did just this in his *Suite delphique*, composed in 1943.[19] To the authentic-sounding melody of Pindar's *First Pythian Ode*, Jolivet gives an awkwardly cacophonous rhythm section. On the other hand, in his attempt at music-historical accuracy he composed his work in the Phrygian mode to convey an appropriate dithyrambic *ēthos* (i.e., mood). In doing so Jolivet ironically exploits the etymological connection between "trumpet" and "dithyramb," the word from which "trumpet" is derived.[20]

This tracing of the history of ancient Greek music and its recreations has now reached the twentieth century and the beginnings of cinema. Early attempts at composing music for films about antiquity were not nearly so carefully devised nor successful as those by Stravinsky and Jolivet. The composers and arrangers made no special effort to establish a musical authenticity, and in this they parallel the feeble attempts at establishing visual and historical accuracy in the films themselves. For most, a grand romantic mood was all that was required. But besides the irony of losing scores not even a century old when there are extant fragments of ancient Greek music twenty-three centuries old, the loss of most of these scores is unfortunate but not critical. One excellent example that typifies the rest is the supplemental score to MGM's 1925 version of *Ben-Hur* which was rereleased in the early thirties with segments from Lizst's symphonic poems. The quotations from nineteenth-century romantic music adequately served the film's need for a grand and romantic musical background to a romantic, nineteenth-century literary epic. *Ben-Hur* closes two decades of silent films set in the ancient world, a fashion which had begun modestly in 1907 with Kalem's *Ben-Hur*, blossomed in 1908 with Arturo Ambrosio's cinematic rendering of *Gli Ultimi Giorni di Pompeii*, and continued with a number of silent epics produced in the United States and, for the most part, in Italy.[21]

When the sound era began, there was some hesitation before any "ancient films" were produced. This hiatus paralleled and resulted from Hollywood's focus on modernity, particularly organized crime and Broadway musicals.[22] Nonetheless Cecil B. DeMille had already made so many successful films in the silent era that he was able to convince Paramount to finance his *Sign of the Cross* (1932) and then *Cleopatra* (1934).[23] As one would expect, the music which accompanies these relatively early sound films accords with the type of nineteenth-century music used to accompany silent films. The credits to *Sign of the Cross* open with

Rudolph Kopp's brass fanfare which leads to the title credit. With this the music shifts to the "sacred, ancient" instrumentation of organ and harp, thus combining the music associated with contemporary American religious services and the ancient world since the era of Verdi's *Aïda*. This instrumentation in turn leads immediately and surprisingly into "The Wild Blue Yonder." The film, not unlike DeMille's silent version of *The Ten Commandments*, begins with a modern prologue to which the rousing Air Force motif applies perfectly. This modern prologue concludes when Hitler is compared to Nero, at which point the film shifts back to antiquity. Accompanying this abrupt historical flashback, the music now reverts to a romantic Sturm und Drang to accompany the burning of Rome. Whereas most ancient lyres contained seven or at most eleven strings, Nero's lyre here boasts twelve. Nonetheless, his lyre is actually mute while the accompanying soundtrack uses a concert harp playing a stereotypical, exotic motif (f#-g#-a#-g#-f#-g# at the root, fifth, and octave). Similarly, the man who plays the double pipes *(biaulos)* in the initial scene by a fountain plays another stereotypically exotic or oriental motif (d-d-g-f-d harmonized at a fourth below).

Rudolph Kopp's overture to *Cleopatra* demonstrates a similar eclecticism. It begins with a romantic theme of three notes played by the full string section, a theme—root, flatted second, third, i.e., halftone plus trihemitone (minor third)—borrowed from the orientalizing and in that sense "exotic" tradition authorized earlier by Ippolitov-Ivanov, Prokofiev, and Khatchaturian. The actual title "Cleopatra" is accompanied by more series of halftones and minor thirds but now played on the requisite Verdiesque harp and flute; in fact, strumming on the harp produces precisely the same progression (in 4/4: major, major, major, another one half higher) as that in the second scene of act 1 of *Aïda*. The rhythm is similarly orientalizing, with a bass drum beaten (in 4/4) every half beat for the first three, then on 4 alone. A martial fanfare both concludes this overture and leads, after a brief interlude on bass clarinet, to a scene with Cleopatra's chariot racing across the desert: this action music differs not at all from contemporary chase scenes in Westerns or other genre films. Similarly, Cleopatra's triumphal entry into Rome, despite some attempt at historical accuracy by the visual presentation of lictors with *fasces*, begins with a quasi-Wagnerian march scored for strings. It culminates with the return of the oriental theme, which appears again with full orchestration in the visually splendid barge sequence.[24]

More than a decade later the United States and Europe had just completed the great war which necessarily obviated any desire to represent the ancient world in the cinema. After the war there was no immediate change of direction. In the 1946 film version of Shaw's *Caesar and Cleopatra* both the playwright and the film-makers maintain a spirit of irreverence toward the historical characters. Consequently, the score by Georges Auric still makes no attempt at accurately recreating an ancient sound. In fact, it represents the type of film-scoring which puts style at a higher value than musical archaeology, whether this applies to an "ancient" or to any historical (or futuristic) film. It is at times capricious, at others stirring, and occasionally takes on an ethereal quality in its clustered but gently orchestrated high-pitched harmonies. This description applies as well to his scoring for Jean Cocteau's *Orphée* (1949), for it was a consciously devised style categorized by contemporaries as the musical style of "Les Six."[25]

After DeMille's extremely successful *Samson and Delilah* (1949), however, the next decade blossomed with a number of large-budget, high-profile films set in Greco-Roman and biblical antiquity. The music for DeMille's *Samson and Delilah* differed little from that which had accompanied his previous productions. Victor Young was a very "tuneful" composer, and he scored so many films that he rarely had the time to focus special attention on any one project.[26] These two aspects of Young's music help to explain his scoring for *Samson and Delilah*. Borrowing heavily from his predecessors, he established with his very overture an enchanting, orientalizing theme of halftones and minor thirds to describe the romance of the two biblical figures.

As mentioned above, in the field of classical music the forties had produced two French pieces, Jolivet's *Suite delphique* and Stravinsky's *Orphée*, which reflected an increasing awareness that a musical archaeology of ancient Greece and Rome was long overdue. No serious composer ever became more conscious of recreating ancient Greco-Roman music in this era than Miklos Rozsa, and this is equally true when applied to film composers. After all, Rozsa's cinematic predecessors had hardly attempted to recreate genuine ancient music. Their interest was to maintain their own style or to create an oriental, romantic, or martial ambience. Established romantic instrumentations and melodic motifs sufficed for this purpose, and such films generally did not demonstrate any serious or consistent attempts by their creators to portray the ancient world accurately.

The task assigned to Rozsa for MGM's *Quo Vadis?* was quite different.[27] Screenwriter Hugh Gray, an Oxfordian educated in the classics, had already filled several notebooks with historically accurate material to be incorporated into the film.[28] Rozsa, too, perceived part of his task to be the accurate recreation of an ancient sound, so he rejected the approach of his immediate predecessors and rethought completely how to score a modern film with ancient music.[29] His solution was to alter normal orchestrations by concentrating on brass, to employ the same authentic ancient modal constructions (tonoi) used less than a decade before by Stravinsky and Jolivet, to avoid triads and counterpoint as much as possible, and to adapt authentic melodies from the extant fragments of ancient Greco-Roman music. He even reconstructed a number of citharae, lyres, auloi, and tubae. For his marches he consciously eschewed the use of strings and built his melodies almost entirely on Pythagorean fourths, fifths, and octaves, although he harmonized this authentic foundation with the sevenths, ninths, and seconds which give his compositions their unique sound.[30] The piece he adapted for Nero's cithara is that from the Seikilos Inscription, a funerary monument found in Aydin (Turkey) a century ago on which is inscribed a dirge with a well-balanced four-line melody.[31] For the otherwise typical dance interlude at Nero's court he incorporated a prestissimo version of Athanasius Kircher's recreation of the music to Pindar's First Pythian Ode.[32] Elsewhere, for the chorus of Christian martyrs in the arena, he adapted the extant Hymn to Nemesis by Mesomedes, court musician to the second-century A.D. Emperor Hadrian.[33]

Rozsa's solution to the quest for musical authenticity might well be labeled the Rozsa synthesis, for he synthesized ancient musical fragments, theory, and instrumentation with melodic lines, harmonies, and orchestrations suitable to modern ears and able to evoke familiar emotional responses from modern audiences. Such a synthesis became for some composers the sine qua non for the scoring of "ancient" films in the fifties. It influenced even such honored film-music composers as Alfred Newman for The Robe (1954) and Bernard Herrmann for Jason and the Argonauts (1963). For Rozsa himself the next decade was filled with assignments to score such ancient films as Julius Caesar (1953), Ben-Hur (1959), King of Kings (1961), and Sodom and Gomorrah (1962), as well as other historical epics: Ivanhoe (1952), Knights of the Round Table (1953), and El Cid (1961). For Ben-Hur he won an Academy Award, the only film score of this genre to be so honored, even though this time he quoted no ancient Greco-Roman musical fragments in his melodies.[34] In addition, it was the first film score to have not only its soundtrack but a second album issued.[35] With the exception of Max Steiner's score to *Gone With the Wind,* which did not win the Academy Award, few films scores had ever been as successful and influential until the advent of John Williams's fully orchestrated "adventure scores" in the seventies.

The scores to the abundance of ancient films that appeared in the wake of the successes of *Samson and Delilah* and *Quo Vadis?* followed Rozsa's solutions to a reasonable extent, particularly in their martial sequences.[36] But several influential composers in the subsequent decade resisted or felt no obligation to adhere to this renewed authenticity in favor of their own musical styles. Film music, after all, is a creative art, and the Rozsa synthesis could influence other composers only to a certain extent, particularly those who would have difficulty adapting their own styles to his model. Also, as Rozsa himself discovered, only a limited number of fragments of Greek music are extant, and *Quo Vadis?* had already consumed the more adaptable ones. As a result, such composers as Dmitri Tiomkin, Alex North, and Nino Rota developed two other noteworthy approaches.

The first is that employed by both Dmitri Tiomkin and Alex North. Tiomkin, who earlier had scored *Land of the Pharaohs* (1955), was hired toward the end of his extremely productive career to score *The Fall of the Roman Empire* (1964). North was considerably younger, and although he had spent his career scoring such challenging and dramatic contemporary masterpieces as *A Streetcar Named Desire* (1951) and *The Long Hot Summer* (1958), he was nonetheless employed for both *Spartacus* (1960) and the notorious *Cleopatra* (1963) that caused a financial disaster for Twentieth-Century Fox.

Predictably, *Spartacus,* the earliest of these three epic scores, begins with a martial snare drum. Its beat, again predictably, supports a melodic fanfare scored primarily for brass, and this melody is still based on fourths and octaves. To this point the influence of Rozsa is marked. But within seconds of this beginning we hear dissonances as North suspends one fourth upon another. He takes us through a series of keys, and each harmonization transcends the simple Pythagorean consonances Rozsa had reestablished for the genre. This and other martial passages were not designed to create grandeur or arouse patriotism for the Roman state. Instead they create a disturbing and perplexing consciousness as befits a score accompanying the screenplay by the once blacklisted Dalton Trumbo. Indeed, this is "the thinking man's epic" which celebrates not the glory and might of Rome but an individual who dared oppose it, a struggle for personal freedom.

When *Spartacus* turns to the plight of the suffering, North's score excels in extracting from the viewer the pathos inherent in such scenes. At one point before the great battle against Crassus' legions, director Stanley Kubrick eliminates all dialogue and leaves us with only images and music to observe the human faces and to experience personal relationships between ourselves and the encamped fugitive slaves. Whereas the martial passages had Rozsa as progenitor, these more intimate sequences have no predecessor, nor could they. They derive from a unique combination of the social sensitivities and rebellion of the 1960s and the tradition of epic films in the 1950s.

For the almost contemporary *Cleopatra* and *The Fall of the Roman Empire*, North and Tiomkin seem to have approached the same problems with essentially the same solution. We must keep in mind here that films such as *Samson and Delilah* and *Quo Vadis?* were by now without direct influence, and that these last two huge and expensive epics were projects conceived and executed after the genre had reached its zenith three or four years earlier. The problem was to allot to these epics something lacking in *Quo Vadis?*, *The Ten Commandments*, *Spartacus*, and *Ben-Hur*. The armies, miracles, and mad emperors that had been the stock-in-trade of ancient epics had all been exploited more than enough, so in *Cleopatra* emphasis was to be given to the love affair between two powerful but ill-destined rulers, while *The Fall of the Roman Empire* was to focus on the love affair between ineffective but benign powers behind the throne of Commodus. The musical solution, then, was to create romantic music of epic proportions. While Rozsa had by no means neglected the romantic elements in *Ben-Hur*, here were two films which were predominantly romantic. Consequently, the Pythagorean intervals, ancient instrumentation, and modal restrictions were all abandoned. The composers found that progressive and at times even avant-garde dissonances scored for large string ensembles could convey both the magnified scope of the romantic protagonists and the depth of the human feelings shared or lost between them, yet at the same time the music of both films gives us an unmistakable sense of isolation from their period of history. The avant-garde harmonies modify our emotional involvement to the extent that we feel only detached sympathy for their plight.

Although the release of *Cleopatra* preceded that of *The Fall of the*

Roman Empire by one year, the former dealt a mortal blow to the ancient epic in the cinema. Cost overruns, the scandalous affair between the costars (Elizabeth Taylor and Richard Burton), and a final product which was not well received by the critics shifted the genre from Hollywood back into the hands of European—especially Italian—directors who better understood the symbolic and artistic possibilities inherent in films set in antiquity and felt challenged by their cultural heritage. Because the very nature of their films differed from those produced in the fifties and early sixties, the music had to emphasize a new, nonepic atmosphere and fresh artistic perspectives. *Fellini Satyricon* (1968) and Pasolini's *Medea* (1968) demonstrate these different perspectives, the former creating a "different" world, the latter a metahistorical, anthropological apologia for Medea's revenge upon Jason and Creon.

For his film version of Petronius' *Satyricon,* Fellini chose two types of music, both intended to belong to what he himself described as a "different" world.[37] Rota composed not his characteristic Neapolitan street and plaintive circus tunes but unfamiliar and synthesized sounds produced electronically. These were complemented by a number of ethnomusical recordings, including frequent segments of *sansa,* the Balinese Ramayana chants for the Minotaur scene, and the central African *niegpadouda* dance. As Kubrick earlier in the decade had rejected the stereotyped glorification of Roman grandeur, so Fellini wished to examine a culture which did not seem familiar to our own. In his own words, the *Satyricon* "is a science-fiction film projected into the past."[38] The one relic of the Rozsa synthesis is Gitone's lyre piece composed on the fourths and fifths of an authentic Dorian mode.

Pasolini also attempted to create a "different" world for his *Medea,* but his approach to antiquity in this film travels into a Bronze Age world in which earth, sun, death, and rebirth still have genuine significance.[39] His Medea slayed her children because child sacrifice had been a part of her Colchian world of ritual sacrifice. Calling upon her grandfather Helios, she performed one last act of ritual sacrifice with divine approval but human horror.

To compose a soundtrack for a film which attempts to describe ancient ritual sacrifice was not possible in Pasolini's opinion, so he, too, selected a number of symbolic ethnomusics.[40] For the rituals in Colchis he selected Tibetan chant for the elders, Persian *santur* music for general Colchian reminiscences, and Balkan choral music (characterized by a female chorus harmonizing at the second) for the women propagating the new crops and fields with the blood of the young, male victim of *sparagmos,* the ritual of dismemberment.

In the wake of the *Cleopatra* fiasco and the shift in popular taste in adventure films from sword-and-sandal epics to "spaghetti westerns" and then Kung-Fu movies, very few "ancient" films of note were made in the period between then and now.[41] There have been a considerable number of TV miniseries, the scores for which are as excessively derivative, tedious, and unimaginative as the four-to-twelve hour teleplays they accompany.[42] There have also been two theatrical releases, the infamous *Caligula* (1979) and *Clash of the Titans* (1981). The most exquisite music of the former derives, ironically, from Khatchaturian's ballet, *Spartacus,* some of which is played in its original orchestral form. (From it, a memorable theme has been adapted into a modern pop song.)[43] The irony here exists not only in that one of the most monstrous Roman emperors has his story told to the music of a ballet about the Thracian slave who could not stomach the *auctoritas* of even the Republican aristocracy, but also in that the musical solution—to use a romantic orchestral piece—is that of the soundtrack created for the *Ben-Hur* of 1925.

Laurence Rosenthal's score for *Clash of the Titans* makes no attempt at authenticity. Finding no use for it in scoring this mythological tale, he easily rejects the marches, lyre solos, and Pythagorean harmonies which Rozsa had employed. The full orchestrations and rousing themes of the film, and particularly the luscious music accompanying Pegasus soaring about the mountains, state Rosenthal's acceptance of the immensely successful style established by John Williams in *Star Wars* (1977), *Superman* (1978), and *Raiders of the Lost Ark* (1981).

The question arises whether there are categorically proper and improper solutions to scoring "Greco-Roman" film music. Selecting the Rozsa synthesis in *Quo Vadis?* as the most "proper," accurate, and influential of "ancient" scores might lead to the assumption that it established the classical form of "ancient" film music and that every score before it was preliminary and thereby inferior, every one after derivative and equally inferior. But this assumption too easily fits a preconceived notion of stylistic development. While it might be noble to have an entire film score consist of actual pieces of ancient music played correctly on properly reconstructed instruments, such musical authenticity might not appropriately reflect the ethos or intent of the film itself. Also, from a more pragmatic perspective, the size of our present corpus of ancient music, only forty brief fragments, and our present lack of knowledge about ancient musical performance techniques greatly limit film composers in their attempt to recreate ancient music.

One reasonable substitute is the solution presently adopted by the New York Greek Drama Company, which has employed Eve Beglarian specifically to score, i.e., compose, "ancient Greek" music based on the Aristoxenian-Ptolemaic *tonoi* and the types of melodic and intervalic movements revealed in the extant fragments.[44] But because these scores accompany academic performances of ancient Greek tragedy and poetry in the original Greek language, they must be as authentic as possible.

When we hear authentic Renaissance masses incorporated into Alex North's score for *The Agony and the Ecstasy* (1965) or the authentic soundtrack of *Amadeus* (1984), we have a secure feeling of historical accuracy. Yet with a musical corpus so generally unrecognizable as that of classical antiquity, our appreciation of the Seikilos Inscription sung by Peter Ustinov (Nero) in *Quo Vadis?* depends not at all on the authenticity or inauthenticity of the words or melody but on the irony revealed in the sycophantic kudos given by his courtiers to this barely tolerable monody sung by a hopelessly untalented tyrant. This rendering of the song is intended to displease us. In fact, it is meant for artistic and political ridicule, and it is indeed worthy of ridicule on both accounts. In a sense, its authenticity is wasted, even detrimental to the employment of ancient Greek musical fragments. On the other hand, we sympathize with Miklos Rozsa, who threatened to leave the *Ben-Hur* project when he was initially instructed to adapt, anachronistically, "Adeste Fideles" for his scoring of the nativity scene.[45]

Rozsa, in the sense discussed above, created a classical perfection against which all other scores to films set in antiquity can be compared. It is not an exaggeration to state that he established the norm in the genre for a decade because of his efforts in *Quo Vadis?* and *Ben-Hur*. But just as Rozsa's music appropriately echoed the well-intended authenticity of MGM's production of *Quo Vadis?*, so did the various ethnomusics effectively convey the artistic messages and unique ambiences Fellini and Pasolini attempted to establish in *Satyricon* and *Medea*. Even the romantically dissonant scores of North's *Spartacus* and *Cleopatra,* the fulsome, winged score of Rosenthal's *Clash of the Titans,* and the orientalizing scores of Kopp's *Sign of the Cross* and *Cleopatra* (1934) appropriately reflect the atmospheres and intended emotional stimuli of these films.

Like the cinema itself, historical film music depends to a large extent on illusion. It is the viewer, not the historian or history itself, who determines the effectiveness of the cinematic recreation of history. But because the viewer's aesthetic judgment ultimately determines the value of the film's historicity, the basis for such a judgment is neither consistent nor universal. John Williams's score for *Star Wars* does not authentically recreate the sound of music on a galaxy far, far away, yet it enhances and is an essential part of the artistic conveyance of *Star Wars*. Along with the special effects, costumes, and other aspects of the film's artistic design, the music helps create for us the illusion of outer space.[46] If the sweep of the film is sufficient, be it the action-packed sweep of *Star Wars,* the romantic sweep of *Cleopatra,* or the religious sweep of *Ben-Hur,* then the viewer will be convinced that the engrossing story is realistically, appropriately, and even authentically represented by the film music.[47]

It is the combination of hearing Rozsa's music and seeing the ancient armaments, costumes, and architectural styles on the large screen that creates the illusion of an ancient setting. Rozsa's music, when it is applied to other periods and when both the brass instruments and the adaptations of actual Greek musical fragments are omitted, sounds stylistically uniform. That is, a hearing of Rozsa's overture to *Ivanhoe,* for instance, would not pass the blindfold test: the hearer exposed to the music alone would easily envision another magnificent setting, medieval or ancient. This applies equally to scores by Rozsa, North, or Rota, and even to baroque operas in ancient settings.

What are the sounds of cinematic antiquity, and how do they strike the viewers? The score becomes "ancient" if the filmmaker creates for the viewer a captivating ambience which successfully establishes a "different" world which is then perceived to be ancient, and if the music itself is an appropriately influential part of this ambience.

Contemporary aestheticians and ethnomusicologists have demonstrated through cantometric analysis that music originates in and creates certain illusions and patterns which are almost always culturally affirmed.[48] It complicates a composer's ability to describe "another," unfamiliar world if the patterns and illusions are equally unfamiliar. But just as speech can be used to communicate intellectual stimuli, music can be used to communicate emotional stimuli. The process of establishing an "ancient sound" depends on the socially interactive process of reality construction.[49] In his score to *Quo Vadis?* Rozsa established just such a process. Once it became familiar enough, it could be reused and adapted by Rozsa and subsequent composers now familiar, as were audiences, with the newly recreated aesthetics of "ancient" cultural norms. Ironically, attempts at musical authenticity became not nearly so important as meeting this new and by now required aesthetic. Rozsa's musical innovations based on his research on ancient music led not to renewed interest in ancient music but to a musical stereotype heard today in parodies of ancient films.[50]

These ideas call into question statements I made in *The Ancient World in the Cinema* twelve years ago. Although writing for a movie-going audience interested in sharing these films with a classicist more than for scholars interested in reviewing films which inaccurately portray events and characters, I summarized there that in general the filmmakers who took greater care to make the ancient film authentic also took greater care to make it better as a whole. Clearly such a statement depends on the bias toward a classical ideal. If authenticity in music belongs to that ideal, then the music of *Quo Vadis?* must be superior to all scores which precede and come after it. But this can no longer be argued convincingly. It was not until Rozsa ceased quoting actual ancient melodic fragments that he was able to write his award-winning and rightly acclaimed music for *Ben-Hur.* Not historical authenticity but the ability to provoke martial, pious, and romantic responses makes his score so outstanding. But since then critics and scholars have developed new intellectual and aesthetic approaches to the arts and employ different criteria. Literal authenticity no longer has the same value as it did thirty to forty years ago. This significantly calls into question the desirability or justification of historical accuracy. The ethnomusics used by Fellini and Pasolini thereby earn a greater critical viability, and so do the romantic scores of the 1930s and the operas of the baroque era. There is no permanent "sound" of cinematic antiquity.[51]

NOTES

1. One might equate the surface chips and fissures in a visual work of art to an alternate reading *(lectio varia)* of a word or phrase in a manuscript tradition, a missing limb

or pottery fragment to a gap in a literary text *(lacuna)*, and the support struts to a line or passage added by a subsequent editor (interpolation).

2. Of which we have only the extensive critique in Aristotle's *Poetics* 1452a21–33, 1452b26–1453a35, 1453b1–33, 1454b8, etc.

3. The musical fragments have been collected in Egert Pöhlmann, *Denkmäler altgriechischer Musik* (Nuremberg: Carl, 1970), and Thomas J. Mathiesen, "New Fragments of Ancient Greek Music," *Acta Musicologica* 53 (1981): 124–32. For the *auloi* fragments, see the bibliography in Denise Davidson Greaves, *Sextus Empiricus: Against the Musicians* (Lincoln: University of Nebraska Press, 1986), 123, n. 5; as well as Annie Bélis, "Auloi grecs du Louvre," *Bulletin de Correspondance Hellénique* 198 (1984): 14–22; and Martha Maas and Jane MacIntosh Snyder, *Stringed Instruments of Ancient Greece* (New Haven: Yale University Press, 1989). For the music theorists, see Thomas J. Mathiesen, *Ancient Greek Music Theory: A Catalogue Raisonné of Manuscripts* (Munich: Henle, 1988).

One attempt at realizing the fragments is by Gregorio Paniagua, *Musique de la Grèce antique* (Recording: Harmonia Mundi 1015); see my review in *American Journal of Philology* 102 (1981): 469–71.

4. An easily accessible video recording of Irish and Turkic bards, whose musical and poetic arts resemble those of archaic Greece, can be found in Michael Woods's *In Search of the Trojan War* (Manchester: BBC, 1985), Part 3.

5. See Mathiesen, "New Fragments," 124–32, and my "*Orestes* 344–45: Colometry and Music," *Greek, Roman, and Byzantine Studies* 18 (1977): 71–83.

6. See Thomas J. Mathiesen, *Aristides Quintilianus: On Music* (New Haven: Yale University Press, 1983), 27–28, n. 135.

7. Some of which no doubt imitated or parodied tragic music. Aristophanes (*Frogs*, 1314) undoubtedly parodies Euripides' unusual proclivity for scoring more than one note to each syllable *(melisma)*.

8. Solon Michaelides, *The Music of Ancient Greece* (London: Faber & Faber, 1978), 294; and Andrew Barker, *Greek Music Writings. I: The Musician and His Art* (Cambridge: Cambridge University Press, 1984), 213, n. 60.

9. The term *archaic* in the study of ancient Greek music has traditionally been misused to refer to almost any period between the close of the Bronze Age and the beginning of the classical period. The antiquarians include [Plutarch], Bacchius, and Alypius. Actually, if we include the extant treatises of [Plutarch], [Aristotle], Cleonides, Ptolemy, Nicomachus, Sextus Empiricus, Philodemus, Gaudentus, Bacchius, and Alypius within this Roman period, the number of antiquarians actively preserving "ancient" music theory is considerable.

10. A Vienna papyrus (*Pap. Wien* G 2315) is the only extant copy of the second stasimon of *Orestes;* Dionysius of Halicarnassus, *On the Composition of Words* 11.58–63, examines the first. Egert Pöhlmann, *Griechische Musikfragmente: Ein Weg zur altgriechischen Musik* (Nuremberg: Carl, 1960), 19–24, points out that the scholia to lines 176 and 1384 also refer to the music.

11. See Thomas J. Mathiesen, "Towards a Corpus of Ancient Greek Music Theory: A New *Catalogue raisonné* Planned for RISM," *Fontes artis musicae* 24 (1978): 119–34. A study of the manuscript tradition of Alypius and Bacchius, both of whose treatises contain ancient Greek notation, will show that only scholars had access to this material. These scholars did not really have any significant effect on the practice of music in the period; see Claude V. Palisca, *Humanism in Italian Renaissance Musical Thought* (New Haven: Yale University Press, 1985), 1–50. It should be remembered that even in ancient Greece very few Greeks could read musical notation.

12. For a recording (of Horace, *Odes* l.1.): Nonesuch HB-73016C.

13. See Claude V. Palisca, *The Florentine Camerata: Documentary Studies and Translations* (New Haven: Yale University Press, 1989).

14. John Towers, *Dictionary-Catalogue of Operas and Operettas* (Morgantown, West Va.: Acme, 1910), s.v.

15. This lack of interest in historical accuracy did not apply to music, particularly theatrical music, alone. In the visual arts as well, it was regular practice to illustrate ancient mythological and historical characters in contemporary costume and style. See, for example, Jacques Bousquet, *Mannerism: The Painting and Style of the Late Renaissance*, trans. S. Tayler (New York: Braziller, 1964).

16. Years after *L'après-midi d'un faune* (1894), Debussy composed *Syrinx* (1910), which depicts the death of Pan. He had also planned operas on Orpheus and Oedipus. In a letter to Robert Godet, Debussy wrote, "Orpheus is the symbol of Power in the world of sound"; see Edward Lockspeiser, *Debussy* (New York: McGraw Hill, 1972), 107–8 and 175. For comparison, see J. Langford, "Berlioz, Cassandra, and the French Operatic Tradition," *Music and Letters* 62 (1981):310; and R. M. Longyear, "Clarinet Sonorities in early Romantic Music," *The Musical Times* 124 (1983): 224–26.

17. And yet in his *Orpheus* (as well as in his *Apollon* and *Oedipus Rex*) Stravinsky intentionally incorporated dotted rhythms in conscious imitation of eighteenth-century style. His purpose, as quoted in a conversation with Robert Craft, *Conversations with Igor Stravinsky* (London: Faber & Faber, 1959), 34–35, was to "build a new music on eighteenth-century classicism."

18. Recording: Nino Rota, *Fellini Satyricon* (UAS 5208, 1970).

19. Recording: EMI OVB 639.

20. Unfortunately, the melody to Pindar's *First Pythian Ode* is a forgery by Athanasius Kircher datable to 1652. See Pöhlmann, *Denkmäler*, 47–49. In the field of classical music there were still other options available. Peggy Glanville-Hicks gives her opera *Nausicaa* a neo-Hellenic sound, while some modern composers who have composed around ancient themes and subject matter remain within their neo-Romantic or modernist style. Included in these categories would be Schoek, Martinu, Scriabin, Satie, Henze, Ussachevsky, and Xenakis. Carl Orff offered a very different solution by attempting in such works as his *Antigone* (1949), *Oedipus Tyrannus* (1959), and *Prometheus* (1968) to recreate not so much ancient but "primitive" sounds of speech and music.

21. Guazzoni's *Quo Vadis?* (1912), *Marcantonio e Cleopatra* (1913), and *Caius Julius Caesar* (1914); Giovanni Pastrone's *Cabiria* (1913); D. W. Griffith's *Intolerance* (1916); the *Cleopatra* (1917) and *Salome* (1918) with Theda Bara; DeMille's (first) *The Ten Commandments* (1923) and *King of Kings* (1927); Ambrosio's *Quo Vadis?* (1925); Palermi's *The Last Days of Pompeii* (1926); and Michael Curtiz's *Noah's Ark* (1929), just to name a few classics. See the narrative listing in my *The Ancient World in the Cinema* (New York: Barnes, 1978), 16–18.

22. Badly timed, therefore, was the establishment of La Itala Film Company di Hollywood and their 1931 production of *La Regina di Sparta*.

Two films from this era which combine the cinematic musical with the tradition of setting films in antiquity are Busby Berkeley's Eddie Cantor vehicle, *Roman Scandals* (1933), and the German musical *Amphitryon* (1937).

23. Wilson Barrett's play, *Sign of the Cross*, had been filmed earlier by Paramount in 1918 and still earlier (1904) in Great Britain. DeMille's *Cleopatra* was the fifth film by that name; earlier versions date to 1899, 1910, 1912, and 1918.

24. Kopp uses the dramatic barge finale to vary his original oriental theme by alternating between the flatted and then the unflatted second.

To this same period belongs RKO's *The Last Days of Pompeii* (1935), the fourth cinematic version of Bulwer-Lytton's novel, for which Max Steiner used some of the same themes he had used two years earlier for *King Kong*. Steiner's score for *Helen of Troy* (1955) is equally inauthentic but appropriately and lusciously romantic.

25. They were labeled as such by Henri Collet, music critic for the Parisian *Comoedia*, in his daily column on 16 January 1920. For a chronological survey of their work, see Richard

Burbank, *Twentieth-Century Music: Orchestral, Chamber, Operatic, and Dance Music 1900–1980* (New York: Facts on File, 1984). The other five were Darius Milhaud, Louis Durey, Arthur Honneger, Francis Poulenc, and Germaine Tailleferre.

26. He scored over 350 films in his twenty-year career, at least eleven in 1949 alone. See Tony Thomas, *Music for the Movies* (New York: Barnes, 1973), 43–48.

27. MGM targeted Henryk Sienkiewicz's 1905 Nobel Prize-winning novel for epic presentation soon after Paramount's very successful *Samson and Delilah*. Earlier acclaimed film versions were those by Enrico Guazzoni in 1912 and Arturo Ambrosio in 1925.

28. Gray also wrote the screenplays to *Ulysses* (1955) and *Helen of Troy* (1955).

29. See Roy Prendergast, *Film Music: A Neglected Art* (New York: New York University Press, 1977), 123–30.

30. For Rozsa's own description of his contribution to the film, see Thomas, *Music for the Movies*, 98–100.

31. See Pöhlmann, *Deukmäler*, 54–57. The words "Oh lamp and flame" are substituted for the original funeral song and thus accommodate Nero's desire to destroy Rome by fire, in this way creating both a new city and a worthy epic poem.

32. See above, n. 20. Rozsa, quoted in Thomas, *Music for the Movies*, 127–28, wrote: "Its authenticity is doubtful, but it is constructed entirely on Greek principles, and it is a hauntingly beautiful melody."

33. See Pöhlmann, *Denkmäler*, 18–19. Rozsa also adapted the hymn to Helios for the music accompanying a chase sequence. See Pöhlmann, 16–19.

34. The other scores in this genre that have been nominated are *Samson and Delilah, Quo Vadis?, David and Bathsheba* (1951—Alfred Newman), *The Silver Chalice* (1954—Franz Waxman), *Julius Caesar* (1953), *Spartacus, Cleopatra* (1963), *The Fall of the Roman Empire, The Greatest Story Ever Told* (1965—Newman), and *The Bible* (1966—Toshiro Mayuzumi). It should also be pointed out that Rozsa borrowed one of his marches from *Quo Vadis?* and reused it in *Ben-Hur*.

35. Recording: MGM 2353 075 Select.

36. For a complete list of these films see my *Ancient World in the Cinema*, 19–21.

37. Dario Zanelli, *Fellini's Satyricon* (New York: Ballantine, 1970), 4–9.

38. *Time*, 12 September 1969, 97.

39. He focuses on the latter, of course, in *The Gospel According to St. Matthew* (1965).

40. Ethnomusicology was becoming generally popular at that time. Folkways and Nonesuch records issued numerous samplings from around the world, and the scholarly journal *Ethnomusicology* had begun publication in 1953.

41. For a complete list of films produced from 1968 through 1977, see my *Ancient World in the Cinema*, 20.

42. These begin with *The Story of David* (1976) and *Moses the Lawgiver* (1976), and then continue with Zeffirelli's *Life of Jesus* (1977), *Masada* (1981), *A.D.* (1985), and, bringing the genre full circle, the sixth attempt at filming *The Last Days of Pompeii* (1984), seventy-six years after the first.

43. The soundtrack was released in 1980 on Penthouse Records 101-CS; Toni Biggs adapted "We Are One."

44. To date, the company has produced Euripides' *Medea* and *Songs of Sappho* on video cassette.

45. Prendergast, *Film Music*, 126.

46. Igor Stravinsky discussed the spatial element in music in Victor Zuckerkandl, *Sound and Symbol: Music and the External World* (Princeton: Princeton University Press, 1956), 69. Film composer Lalo Schifrin commented: "Playing music without the picture is often like playing a two-part Bach invention with one part missing." See Thomas E. Backer and Eddy Lawrence Manson, "In the Key of Feeling," *Human Behavior* 7, no. 2 (1978): 63–67.

47. On authenticity in opposition to emotional response see Peter Kivy, "On the Concept of the 'Historically Authentic' Performance," *The Monist* 71 (April 1988):278–90.

48. Alan Lomax, "Song Structure and Social Structure," in *Readings in Ethnomusicology*, ed. David P. McAllester (New York: Johnson Reprint Corp., 1971), 227–52, esp. 251; and Steven Feld, "Communication, Music, and Speech About Music," *Yearbook for Traditional Music* 16 (1984):2–6.

49. See Charles Seeger, *Studies in Musicology 1935–1975* (Berkeley: University of California Press, 1977), 16–44.

50. Such as *Monty Python's Meaning of Life* and *The Three Stooges Meet Hercules*. See Richard Taruskin, "Symphonies . . . The New Antiquity," *Opus* 107 (October 1987):31–63.

51. I am grateful to Kathleen Higgins, University of Texas, for her bibliographical assistance and general expertise in musical aesthetics.

Notes on Contributors

FREDERICK AHL is professor of classics at Cornell University. He is the author of *Lucan: An Introduction, Metaformations: Wordplay and Soundplay in Ovid and Other Classical Poets*, and *Sophocles' Œdipus: Evidence and Self-Conviction*. He has also translated three plays of Seneca *(Phaedra, Medea, Trojan Women)* and published articles on ancient music, theater, and religion.

JAMES R. BARON is associate professor of classical studies at the College of William and Mary, where he frequently teaches courses on the classical tradition in European and American culture, often with special attention to Scandinavian authors. He is completing a book entitled *Ingmar Bergman and the Classical Tradition*.

MARY-KAY GAMEL is associate professor of classics, comparative literature, and theater arts at the University of California, Santa Cruz. She has published essays on Ovidian poetry, has translated Euripides' *Medea, Alcestis,* and *Electra* for the modern stage, and stages annual productions of ancient drama on the UCSC campus.

ERLING B. HOLTSMARK is professor and chair of classics at the University of Iowa. His research interests include Greek and Latin poetry and linguistics and the reflections of classical literature in modern popular culture. He is the author of *Tarzan and Tradition: Classical Myth in Popular Literature*.

MARIANNE MCDONALD is adjunct associate professor of theater at the University of California, San Diego. She is the founder of the *Thesaurus Linguae Graecae* project and has published several concordances to Euripides. She is the author of *Terms for Happiness in Euripides* and *Euripides in Cinema: The Heart Made Visible*. Currently she is working on *From Parnassus to High Rise: Ancient Greek Drama in Modern Settings*. She has also published articles and frequently lectures on ancient Greek drama, particularly in modern productions.

J. K. NEWMAN is professor of classics at the University of Illinois and holds Oxford degrees in both Litterae Humaniores and Russian. His books include *Augustus and the New Poetry, The Concept of Vates in Augustan Poetry, Pindar's Art* (with F. S. Newman), *The Classical Epic Tradition,* and *Roman Catullus* (forthcoming). He is currently working on *Russian Literature: The Classical Impulse.*

KRISTINA M. PASSMAN is assistant professor of classical languages and literatures at the University of Maine. She has written on Vergil and feminist theory and is currently at work on a book with Kathleen N. March on the figure of the Amazon in the conquest of Latin America.

PETER W. ROSE is professor of classics at Miami University of Ohio. He has published articles on Pindar, Homer, and Sophocles in scholarly journals and analyses of films in various leftist political newsletters. His book on ancient Greek ideology and literary form, *Sons of Gods, Children of Earth,* is forthcoming.

JON SOLOMON is associate professor of classics at the University of Arizona. He is the author of *The Ancient World in the Cinema* and is currently working on a translation and commentary on Ptolemy's *Harmonics.*

J. P. SULLIVAN is professor of classics at the University of California, Santa Barbara, and was once a film reviewer for *The Oxford Magazine.* He is the author of *Ezra Pound and Sextus Propertius: A Study in Creative Translation, The Satyricon of Petronius: A Literary Study, Literature and Politics in the Age of Nero,* and other books and articles.

MARTIN M. WINKLER is associate professor of classics at George Mason University. He is the author of *The Persona in Three Satires of Juvenal* and has published articles on Roman literature, the classical tradition, and mythology in film.